Romance
101

Lessons In Love

Also by Gregory J.P. Godek

1001 Ways To Be Romantic®

and

1001 More Ways To Be Romantic

Casablanca Press,™ Inc.

Boston ✦ Sydney

Bookstore distribution: Login Publishers Consortium
800-626-4330

Giftstore distribution: Sourcebooks
800-798-2475

1001
WAYS TO BE
ROMANTIC

Romance
101

Gregory J.P. Godek

First printing.
Printed in the United States of America.
10 9 8 7 6 5 4 3 2

Published by
Casablanca Press, Inc.
P.O. Box 226
Weymouth, Massachusetts 02188-0001
617-340-1300

Cover illustration by Maria Thomas at Pendragon Ink, 508-234-6834
Cover design by Mary-Lynne Bohn at Accent Design, 617-364-0084
Logo design by Josephine Fatta

Publisher's Cataloging in Publication Data

Godek, Gregory J.P., 1955-
Romance 101: Lessons in Love

Includes index.
1. Self-help. 2. Psychology. 3. Relationships. 4. How-to. I. Title.

Library of Congress Catalog Card Number
93-73298

ISBN 0-9629803-8-2 (softbound)
ISBN 0-9629803-9-0 (hardbound)

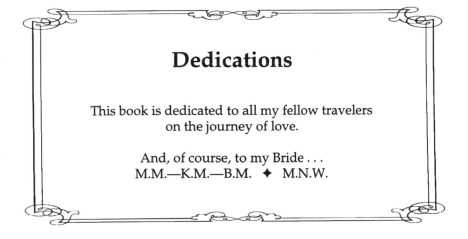

Dedications

This book is dedicated to all my fellow travelers
on the journey of love.

And, of course, to my Bride . . .
M.M.—K.M.—B.M. ✦ M.N.W.

✦ Table of Contents ✦

Acknowledgments

Tracey Ellen Godek
Keith Taylor
Sam & The Group
Craig Schreiber
Timothy Corbett
Gregory Corbett
Mary-Lynne Bohn
Dominique & Mitch & Ben
Maria Thomas & Pendragon, Ink
Suzanne Heiser
Andy Pallotta
H.S.
Bill McHugh
Mark Evans
Dot Bernier
Gil Friedman
Wolfgang Amadeus Mozart

About the Author

Gregory J.P. Godek is a writer, lecturer and newlywed (*still*—after three years of marriage). He is the author of two bestselling books (*1001 Ways To Be Romantic* and *1001 More Ways To Be Romantic*) based on his 12 years of teaching Romance Classes. ✦ *Romance 101* is his third book in three years. Greg has appeared on *The Donahue Show* ("Is Your Lover Among the Romantically Impaired?") and on hundreds of other TV and radio shows. Thousands of people have attended his Romance Classes, and nearly half a million know him through his first two books. ✦ Greg confides that he is a "natural-born" romantic. He never went through that stage when most little boys *hate* girls. He always went "steady" in high school. He never dated-around much because it was the *relationship*, not the *chase*, that compelled him. ✦ He now resides in Boston with his wife Tracey and their three books.

Greg has been called "America's #1 Romantic" by media nationwide, but he resists high-blown labels, preferring to be called a "fellow traveler on this journey of love"—but that's *much* too long to fit onto a business card. ✦ Greg speaks nationally and internationally, presenting keynote speeches and seminars on love and relationships. His qualifications? "I'm a hopeless romantic, incurable writer, intense listener and passionate speaker."

Author's Note

I believe that *everyone* wants more romance in their lives. (Some people just don't *realize* it yet.) I *know* that everyone is capable of expressing more love. There is only one requirement if you want to be more romantic: *You need a little willingness.* If you have *that*, then everything else will follow—the time, the creativity, the money, the partner! ✦ I believe that we all have the potential to transform our lives radically and positively. The changes that transform our lives are rarely achieved easily, and we each seem to have our own unique path, process, and timing. ✦ I believe in looking for the positive, giving the benefit of the doubt, and hoping beyond hope. I believe in looking for connection where none seems to exist. ✦ I believe that *expressing love* is our Purpose. The variety of ways we express love in the world is nearly *endless*: Through words and thoughts and actions; through our Calling; and by raising children lovingly, working honestly, expressing feelings, helping others and creating intimacy. From the everyday, commonplace activities of our lives to the "peak experiences" and rare occurrences, it's all about expressing love. ✦ The rewards of a truly loving, intimate relationship are *beyond all description*.

The Big Question is, Will this material translate well onto paper? I've tried hard to retain the feeling—the *spirit*—of the Romance Class. I hope you'll hear my *voice* behind these words. The process leads me to mangle the English language [Sorry, Mrs. Wilcox], and juxtapose very serious observations with humorous thoughts and oddball ideas. It somehow works in the Class. ✦ I don't believe I have all the answers. I don't insist that you follow any order in reading the book. I encourage you to cheat while you're doing the lessons—by looking at your partner's paper, and talking in class, and passing love notes during lectures. ✦ Please join me and Tracey . . . and bring *your* lover along—Because the journey is so much more *fun* and *fulfilling* and *meaningful* and *rewarding* when you travel through life as a *couple*.

Namaste,

~ G.J.P.G.

Publisher's Note

We believe that *Romance 101* represents a new approach—a new paradigm, if you will—for self-help/psychology/relationship books. It takes the material, but not *itself*, seriously. It respects the reader's intelligence. It's written in a conversational style that "sounds good" on the page, and speaks to the heart as well as the head. ✦ And even though our accountant advises against it, we're going to repeat our "free book" offer: If you find any errors in this book, drop us a note. We'll correct them in the next edition, and send you a free copy of Greg's first book, *1001 Ways To Be Romantic*. Please note: Punctuation is *off-limits*, since Mr. Godek insists on (gleefully) ignoring the rules that Every Other Writer In The Known Universe accepts. Thank you.

Some readers have already written to inquire about Greg's *LoveStories* book, which was originally scheduled for publication in the Autumn of 1993. *LoveStories* is a work in progress still (and Greg welcomes *your* stories). ✦ The novel? We have *no* idea. ✦ The calendar? Yes, that's done. The *365 Days of Romance* daily calendar is available in bookstores and giftshops. ✦ The audio cassette tapes? Probably next year. ✦ Thank you for your interest.

Introduction

A description of Greg's Romance Class, from a participant: "A little theory; a little lecture; a little sharing; a little homework. A lot of fun; a lot of insight; a lot of ideas; a lot of love." ✦ This book has two goals. First, to bring the content and *spirit* of the Romance Class to people around the world. And second, to help *you* re-create the spontaneous affection and deep passion that you felt and expressed early in your relationship.

This book has been 12 years in the making. It's based on the seminar "1001 Ways To Be Romantic," taught by Gregory J.P. Godek. In many ways, *Romance 101* should have *preceded* the first two books (*1001 Ways To Be Romantic* and the cleverly-titled sequel *1001 More Ways To Be Romantic*) because it creates a *context* for those two books. ✦ The first two are *idea* books, while *Romance 101* is a *lesson* book. While this book is essentially a self-directed Romance Class (complete with homework), it does *not* approach the challenge of conveying information in the typical linear manner. You are encouraged to flip through the book, stopping when something interesting catches your eye. ✦ These 64 lessons are, by no means, the *only* lessons you need to master in order to create and maintain a romantic, passionate, intimate relationship—but we think it's a good start! And, these lessons are not complete. You can find entire *books* on nearly every topic discussed here. We encourage you to seek out those books/tapes/seminars that deal in depth with the issues that touch you, trouble you, intrigue you.

This book is not about "Doing it right" or "Doing it Godek's way"—it's about discovering *your* way; feeling *your* feelings; improving *your* life and *your* relationship. This book is not a philosophical, psychological or theoretical book. It's about an *experience*. The experience—*your* experience—of Love. Thus, the exercises, homework and suggestions are the heart of the book. The important thing is what you do *after* you put this book down. ✦ *Romance 101* is meant to be interactive as well as contemplative. You will benefit *more* if you include your lover in the practice of these lessons. ✦ *Enjoy!*

Romance 101 . . .

. . . Book #3 in the  *series*

Reprinted with permission of NEA, Inc., Arlo & Janis © 1993

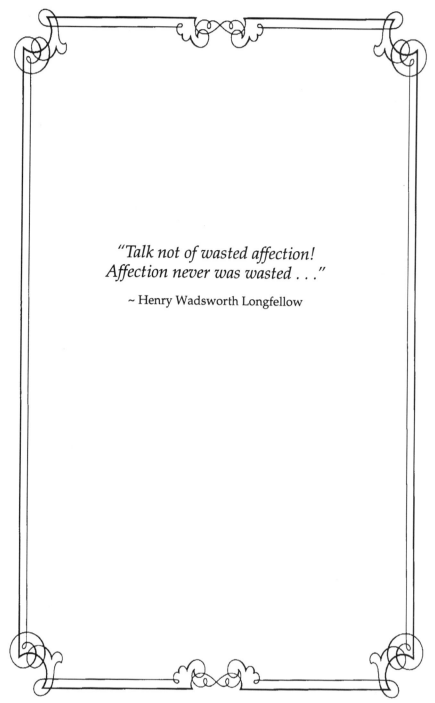

"Talk not of wasted affection!
Affection never was wasted . . ."

~ Henry Wadsworth Longfellow

Affection

How do you express affection? How *often* do you express affection? *Do* you express affection? ✦ Affection is the first cousin of Romance. While romance is the expression of love, affection is the expression of caring. Another definition, from Marisa G., a Romance Class participant, is that affection is "little romance." ✦ Many people, especially the workaholics and skeptics among us, who are somewhat threatened by the enormity of romance, feel they *can* manage to squeeze in a little affection. Great! You gotta crawl before you can walk. [Note: The true goal of this book is to help you *fly*.]

Tip: Minimum Daily Reqirement

The Minimum Daily Requlrement of affection for a healthy relationship is three doses per day. The "minimum" is defined as one kiss per dose, or its equivalent. Some equivalencies, as established by an Expert Panel of Romance Class participants:

➤ 3 hugs = 1 kiss
➤ 1 "I love you" = 1.5 kisses
➤ 1 greeting card (sentimental) = 1.25 kisses
➤ 1 greeting card (humorous) = 0.5 kiss
➤ 1 call from work (1-minute in duration minimum) = 1 kiss
➤ 1 "love note" = 1.3 kisses

Some adjustment may be necessary for: 1) Self-esteem factors, 2) Workaholics, 3) Menstrual cycle timing. Check with your local Love Doctor for details.

Homework: A Written Assignment

Expressing your affection verbally is fine, but expressing it in *writing* is *really* something! "Feelings on paper" can be saved, savored and re-experienced. ✦ For 10 minutes, put some of your feelings on paper: "Why I love you." "My favorite memory of us is . . ." "When I'm with you I feel . . ." ✦ We're not striving for *eloquence* here—merely *expression*. Grammar don't matter. Neither does speling. Neither/does; punctuation or—usage—;or penmanship; or sentence structure. ✦ Just try to put those private, intimate feelings on paper. This is a pass/fail exercise. No grading allowed. But in order to pass, you must give your assignment to your lover.

Affection is simple. Affection is small. Affection has no motive beyond expressing appreciation and caring. Affection that comes with strings attached is no affection at all. ✦ Actually, affection that comes with strings attached is manipulation in disguise. Perhaps it would help to think of affection in the context of "unconditional love." Unconditional affection, spontaneous affection, joyful affection—these describe the true meaning and intent of affection. When encumbered with ulterior motives, affection becomes an unwitting dupe in a game that resembles love but in truth is not.

Question: What's Your Style?

❋ What's your *style* of showing affection? Do you stick to the "basics" or do you prefer the "frills" ? (There's no right or wrong answer here—just your personal preference.)

  ✓ Those who stick to the "basics" tend to verbalize their love. They tend to give gifts like flowers and jewelry.

  ✓ Those who like the "frills" tend to express their love through small, meaningful gestures. They like to create surprises. They like to do different, creative kinds of things.

❋ Focus on your natural style, but don't stay stuck in it. Experiment with the style that's a little foreign to you. It will stretch your repertoire, and your lover will probably appreciate an occasional change of pace.

"When you express your anger constructively,
you make room for affection."

~ Jay Uhler

Do you know how to be affectionate without being sexual? Do you know how to be assertive without being aggressive? Do you know how to give without giving-in?

Before the Romance Class began one evening, someone had written this on the blackboard, without giving its author. I assume it's either by that great, prolific writer Anonymous, or by the class member who wishes to remain incognito. I hope you don't mind if I share it with the world:

> *We express friendship and respect always.*
> *We are affectionate often and regularly.*
> *We make love at special times.*

I've asked *thousands* of people over the years why they're not more affectionate with their partners. ✦ Men tend to say "Affection is 'kid stuff'—it's fine while dating, but we're adults now," or "What *exactly* do you mean by 'affection'?" Women tend to say "I'm afraid he'll interpret all of my affectionate gestures as a prelude to sex." ✦ Do you think you're affectionate enough? Do you think your partner is affectionate enough? What does your partner think? ✦ In most relationships, it's a relatively easy matter to generate more affection simply by talking about it.

Homework: Clarifying Some Terms

It will help your partner tremendously if you clarify what the differences are—*for you*—between these words and phrases.

➢ What's the difference between *affection* and *courtesy*?
➢ What's the difference between *sexuality* and *sensuality*?
➢ What's the difference between *having sex* and *making love*?
➢ What's the difference between *talking* and *communicating*?
➢ What's the difference between *assertiveness* and *aggressiveness*?

Resources

☆ *This Is My Beloved*, by Walter Benton
☆ *A Time for Caring: How to Enrich Your Life Through an Interest and Pleasure in Others*, by George Back & Laura Torbet
☆ *For Each Other: Sharing Sexual Intimacy*, by Lonnie Barbach

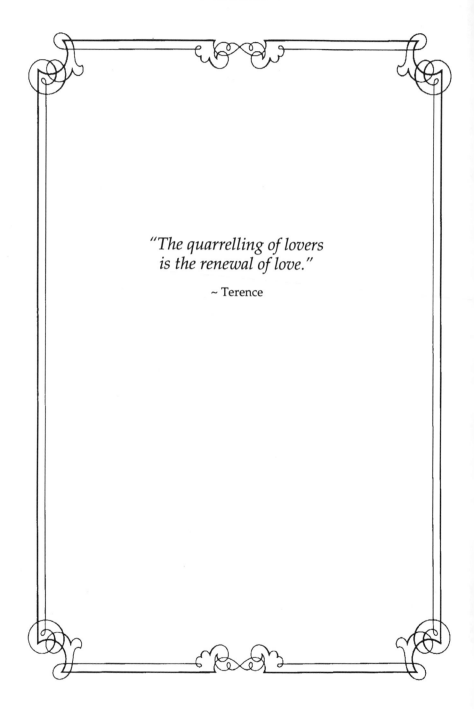

*"The quarrelling of lovers
is the renewal of love."*

~ Terence

Arguing

A young woman in the Romance Class declares, "My fiance and I have a *great* relationship—we've *never* had an argument!" Godek's infallible crystal ball reveals that either she's lying, or this couple is afraid to face-up to the difficult, complex and painful issues that all of us must deal with, or they just have an immature or shallow relationship. [Either this, or these folks are actually the world's first Perfect Couple. A rare species, never actually observed or captured.] ✦ Granted, early in a relationship, you may experience no conflict. Infatuation is a wonderful period in which you both bask in the delightful feeling that you're just *perfect* for each other! ✦ All healthy people argue. We all come into conflict: Our ideas, desires, needs, hopes, etc. If you don't argue, I guarantee that one of you is holding back.

A common trap is to start viewing your partner as an enemy, a competitor; someone you don't trust. You must have *mutual goodwill* in order for any arguments, fights or simple disagreements to have a chance of being resolved, much less leading to intimacy.

Homework: What Bugs You?

↦ List five things that bug you about your partner.
↦ Now, toss-out that list, and write-down the five things that *really* bother you about him or her.—The things that you've swept under the rug; the things that, for whatever reason, are difficult to deal with.
↦ Choose one of these items—just *one*, hear me?!—and talk with your partner about it.
↦ Rules: No blaming. No raised voices. No arguing about who's right and who's wrong.

Many people find it insightful and comforting to see that all of their arguments fit into certain patterns that we all share. An excellent book called *The Seven Basic Quarrels of Marriage* offers explanation and help. According to authors William Betcher and Robie Macauley, these are the seven quarrels: 1) Gender, 2) Loyalties, 3) Money, 4) Power, 5) Sex, 6) Privacy, and 7) Children.

What's your *style* **of fighting?** You won't get a fair fight if you put a boxer and a Sumo wrestler in the ring together. You also won't get a fair fight if your style of arguing differs radically from your partner's. What's an unfair fight? You argue; she bursts into tears. You scream at the top of your lungs; she remains calm and understanding. You're totally emotional; she's totally rational. ✦ Now, realistically, you're probably not going to match your partner's style perfectly. But being aware of your different styles will help you get through your difficulties. ✦ Another difference in style can be each person's tolerance for misunderstanding, and the desire to settle the argument. Some people *hate* to be in the midst of any misunderstanding or argument. They often give-in before things have really been resolved, or they patch things up prematurely. Other people need to discuss every nuance. ✦ Yet another difference is our speed of "recovery." Some people bounce back pretty quickly. They can be fighting one minute and kissing the next. Other people need time to digest an argument, time to cool off. They probably need some time alone before they can be civil with their partners. Neither way is right or wrong.

FYI: Rules for Fighting Fair

- ♠ *Stick to the issue.* Don't drag in every problem you can think of.
- ♠ *Stay in the **present**.* Don't drag in the past!
- ♠ *Say what you feel when you feel it.*
- ♠ *Don't generalize* ("You always . . ." "You're just like your mother . . .")
- ♠ *No threatening allowed.* (Either verbally or physically.)
- ♠ *Absolutely, positively **no violence**.* (Men: Not even the *slightest* touch. Women: This includes slapping his face.)
- ♠ *State your needs as specific requests for different behavior.*
- ♠ *Work toward resolution.* Don't escalate the fight.

Some good news: Arguments and disagreements are *not* necessarily signs that your relationship is bad or that your love is fading. It's all in *how* you practice the Art of Arguing. For some couples, arguing is a sign that each person is expressing his or her individuality—a healthy thing. For others, arguing is a substitute for true communicating. How can you tell the difference? Ask yourself: 1) Are we having the same argument we've had over and over again? 2) Do our arguments "spiral upwards" toward solutions and intimacy, or "spiral downwards" toward stalemate and bitterness?

One of the dumbest things people say: "You're *just not the same person* I married 20 years ago!" Good Lord, let's *hope* he/she's not the same inexperienced, insecure person he was way back then! Change and growth are *supposed* to happen.

FYI: Behind-the-Scenes

✳ Arguing about money is rarely about money. It's about *power.*
✳ Arguing about sex is rarely about sexuality. It's about *intimacy.*
✳ Arguing about chores is rarely about the chores. It's about *fairness.*
✳ Arguing about the kids is rarely about the kids. It's about *control.*
✳ Arguing about jealousy is rarely about fidelity. It's about *maturity.*
✳ Arguing about work is rarely about the work. It's about *time.*
✳ Arguing about relatives is rarely about them. It's about *expectations.*

News Flash! "Nasty marital arguments—especially those knock-down drag-out fights—can be hazardous to couples' health." ✦ A recent study by the Ohio State University Medical Center shows that "the more negative behaviors displayed while arguing, the more the immune system is affected." Among those negatives are sarcasm, put-downs, interruptions, excuses and denying responsibility.

Note: Myths and Other Fallacies

➤ "Nice girls don't get angry."
➤ Couples who never argue are stronger than those who do.
➤ Anger ignored will simply go away.
➤ My rage is so strong that it will blow my partner away.

Resources

☆ *From Conflict to Caring: An In-Depth Program for Creating Loving Relationships,* by Jordan & Margaret Paul
☆ *The Intimate Enemy,* by George Bach & Peter Wyden
☆ *We Can Work It Out: Making Sense Of Marital Conflict,* by Clifford I. Notarius and Howard J. Markman
☆ *If You Could Hear What I Cannot Say,* by Nathaniel Branden

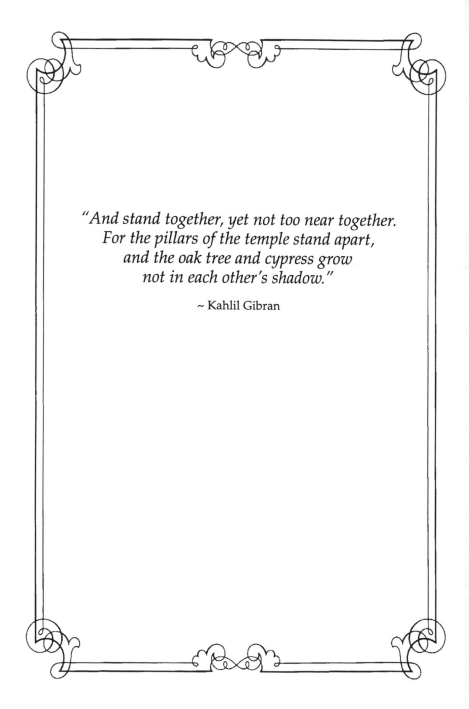

"And stand together, yet not too near together.
For the pillars of the temple stand apart,
and the oak tree and cypress grow
not in each other's shadow."

~ Kahlil Gibran

Balancing

Do you remember those guys on the *Ed Sullivan Show* who balanced 300 spinning dishes on wobbly poles while riding a unicycle and juggling 15 bowling balls all at the same time? That's what relationships are like.

FYI: Your Balancing Act

How you choose to spend your time and energy determines the quality of your life. Are you aware of

* Independence & interdependence
* Fear & love
* Togetherness & solitude
* Responsibility & fun
* Time & money
* Family & friends
* Desires & wants & needs
* Commitment & freedom
* Work & play
* Strengths & weaknesses
* Giving & taking
* Competition & cooperation
* Control & letting-go
* Forcing & flowing
* Power & sharing
* Values & expectations

Why strive for balance at all? What's wrong with having an imbalance of power in a relationship? Why can't one person be the logical one while the other is the emotional one? ✦ Why? Because things simply work *better* when they're balanced! This isn't Godek's Rule . . . it's a Law of Nature, or something like that. ✦ 1) Imbalanced things get stuck—like when a fat kid gets on the teeter-totter. 2) Non-moving things lose their balance and fall down—like a child's spinning top. 3) Imbalanced things are unhealthy—like a diet comprised of carbohydrates and nothing else. ✦ Imbalanced realtionships often fail. Sometimes one person is happy, while the other is miserable. Imbalanced relationships develop unhealthy undercurrents. "Head games" and guerilla warfare often result. Yes, it's true that many unbalanced relationships last a lifetime. But are those lives happy, exciting, creative, passionate, fulfilled?

Note: A Question of Balance

→ Do you balance *your* needs with your *partner's* needs?
→ Do you balance the needs of your *relationship* with each of your *individual* needs?
→ Do you balance your *personal* life, *professional* life and *social* life?
→ Do you balance your *emotional* needs with your *practical/logical* needs?
→ Do you balance your short-term needs and your long-term goals?
→ Do you balance your *emotional, spiritual* and *physical* needs?

The most basic concepts we have to balance in our lives are *Yes* and *No*— what you say *yes* to, and what you say *no* to. For example, in our everyday lives many of these yes/no decisions involve balancing assertiveness and aggressiveness. It's not easy—for any of us. ✦ Assertiveness is a tricky concept, one that deserves more respect and more practice. It is often difficult to be assertive without also being angry, or without the assertiveness turning into aggression. ✦ The problem, you see, is that very often we need the power of our anger to push us into being assertive. I think this is fine at the outset, because if you're not used to asserting yourself, you'll need that extra kick that anger provides. Anger can empower you! Anger can help affirm you! But you can only use your anger for so long to help you out. This is part of the reason why assertiveness is a hard skill to learn. It's deceptively easy to let loose with your anger and call it "assertiveness." ✦ In our culture at this time, women are making great strides toward claiming their assertiveness. Yes, I know that many men still react defensively, but keep it up, ladies! However, I feel a need to add some balance to this discussion by reminding you that not all men are assertive, either! Let's watch those stereotypes, okay? 'Nuff said.

Homework: A Balancing Exercise

✳ Just how balanced *is* your life? Let's be analytical for a moment.
  ❑ Grab a pad and pen. Write a list with these headings:
    1) Work, 2) Sleep, 3) Chores, 4) Parenting, 5) Recreation,
    6) Community, 7) Meals, 8) TV, 9) Personal Projects, 10) Other.
  ❑ Add up the number of hours you spend on each activity *per week*.
  ❑ Are you surprised by how much time you spend on any of them?
  ❑ How does your list compare with your partner's list?
  ❑ What are you satisfied with—and what would you like to change?
  ❑ Brainstorm some strategies for creating a new balance in your life.

"When I think of balance, I think 'boring'," challenged Gary G., in one Romance Class. [There's one in every crowd!] ✦ Gary was focusing on *outer* balance instead of *inner* balance. His interpretation of balance in his life was to make sure the scales were balanced between himself and his wife. This mindset causes problems because it puts unreasonable expectations on your partner; because you give-away your own responsibility and power in the relationship; and because it promotes scarcity-thinking instead of abundance-thinking. When you're focused on balancing the scales, you never really give much, because you're always waiting and wondering if your partner will want to, or be able to, match your effort. The net result of this kind of thinking is a boring, flat life. ✦ Here's the way out: Shift your view of "balance." Don't strive to balance the *relationship*—strive instead to balance *yourself*. If you're centered, secure and strong, you'll be better able to give love and express yourself freely. Those who are balanced internally are not only better able to withstand life's ups and downs, they are able and willing to create their *own* thrills! And part of what romance is all about is keeping the thrill in your relationship!

Balance is a dynamic process—it's not a static state.

In order to balance, you must be *flexible*. You must be able and willing to choose from a variety of responses and options. Rigid, dogmatic people who are fearful of change aren't very good at balancing. They strive for a steady state; what they achieve is boredom. They insist on the status quo; what they get is mediocrity. ✦ Flexible people are able to go with the flow. They embrace change and welcome spontaneity.

Resources
☆ *Parallel Lives*, by Phyllis Rose
☆ *Peace of Mind*, by Joshua Liebman
☆ *The Anatomy of Relationships*, by M. Argyle & M. Henderson
☆ *Flow: The Psychology of Optimal Experience*, by M. Csikszentmihalyi

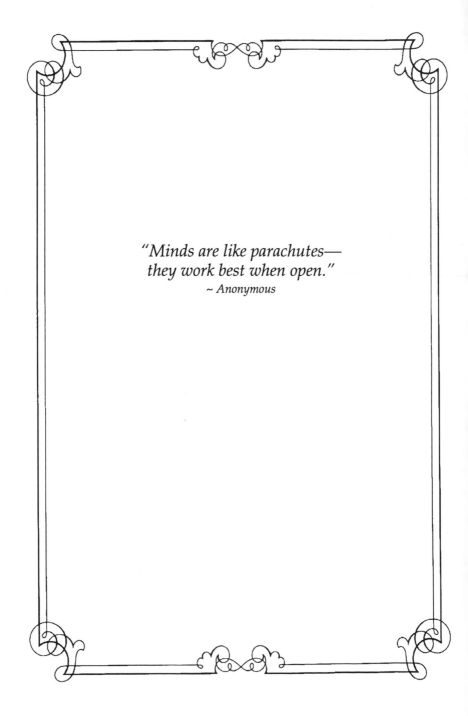

*"Minds are like parachutes—
they work best when open."*
~ Anonymous

Brainstorming

Brainstorming: A process of focused fantasy, in which your natural playfulness is released by suspending judgment—leading to a free flow of creative ideas.

Note: A "Romantic Brainstorming Party"

❖ You can certainly brainstorm by yourself—but it's more fun, and often more productive, when you do it with others. Include your lover. Include your friends. Why not hold a "Romantic Brainstorming Party"?!

❖ Here's the set up:
- ❏ You need a comfortable space and a few hours of uninterrupted time.
- ❏ A flip chart or large pads of paper and a tripod.
- ❏ And lots of colored markers.
- ❏ And smaller pads of paper and markers for each participant.
- ❏ Food! You need food and drink to fuel this process!

❖ Here are some guidelines:
- ○ Choose one person to be the facilitator. He or she is in charge of keeping the process going—without directing or controlling the flow—and is the official scribe, in charge of recording ideas on the pads.
- ○ The one key Rule in brainstorming is: No judging, no criticisms, and no value judgments are allowed! No idea is too silly, stupid, unrealistic or impractical to be mentioned and recorded.
- ○ Laughing, joking and general silliness are strongly encouraged.
- ○ Build on each other's ideas. Use them as springboards to additional ideas.
- ○ The goal is to generate ideas—*lots* of ideas! When you're through, the walls should be covered with dozens of sheets full of ideas!

❖ To begin the brainstorming, the facilitator asks the group to come up with a question to guide the session. For example:
- ❏ "How can we keep romance in our relationship forever?"
- ❏ "How can we make more time for each other?"

❖ Brainstorm for two to four hours. Take five-minute breaks every 1.5 hours. If you can eat and think at the same time, do so!

❖ The *last* step in brainstorming is to choose three of the best ideas from the hundreds you've generated. Brainstorm different ways to turn these crazy ideas into practical and affordable plans.

FYI: Brainstorming Strategies

Romantic ideas are *not* hard to come up with! These tips will help focus your efforts and give you some direction.

☞ **Playfulness**. If you're not having fun, you're doing it wrong! Creativity is stymied by too much seriousness, and released by a playful spirit.

☞ **Volume!** The more ideas you generate, the better chance you'll have of coming up with a great one.

☞ **Avoid logic!** Ideas are often generated by intuitive leaps, emotional responses and paradoxical thinking.

☞ **Don't rush!** Don't be in a hurry to find "The" answer, or the best-of-all-possible ideas. The best ideas often turn-up later in the process!

☞ **Look elsewhere**. If you look in the same old places, you'll find the same old things. Read different magazines. Shop in different stores.

☞ **Time**. Give yourself enough time to think! Yes, sometimes we work well under deadlines, but the best ideas take time to incubate.

☞ **Role play**. How would a person of the opposite sex approach this challenge? How would Einstein view it? Cleopatra? Bill Cosby? Elvis?

☞ **Sleep on it**. And then pay attention to your dreams. Very often our unconscious minds will generate some fabulous ideas!

☞ **5 senses**. View the question through several different senses. If you're a *visual* person, "hear" the problem; "feel" the challenge.

☞ **Unlearn**. What you already know may block some creative avenues that you'd never consider exploring. Challenge your assumptions!

☞ **Draw it**. Grab a pad and pen—or better yet, some crayons!—and *draw* the problem. Draw some solutions. You don't have to be artistic!

☞ **Wrong answers**. Look for wrong answers and stupid ideas—on purpose! Very often they are the flip-side of great ideas and clever solutions.

☞ **Laugh!** A humorous frame of mind enhances creativity. Funny things are often those that juxtapose unusual things—a great help in creativity.

☞ **Analogies**. Look for analogies in unrelated areas: Nature, history, sports, architecture, movies, fashion, food, computers, children, politics.

☞ **Paradoxes!** Can you hold two different and contradictory ideas about the same thing in your head at the same time? It will enhance creativity.

☞ **Intuition**. Do you pay attention to your "hunches"? Can you sense when an idea "feels right"? Practice listening to your "Inner Voice."

FYI: From a Romance Class Brainstorming Session

Greg: Speaking of *time*—how do we keep track of it?

Barb: Clocks and watches.

Linda: Calendars, too! Watches keep track of the short-term. Calendars are for the long-term.

Greg: How might we use these "time-trackers" as romantic tools?

John: Set your watch to buzz every hour, as a reminder to tell your partner "I love you!"

Gary: Cover the faces of all the clocks in the house with notes saying "Time for love!"

Kristin: Write-in your birthday and anniversary dates in his business calendar.

Warren: And write a *reminder note* in the calendar one week ahead of the date—so he has some advance notice!

Judy: How about getting one of those poster-sized wall calendars that you can write on . . . and plan-out some romantic activities months in advance.

Kevin: Yeah! It not only would help you plan better, but it will be a visual reminder of things you'll be looking forward to.

Pete: I'd mark-in some "Mystery Dates."

Marisa: I'd create a secret code that only my husband and I could understand—so the kids wouldn't know what we're up to!

Steve: That's *great* for planning "Lovemaking Dates"!

"Discovery consists of looking at the same thing as everyone else and thinking something different."

~ Roger von Oech

Resources

☆ *A Whack on the Side of the Head: How You Can Be More Creative*, by Roger von Oech

☆ *Thinkertoys: A Handbook of Business Creativity for the 90s*, by Michael Michalko

☆ *Intuition*, by R.B. Fuller

☆ *New Think: The Use of Lateral Thinking*, by E. DeBono

☆ *The Artist's Way*, by Julia Cameron

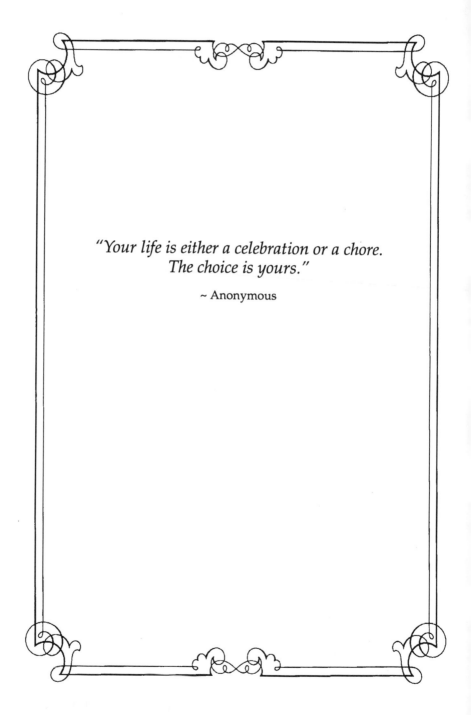

"Your life is either a celebration or a chore.
The choice is yours."

~ Anonymous

Celebrating

Romance *itself*— being the expression of love—is, in fact, a celebration. Romance isn't a chore, a responsibility or something imposed on you from outside. Romance is a celebration of the life you live as part of a couple. It springs naturally and joyfully from inside of you . . . *if* you'll give it access to your creative energies.

Have you ever yelled, at the top of your lungs, *"I LOVE YOU!"* to your lover? Try it. It's exhilarating. ✦ Try it indoors. Try it outdoors. Try it on a roller coaster. Try it while singing at a Karaoke bar. Try it on a mountain top, for the echo effect!

Romance is the appreciation of two people who are celebrating the lucky coincidence that they found each other.

Not only are you and your lover unique—your *relationship* is unique. Yes, of *course* you follow some universal and predictable patterns—some are pre-programmed biological/sexual patterns and some are cultural patterns—but you and your partner take all of these factors like clay and form your own new and unique creation. ✦ Sounds like reason enough to celebrate to me!

Don't wait for some *reason* to celebrate. The fact that you're alive and reasonably healthy, fairly good-looking, adequately wealthy—and *fabulously* in love are reasons enough to celebrate! ✦ The calendar is full of dates when you're supposed to celebrate. True romantics create their own calendars, and celebrate whenever their hearts are singing.

Idea: For Celebrating Award-Winning Lovers
Does she deserve a Blue Ribbon for staying by your side through thick and thin? Should he be awarded a Loving Cup for being a great lover? How about a trophy on your anniversary or a plaque for a birthday? ✦ Call for a catalog full of ideas from the Emblem & Badges Company: 800-875-4444.

When you see the poetry in your relationship, then you'll truly see what you have to celebrate. You don't need to be a *poet* in order to live poetically. You just have to see the beauty in the little things; appreciate every moment for what it has to offer; feel your feelings for your lover with all the intensity of your heart; and strive always for the awareness of your connection to all things. ✦ Veronica Hay celebrates life and love through here words. I'd like to share a few of them with you:

Passion

*The difference between a job and a **career***
*The difference between an actor and a **star***
*The difference between a song and a **symphony***
*The difference between a painting and a **work of art***
*The difference between caring and **intimacy***
*The difference between romance and **rapture***
*The difference between intelligence and **genius***
*The difference between living and being **alive***

From *In A Dream, You Can Do Anything, A Collection of Words*

Veronica creates wonderful hand-made books and other romantic things from her home in Calgary, Canada. Write for more info: Rebecca Ryan Resources, Highstreet Business Centre, #700, 933 Seventeenth Avenue S.W., Calgary, Alberta, Canada T2T 5R6. Or call 403-245-6815.

Note: Different Kinds of Celebrations

Not only are there many different *things* and *occasions* to celebrate, there are many different *kinds* of celebrations.

❑ Spontaneous celebrations—and planned celebrations
○ Private celebrations—and public celebrations
❑ Solemn celebrations—and joyful celebrations
○ Yearly celebrations—and once-in-a-lifetime celebrations
❑ Ritual celebrations—and spontaneous celebrations
○ Quiet celebrations—and loud celebrations
❑ Big celebrations—and little celebrations

FYI: 1001 Things To Celebrate

❖ Weekends together
❖ Sunsets
❖ You've found each other!
❖ "Your song"
❖ Snuggling in bed
❖ Christmas
❖ Your first date
❖ *The Prophet*, by Kahlil Gibran
❖ Chocolate!
❖ Hot oatmeal
❖ Summer camp for the kids
❖ Hugs
❖ Your baby's first step
❖ The first day of spring
❖ Lemonade on a hot day
❖ Hallmark
❖ Pepperoni pizza
❖ Your parents
❖ Macintosh computers
❖ America
❖ Beer
❖ Bookstores
❖ Saturday
❖ Your faith
❖ The first snowfall
❖ Puppies
❖ Carly Simon
❖ Mozart

❖ Vacations
❖ Sex
❖ Your health
❖ The way she looks into your eyes
❖ Birthdays
❖ Orange sherbet
❖ Red roses
❖ The Poconos
❖ Lingerie
❖ Charge cards
❖ Finding that missing sock
❖ Ice cream sundaes
❖ A new job
❖ Valentine's Day
❖ The Moody Blues
❖ Massages
❖ Lazy Sunday afternoons
❖ Bicycles
❖ *Casablanca*
❖ Soaking in a hot tub
❖ The mystery of life
❖ Walking barefoot
❖ Today
❖ Hershey's Kisses
❖ Pierre-Auguste Renoir
❖ Graduation
❖ Candlelit dinners
❖ Calvin & Hobbes

Resources

☆ *Live Your Dreams*, by Les Brown
☆ *Celebrate Your Self*, by Dorothy Corkville Briggs
☆ *Living, Loving & Learning*, by Leo Buscaglia
☆ *The Power Of Positive Thinking*, by N. Peale
☆ *The Pagan Book of Days: Celebrating Festivals & Sacred Days Through the Millenium*, by Nigel Pennick
☆ *Myth, Ritual & Religion*, by Andrew Lang

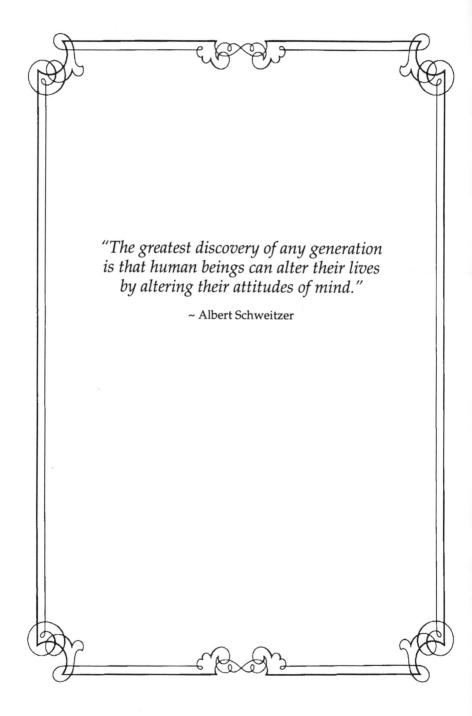

*"The greatest discovery of any generation
is that human beings can alter their lives
by altering their attitudes of mind."*

~ Albert Schweitzer

Change

"Don't ever change—I love you just the way you are!": A lovely sentiment …and an attitude guaranteed to cause untold grief later in the relationship. We *all* change! [And some of us even *grow*…but that's a different chapter.] Change is natural, change is inevitable. If our love is based on a stagnant relationship, we're setting ourselves up for failure and misery. ✦ The challenge, of course, is to change together. Notice I didn't say to "change *identically*," but *together*. If I develop a fondness for Reggae music, and you continue to prefer a little Mozart, it doesn't—or shouldn't—signal the end of our relationship! (Although some divorce cases seem to be based on such silly differences!)

You can't change another person. You can only create a climate that is *safe* for change; that is *supportive* of change; that is *patient* with the time it will take to change; that is *flexible* with the ups and downs the process will require.

Questions: Your Kind of Change

➤ How does change happen in your life?

    ✳ Is it sudden and dramatic? Or does it happen slowly, more like an evolutionary process?

    ✳ Do you *embrace* change, welcome its mystery? Or are you *stubborn*, clinging to more familiar ways?

    ✳ Does change come about through your conscious effort and action? Or does change sneak up on you like an unwanted visitor?

    ✳ Do *you* change? Or do things change around you?

Nature has conveniently created two ways in which change can come about—one for people who are "thinkers/analyzers/talkers," and one for those who are "doers/action-oriented." You can create change through 1) Insight, or 2) Action. ✦ *Insight* people respond well to discussions, insight-oriented therapy and *introspective* self-help books. *Action* people respond well to action by loved ones, behavior-modification therapy and *practical* self-help books.

Homework: Change Something!

Let's change something about your life. Something—*anything*. Let's shake up your life and see what happens. (Don't forget to take your partner along!)

✤ Get up an *hour earlier* every day this week. Now, think about what you could do with that hour . . .
  - ✢ You could make love.
  - ✢ You could lie in bed and talk with your lover.
  - ✢ You could give her a massage.
  - ✢ You could go for a walk.
  - ✢ You could cook an *awesome* breakfast.
  - ✢ You could have breakfast in bed.
  - ✢ You could read an inspirational passage aloud.
  - ✢ You could meditate or pray together.

✤ Take a half-day off work this Friday. What kind of fun could you have with your lover during that time?

✤ Trade roles with your partner this weekend. You do *her* chores, and she'll do *yours*. What else would you do differently if you were your partner?

✤ Change the way you greet each other. Do it with a passionate kiss. Greet each other in French. Or simply slow down . . . hold hands and gaze into each other's eyes silently.

One mistake that people often make is to approach personal change from a purely *individual* point-of-view. They forget that any changes they make will affect their partner and the relationship, too. This is where "Couple Thinking" comes into play. You've got to remember that you're part of a couple; and that your actions profoundly affect your partner. ✦ I'm all for individual growth and self-discovery. In fact, it nearly *always* precedes any growth the couple may undergo. The danger here is that one partner will change far more than the other. Couples who are truly committed to *staying* together attempt to *change* together. Of course, the two of you are not always going to be in perfect sync. That's not the point. I'm merely promoting "togetherness" in our growth processes. [And if your partner refuses to come along for the ride, refuses to join you in couples counseling, or actively resists *your* changes, I say leave him or her behind. You have a Life to live!]

Don't change! That is, don't change just to suit someone else. Now, keep in mind that we all must *compromise* and *adjust* in a relationship. But you shouldn't try to change yourself into someone else for the sake of "love." If your partner can't accept you without some major change, I suggest you change *partners* instead.

Tips: Do's & Don'ts

☛ Don't nag. Don't whlne. Don't criticize.
☞ *Do* ask for specific changes in behavior.
☛ Don't be vague about your desired changes.
☞ *Do* make constructive suggestions.
☛ Don't try to make your partner feel guilty.
☞ *Do* offer to take the first step.

There are many different ways to approach the challenge of making change happen in your life. ✦ One way is to focus on the desired changes themselves. *Another* way is to focus on the things that block you or interfere with the accomplishment of your goals. Another way is to focus specifically on the *behavior* you want to change. Another way is to focus on the *psychological motivations* for your behavior. Another way is to ask for help—whether from your lover, your friends, or a counselor. Another way is to research and read about possible solutions. Another way is to join some kind of support group. Another way is to embark on a "crash course" to bring about quick change. Another way is to allow slow, evolutionary change to take place. Another way is to impose a structure to help discipline yourself. Another way is to let change come about naturally and organically. ✦ How do you know which way is best for you? You *don't!* You have to explore and experiment.

Resources

☆ *Helping Couples Change: A Social Learning Approach to Marital Therapy,* by Richard Stuart
☆ *Pathfinders: Overcoming the Crises of Adult Life and Finding Your Own Path to Well-Being,* by Gail Sheehy
☆ *Step by Step: A Guide to Creating Change for Families,* by Virginia Satir & Michele Baldwin
☆ *The New Male-Female Relationship,* by Herb Goldberg
☆ *Phoenix,* by Meribeth Anderson and David Gordon

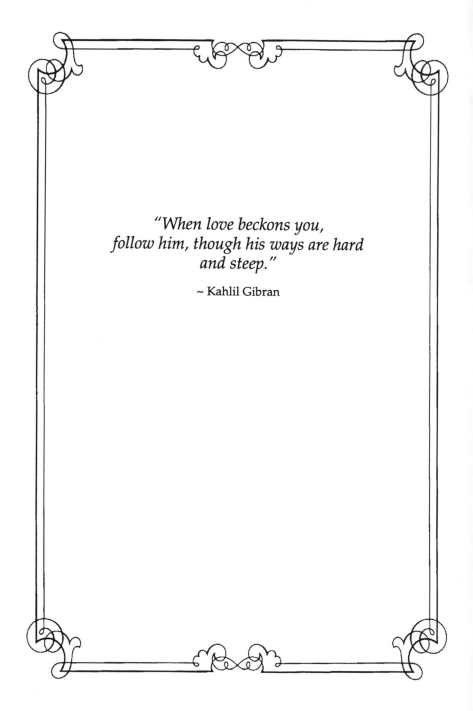

*"When love beckons you,
follow him, though his ways are hard
and steep."*

~ Kahlil Gibran

Commitment

"Dear Greg . . . I came within an inch of throwing away my 25-year marriage last year. We'd been fighting a lot, I was away on business, and I thought, *What the hell, I'm going to the bar and see if I can get lucky.* As I headed out my hotel door I paused to remove my wedding ring. It took me nearly five minutes to get it off. As I fought with the damn thing, it occurred to me that I had *never had that ring off my finger in 25 years.* I stood in the doorway holding that ring. Thinking about how the good times far outweighed the bad times. I went back inside, sat on the bed and cried. I then called my wife, told her I'd be home a day early, and that if she couldn't find a babysitter for the kids for the entire day, that I was going to sell them to the circus . . . I heard you on the radio last night, and thought my story might make it into one of your future books." {Special thanks to C.T. & G.T.}

Ideas: Showing Commitment

* Memorize your wedding vows.
* Tattoo a ring on your finger. {Jim C., of Cincinnati, Ohio, has a tattooed wedding band!}
* Write a love letter that describes all the reasons you're committed to your lover and to your relationship.
* Create your own unique rituals. (See the Rituals chapter.)

There is a key difference between making a commitment to a *relationship* and making a commitment to *anything else*. With anything else, your commitment is an individual, solitary decision. You make a commitment to excellence in your work; you make a commitment to serve our country in the armed forces.   ✦   But when you make a commitment to a *relationship*, it's a *joint* decision. Either you *both* agree, or you don't *really* have a relationship—you have one person believing in a fantasy, and one person withholding or wandering off.

Commitment requires daily renewal. A promise kept, an action made, over and over and over and over and over again.

We all make many emotional commitments, or "emotional contracts" with one another. We depend on each other to be there when we're in need; we promise to listen with love; we plan to share "the good times and the bad." ✦ Emotional contracts are fine—*if* they're clear, understood by both partners, and realistic. Problems arise when our contracts are unrealistic, unhealthy, or when they are *unspoken* contracts. ✦ *Unrealistic* contracts include "I'll be understanding *all the time* if you'll be strong *all the time*." *Unspoken* contracts include "I'll support you economically if you'll support me emotionally." Unhealthy contracts are those that create co-dependency; they promote the belief that each of you is responsible for the other's happiness. ✦ Healthy emotional contracts can only be entered into by two mature, independent, loving and equal people who freely choose to join their lives together. To the extent that any of those factors are missing, damaged or incomplete, your emotional contract will be weak or full of loopholes. ✦ It is critically important for the long-term success of your relationship to bring your unspoken contracts into the open. Tracey and I know from personal experience how difficult and threatening this can be. We also know how rewarding it can be!

Exercise: Emotional Contracts

➤ Pad and paper poised?
➤ List at least five emotional contracts that you have with your partner.
  ✳ Label them "Spoken" or "Unspoken."
➤ Compare lists with your partner.
➤ How many *different* contracts do you have listed?
➤ Do you each agree with the contracts on your partner's list?
➤ Are you surprised/angered/resentful/amused by any of your contracts?
➤ Which contracts are *good*? These, you'll keep.
➤ Which contracts need modification/re-negotiation?
➤ Which contracts are just plain *bad*? (Those that harm, demean, demoralize or devalue either one of you?)
➤ Make time to discuss and re-negotiate these contracts. Handle them with care—they're very emotionally-charged.

One guy whispering to another in the Romance Class, when they thought I wasn't listening: "Yeah, we're committed. *I'm* committed to putting up with her, and *she's* committed to making my life miserable." ✦ We reassigned him to the beginners' class.

How can you be committed to your wedding vows
*if you don't even **remember** your wedding vows?*

One couple in the Romance Class was terribly distraught when we talked about wedding vows, because they couldn't remember their vows (and they'd only been married for a year).   ✦   We came up with a great, creative solution: They wrote *new* vows! Actually, we only *started* the process in the class. They wrote to me several months later explaining that they enjoyed the exercise so much that they'd decided to make it an *ongoing* process. They sit down together every two weeks and re-read, edit, and add to their vows. They're also planning a re-dedication marriage ceremony for their fifth anniversary!

How do you make a marriage last for half a century or more? *Commitment!* A recent PBS documentary called "For Better or For Worse" illustrated this well, as it took an intimate look at five couples who have been together for more than 50 years. Catch it on reruns if you can.   ✦   Some quotes from the show: "We allow ourselves to be ourselves—which isn't very civilized, perhaps. But we're *we*." "Almost from the very beginning, we both had the same kind of ideal." "We don't go to sleep at night without saying we love each other."

Resources

☆ *Challenge of the Heart*, by J. Wedgewood
☆ *Pairing*, by G. Bach and R. Deutsch
☆ *The Art of Staying Together*, by Michael Broder

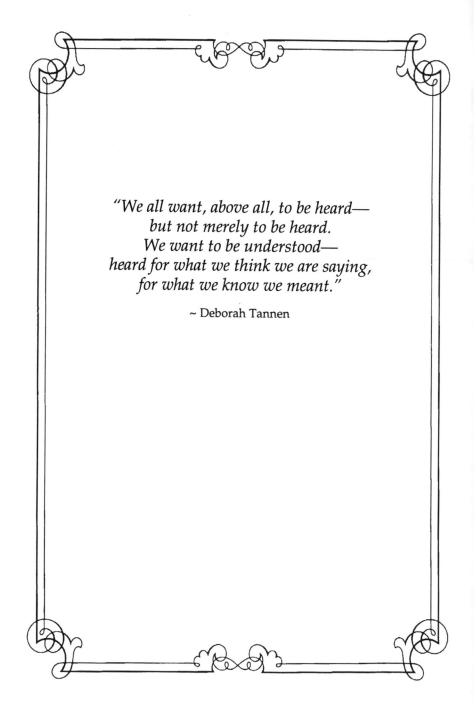

"We all want, above all, to be heard—
but not merely to be heard.
We want to be understood—
heard for what we think we are saying,
for what we know we meant."

~ Deborah Tannen

Communicating

Today's lesson is "Communicating." In *three easy steps* I'm going to teach you *everything* you'll ever need to know about communicating effectively with your partner—and achieve everlasting bliss. [. . . And if you believe *that*, I've got a bridge in Brooklyn I'd like to sell you.] ✦ Communicating *isn't* easy! There are *whole books* written on this one subject (and a few of them are even worth reading). It's a big topic, worthy of serious study; one that takes lifelong practice. So let's be realistic, shall we?—We'll explore some important aspects of communicating, but we're not going to wrap it into a neat-and-easy package.

Note: Let's clarify a few things

➤ When I say "communicating," I mean "communicating *effectively*."
➤ Talking isn't necessarily communicating. (Got that, guys?)
➤ Sharing feelings isn't necessarily communicating. (Got that, gals?)
➤ *How* you say what you say is just as important as *what* you say.
➤ Half of communicating is *listening*. [And I don't mean "*just* listening"—I mean *active, reflective* listening.]
➤ *Communicating* in an intimate relationship is 10% about relating facts, and 90% about relating feelings. ("Head-to-head" communicating vs. "heart-to-heart" communicating.)

Exercise: Repeat After Me . . .

I know you've all heard this before, but it really, *really* works: When communication starts to break-down, *switch roles*—repeat back to your partner what he or she is saying. This effort accomplishes several things. It will slow both of you down. It will help straighten-out misinterpretations between the two of you. It will start to generate understanding—if not empathy—for the other person's point-of-view. "Walking a mile in another's shoes" is simple but powerful advice. ✦ This exercise works best when you refrain from judging your partner's motives; from adding in your own editorial comments; from playing "Yes-but . . ."

It is becoming increasingly apparent that men and women have different communication styles. A number of books do an excellent job of exploring this topic. I believe that most of us have a lot to learn in this area. But I do have one little warning to sound. ✦ Let's be careful of stereotyping one another, and of viewing the communication styles along gender lines only. It is *not* true that all men view communicating as a power struggle; and it is *not* true that all women value relationship-building over information transfer. I've had many Romance Class participants express great indignation that they were being categorized. Especially the guys. They resent the implication that they are being "feminine" when they express feelings or sensitivity. {"If somebody tells me I'm being *feminine* when I'm gentle and loving with my four-year-old son, I'll *pound them into the ground!*" Steve P., Boston} ✦ As far as I can tell, the line between masculine and feminine—between the yin and yang—is not sharp, definite, or unchanging.

Homework: Communication Tools

How could you use each of these items to help you communicate with your lover? Plan to use one a week. (What *other* tools can you create?)

- ❑ A *Peanuts* comic, cut from today's newspaper
- ❑ One red rose
- ❑ One daisy
- ❑ One egg
- ❑ One bottle of *Incognito* perfume
- ❑ Her favorite magazine
- ❑ A toolbox
- ❑ A bicycle
- ❑ An Elvis postage stamp
- ❑ A calendar
- ❑ One sock
- ❑ A bookmark
- ❑ The laundry basket
- ❑ Her car
- ❑ A bag of peanut m&m's

For example: Cut-out headlines from a magazine and paste them together to form a funny message. ✦ While folding the laundry, tuck little notes in her underwear. ✦ Float rose petals in a hot tub for her.

FYI: Enemies of Communication

❥ Resentment
❥ Stereotyping your partner
❥ Withdrawal—both emotional or physical
❥ Inflexibility
❥ "Humoring her"—not really engaging your partner
❥ A superior attitude—staying "above it all"
❥ Blaming—refusing to take responsibility for your part
❥ Assuming a parental role
❥ Escalating discussions into arguments
❥ Evading important issues
❥ Leaving insufficient time
❥ Distractions (kids, phones, chores)

FYI: Friends of Communication

♥ Respect for your partner
♥ Empathy—putting yourself in your partner's shoes
♥ A good counselor/therapist/pastor
♥ Focus
♥ Adequate time
♥ Goodwill—giving your partner the benefit of the doubt
♥ An environment conducive to communicating
♥ Listening—"Active listening" and "Listening with your heart"
♥ Eye contact and physical contact

FYI: A Quiz

✛ Communication fosters: a) Intimacy, b) Higher phone bills,
   c) More problems than it solves, d) Respect and understanding.
✛ Intimacy is at its greatest when: a) Making love, b) Disclosing feelings,
   c) You're dating, d) You've been together for years.
✛ Men express feelings: a) With difficulty, b) During commercials only,
   c) Once in a Blue Moon, d) With encouragement.

Resources

☆ *A Couples' Guide to Communication*, by John Gottman
☆ *If You Could Hear What I Cannot Say*, by Nathaniel Branden
☆ *Passage To Intimacy*, by Lori H. Gordon
☆ *You Just Don't Understand*, by Deborah Tannen
☆ *Men Are From Mars, Women Are From Venus*, by John Gray

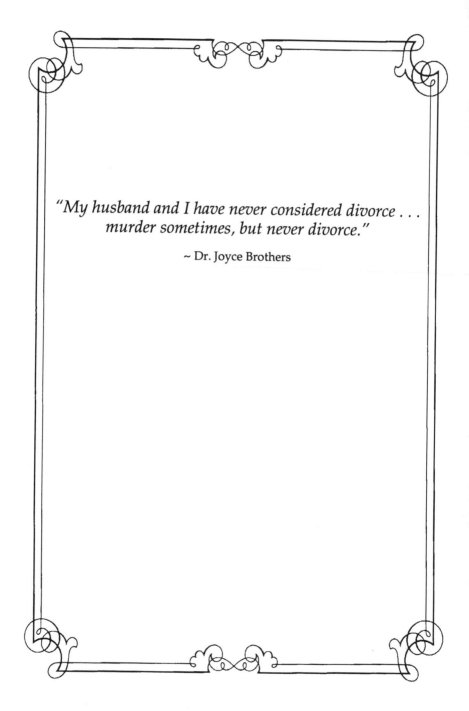

"My husband and I have never considered divorce . . . murder sometimes, but never divorce."

~ Dr. Joyce Brothers

Compromise

Compromise. It almost sounds like a *dirty word*, doesn't it? I nearly changed the name of this chapter to "Cooperation" in an effort to be more gentle about the topic—but I decided that the emotional impact of the word "compromise" would make the lesson more interesting. ✦ Who wants to *compromise*? *Nobody*! It feels like losing, doesn't it? Usually, when two people compromise on something, they both feel like they're losing. If this happens, you're using a bad model of what compromising is. The "Win-Lose" model may work in the outside world, but it wreaks havoc inside intimate relationships. In fact, what often happens when one partner insists on a "Win-Lose" model is that you end up with a "Lose-Lose" situation! ✦ The "Win-Win" model is the only one that promotes healthy relationships.

*When **one** person compromises, he loses.*
*When **two** people compromise, you both win.*

Perhaps a "Vocabulary Lesson" would help. The *Random House Dictionary* defines compromise as "a settlement of differences by *mutual* concessions; an agreement reached by . . . *reciprocal* modification of demands." [Italics are mine.] Compromise is either a two-way street, or one of you gets run over. ✦ When you compromise you don't make demands of your partner, you make requests. When you compromise, you do so from a base of trust and goodwill. Otherwise, you're not really engaging in compromise, but in a negotiation. It's the difference between a couple compromising, and a divorced couple negotiating.

*The goal of **negotiating** is to get as much as you can for yourself.*
*Whereas the goal of **compromising** is to give as much as you get.*

In order to compromise successfully, you must have four conditions: 1) A sense of fairness, 2) A clear idea of what you want, 3) An understanding of what your partner wants, and 4) A desire to create a win-win solution.

Compromising with your lover is unlike compromising and negotiating with anyone else in the world. Why? Because there are not just two parties involved, there are *three*. There's *you* and *me*—and *us*. "Us" is a third "entity" that comes into being when a "me" and a "you" decide to become a couple. ✦ When you're compromising in your relationship, there's more at stake than *my* happiness, or *your* desires. There's also what's best for the *relationship* to be considered. When the *relationship* wins, *you both win*. If you don't feel that way, it's an indication that your commitment to the relationship isn't as strong as you'd thought it was.

Homework: Identifying Core Issues

When you and your partner are faced with a difficult issue that requires compromise:

➤ Discover who feels the most strongly about the issue. It will rarely be a 50/50 situation. This gives you a place to start. It does not mean that the person who feels less strongly automatically gives-in!

➤ Consider the trade-offs that you could make: "I'll do this for you, if you'll do that for me."

➤ Maintain an attitude of fairness and equality.

➤ In the middle of your negotiating, trade roles temporarily. What insights does this generate?

  ❐ You can only do this if you truly have your partner's best interests at heart.

  ❐ This is where compromising with your lover differs from negotiating a business deal. The mindset and trust level are totally different.

Compromising isn't the same thing as "giving in"! [There's an audible sigh from the guys in the Romance Class when I say this.] However, it sometimes *does* involve delayed gratification. But mature adults are supposed to be able to deal with delayed gratification. (In fact, some experts feel that the ability to responsibly handle delayed gratification is the key defining attribute of maturity!)

Overheard in the hallway before the Romance Class:
"Cooperate—*Do it my way!*"

"My wife and I used to argue quite a lot until we learned that I'm a strawberry and she's a grape," announced one fellow in the Romance Class one night. In answer to our puzzled expressions he pulled out of his wallet a yellowed piece of paper that he said he's been carrying around since World War II, and he read to us . . .

> *"He who knows nothing, loves nothing.*
> *He who can do nothing understands nothing.*
> *He who understands nothing is worthless.*
> *but he who understands also loves, notices, sees . . .*
> *The more knowledge is inherent in a thing, the greater the love . . .*
> *Anyone who imagines that all fruits ripen at the same time*
> *as the strawberries knows nothing about grapes."*

~ Paracelsus

Don't compromise yourself! ✦ You can *give* yourself, *share* yourself, *extend* yourself, *express* yourself, *risk* yourself—but don't *compromise* yourself. Don't settle for less in your life. If there's one really bad trade that people commonly make, it's this: They settle for feeling neutral or empty in order to avoid feeling hurt or alone.

Resources

☆ *'Til Death Do Us Part: How Couples Stay Together*, by Jeanette C. Lauer

☆ *Getting to Yes*, by R. Fisher and W.Ury

☆ *Marriage Contracts and Couples Therapy: Hidden Forces in Intimate Relationships*, by Clifford J. Sager

☆ *The Fragile Bond*, by A. Napier

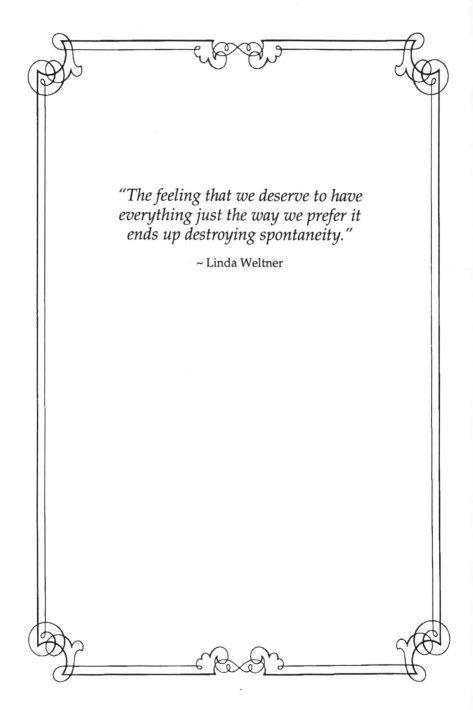

*"The feeling that we deserve to have
everything just the way we prefer it
ends up destroying spontaneity."*

~ Linda Weltner

Control

Just what *is* it you're trying to control? Yourself? Your partner? Your environment? Your future? Your family? ✦ The more I explore this concept of control, the more complex it becomes. One thing I know for sure, though: Being in control of one's self is a full-time job! Most people seem to require just about one complete lifetime in order to understand themselves, love themselves, and discover and pursue their Purpose in Life. [Pretty cool, the way the timing works out, huh?!] ✦ So what does this have to do with Romance? Just this: Too much control (of any type) squeezes the Life out of your life; it puts undue stress on your relationship; and it drives your partner away from you.

FYI: Control Strategies

Here are some strategies that people use to control one another (do you recognize anyone you know?!):

✗ Maintaining a logical stance when your partner is expressing emotion.
✗ Breaking down in tears at the first sign of disagreement.
✗ Being *parental* instead of simply *adult*.
✗ Putting your partner on a pedestal.
✗ Overwhelming your partner with anger.
✗ Feeling "above it all."
✗ Refusing to take your fair share of the blame.
✗ Being jealous.
✗ Being "nice" all the time.
✗ Knowing your partner's vulnerable spots—and pushing those buttons.

You can't control a relationship.
It's not like driving a car—It's more like flying a kite.
You have some say in where it goes, but not a lot!

Efforts to change or control your partner ultimately suffocate the true uniqueness that attracted you to her in the first place! We often take on the task of changing—"improving"—our partner. ("For her own good!" —Yeah, *right!*) Any effort to limit or control your partner diminishes her, weakens your relationship—and ultimately hurts *you.*

Homework: Who's In Control Here?

Here are some exercises to help you become more aware of your unconscious attitudes about control, and of how you as a couple deal with issues of power and control.

➤ Trade roles for a day or two. Do each other's chores. Handle each other's responsibilities. *Act* like your partner.

❖ What insights are generated?

❖ What did you *like* about being your partner? What did you *dislike*?

➤ Take turns being in control. For one entire week, *one* of you makes *all* the decisions that affect the two of you. Change roles the following week.

❖ Are you comfortable being in control?

❖ When you're *not* in control, do you worry and second-guess your partner? Or do you relax, knowing you have no responsibility?

Most couples who do these exercises come away with a heightened awareness that their relationships work better when they *share* responsibilities and control. Even the "control freaks" usually understand that they're putting tremendous pressure on themselves when they try to control everybody and everything around them.

"Love can be very *controlling*, can't it?" asked Marie M. "The power of love can be abused if you're not careful." Marie is right—kind-of. It *is* true that people in relationships can be controlling, and that we can abuse the privileges of intimacy with one another. But it's *not* true that *love* itself is controlling, or that *love* can be abused. ✦ This distinction— between "love" and our own unloving actions—is very important. If you start blaming things on love, you corrupt the very *concept* of love. ✦ That kind of thinking leads some folks to be cynical about people, relationships and life in general. It leads others to give up. It leads others to insulate themselves from the "cold, cruel world." (If you don't believe in love, it *is* a cold, cruel world! You create your own reality with your beliefs.) ✦ Love is *tremendous*. It is giving, trusting, strong, creative and dynamic. When our lives do not reflect these attributes, it is because we are falling short of love's potential. This is not to say that we are *failing*! It simply means that we are *human*. And part of what being human is all *about* is striving and reaching and falling down and picking ourselves back up and trying again and learning and laughing and screwing things up and patching them back up and moving on and doing it all again. Sounds like fun, doesn't it?

The twin issues of power and control are explosive issues, so be extra *careful* when you talk about them with your partner. The urge to assign blame and attack is hard to resist. The so-called Battle of the Sexes comes into sharp focus when power and control are discussed. When we talk about these issues in the Romance Class I usually end up playing the role of referee rather than facilitator. These are *hot* issues.   ✦   I'm *serious* when I ask people to refrain from beating each other over the head with the latest sex survey or psych book. It's so easy for us to wield information as weapons against each other. It's dangerous! ✦ Recently, one guy in the Romance Class tried to use a copy of *The Myth of Male Power* to hammer home his point that it's men—not women—who are the oppressed sex.   ✦   Now, I happen to think that psychologist Warren Farrell makes some valid points in the book. (Men have bought into a false definition of power—one that keeps us slaving at unsatisfying jobs, falling prey to stress-related diseases, and dying seven years sooner than women. Men also feel trapped by the social pressure to be tough and not express emotions.) But I think you can easily see how this material could be used to set a roomful of women aflame!   ✦   Placing blame and ranting and raving makes for entertaining TV talk shows, but it makes for *miserable* relationships. What happens is that you enjoy a short-term "victory" by "proving" that men (or women)—or *you* (not *me!*)—are to blame for whatever it is you're arguing about. This Win-Lose scenario always backfires because the "loser" either attacks later, or goes underground and wages a nasty—but effective—guerilla campaign. Is *this* what our relationships are all about?!   ✦   Don't look for a simple answer here, because there ain't one! Here's an idea, though. When you discuss power and control, first remind yourselves and each other that first and foremost, you love and respect each other. With that as a base, go at it! (*Gently.*)

Resources

☆ *Flow: The Psychology of Optimal Experience*, by M. Csikszentmihalyi
☆ *The Intimate Enemy* , by George Bach & Peter Wyden
☆ *How To Get People To Do Things*, by Robert Conklin
☆ *How To Win Friends and Influence People*, by Dale Carnegie

---

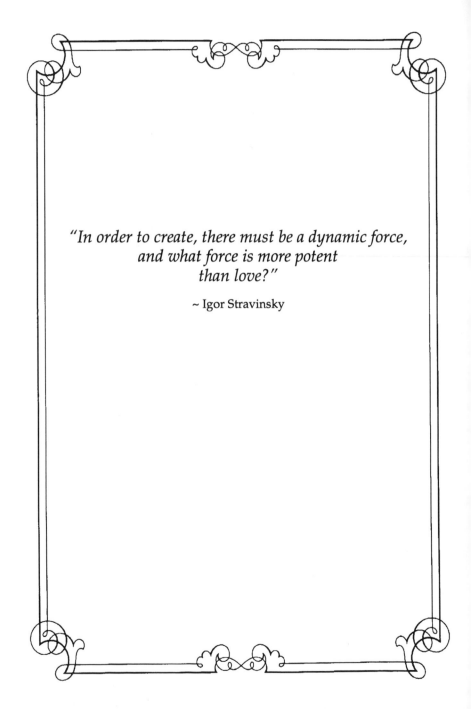

"In order to create, there must be a dynamic force, and what force is more potent than love?"

~ Igor Stravinsky

Ross,

Enjoy! And,
I hope you
don't already
have it.
Merry
Christmas.
Tana

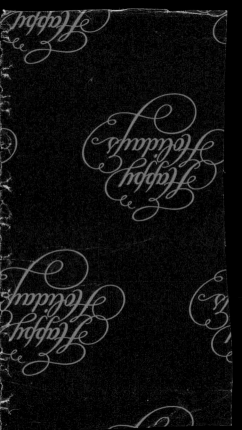

Creativity

Creativity arises out of a dynamic tension: Between freedom and discipline; between chaos and order; between old and new; between imagination and reality; between the known and the unknown; between comfort and pain; between passion and routine; between knowledge and faith. Artists are familiar with these dynamics. We—as regular folks and loving couples—could learn a thing or two from the artists among us. ✦ Relationships contain all of the tensions and challenges listed above. Re-read them with your relationship in mind. —See what I mean? Now, here's the difference between romantics and everybody else: Romantics embrace these tensions as creative challenges; others see them as problems or threats—or try to ignore them altogether. ✦ I invite you to become an artist of your relationship!

"To live a creative life, we must lose our fear of being wrong."

~ Joseph Chilton Pearce

Don't feel bad if you're not very creative. Chances are, you were never *taught* to be creative. Our educational system stresses facts and memorization over problem-solving and thinking skills. ✦ The good news is that creativity *can* be taught—nourished, encouraged and unleashed! Actually, the process of "learning" creativity is more about *unlearning* habits that limit your thinking, than it is about learning new ideas. You were *born* creative. We're simply going to dip into the immense reservoir of creativity that's inside of you.

Creativity Blockers
▼ Following the rules
▼ Looking for one right answer
▼ Logical thinking
▼ Fear of failure
▼ Fear of embarrassment
▼ Belief that you're not creative

Creativity Enhancers
▲ A playful attitude
▲ A belief that you're creative
▲ Ability to handle ambiguity
▲ Risk-taking
▲ Changing the Rules
▲ Humor

What's the biggest difference between creative people and non-creative people? It's that *creative people* **believe** *they're creative*! This has been demonstrated by numerous psychological studies. The lesson is obvious!

Ideas: Inspiration from Books

♥ After reading *The Bridges of Madison County* . . .
>   ➣ One couple in the Romance Class was inspired to take up photography.
>   ➣ Another couple decided to go on vacation to Madison County, Iowa!
>   ➣ And another couple was inspired to create their own personal fantasies based on the book! ("Quick!—Where's my camera?")

♥ After reading *Griffin and Sabine* . . .
>   ➣ You could start your own series of correspondences—either real or fictionalized!
>   ➣ You could create your own book/journal/scrapbook based on the format of *Griffin and Sabine*.
>   ➣ You could act-out the meeting of Griffin and Sabine.

A relationship is an act of creativity.
You either re-create your relationship each and every day,
or you're stuck with something old, inadequate and,
ultimately, boring.

What area of your life needs a little more creativity? Your work? Your tennis game? Your family life? Your relationship? Your sex life? ✦ If you didn't answer "All of the above," then your thinking is too narrow. The fact is that most everyone would be more effective, more efficient and more satisfied in every area of their lives if they approached things with more creativity. ✦ I've had people leave the Romance Class who were more inspired to be creative than to be romantic. Guess what? Without fail they all reported back that the more creative they were at work, the happier their home lives became. ✦ Creativity has a lot in common with love. They both are expansive, life-enhancing and expressive. They're both inborn characteristics that are intimately connected to our true selves and core personalities. To be loving is to be creative; and to be creative is to express love.

Exercises: Q&A

♥ How could you celebrate her birthday *more creatively?*
- → Hire a barbershop quartet to sing "Happy Birthday" to her.
- → Hire a "celebrity look-alike" of her favorite actor to entertain at her birthday party.
- → Write new lyrics to her favorite love song—then hire a local musician to record a cassette tape for her.
- → *Your* ideas: _____

♥ How could you celebrate your anniversary more creatively?
- → Write a love sonnet.
- → Write a one-page essay celebrating each year of your life together.
- → Create a 10-foot-tall anniversary card.
- → *Your* ideas: _____

♥ How could you creatively liven-up your relationship this month?
- → Take inspiration from the airlines' Frequent Flyer programs: Create a *Frequent Lover Program!* Make membership cards, give "Bonus Points," and award prizes!
- → Decide to go on a second honeymoon next year. Start planning and anticipating it *now!* Buy some books on your destination. Start shopping for your vacation wardrobe this weekend!
- → *Your* ideas: _____

"Why should we all use our creative power . . . ?
Because there is nothing that makes people so generous,
joyful, lively, bold and compassionate, so indifferent to fighting
and the accumulation of objects and money."

~ Brenda Ueland

Resources

☆ *A Whack on the Side of the Head: How You Can Be More Creative*, by Roger vonOech
☆ *The Five Day Course in Thinking*, by E. DeBono
☆ *The Artist's Way*, by Julia Cameron
☆ *Mental Aerobics: Exercises for a Stronger, Healthier Mind*, by B. Alexis Castorri
☆ *The Courage to Create*, by Rollo May

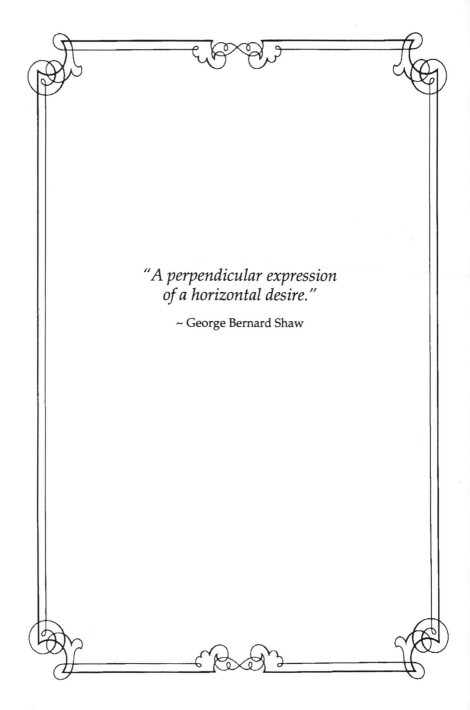

*"A perpendicular expression
of a horizontal desire."*

~ George Bernard Shaw

Dancing

Life is a dance. A joyous, rhythmic, energetic swirl of activity. Sometimes we dance alone. Sometimes we dance in groups. But most often we dance as couples. ✦ What kind of dance are *you* dancing? Sometimes we're Waltzing: Comfortably-paced and elegant. Sometimes we're Rockin': Wild and free-flowing—(but not touching). Sometimes we're doing the Tango: Sensuous and pulsing. Sometimes it's Ballet, and sometimes its Square Dancing!

When the two of you come together to form a couple, it's not simply a straightforward dance of two people. There's a whole *crowd* of "secret partners" jostling for position: Your parents, your "Inner Child," and a whole "Inner Cast of Characters," who represent various facets of your personality. (The Eccentricity Chapter describes this concept.)

Suggestion: Dancing With Your Lover's Characters

☞ Each of you write a list of your "Inner Characters." (See the Eccentricity Chapter.)

☞ Mix and match your characters with your partner's.
- ❑ Which characters get along well together?
- ❑ Which combinations are surefire disasters?
- ❑ How do your daily interactions reflect your characters?
- ❑ How might you introduce a new character into an old situation—to produce a better outcome? (Instead of your "Grump" returning home from work, to be greeted by her "Bitch," try bringing home your "Hero" to meet her "Girl Next Door.")

"Dancing is a great metaphor for living—for being—in harmony, since the whole universe, the sum total of energy moves as in a dance. The person dancing is the person at one with the universe. The person dancing is fully alive."

~ John Travis & Regina Sara Ryan

Metaphors aside, dancing is a *very* romantic thing to do. Whether it's the two-step or the Jitterbug, dancing is a *great* couple activity. Out of practice? Take some dance lessons together! (A medical mystery: Why are more men than women born with two left feet?) ✦ Historical note: When the Waltz was introduced it was considered lascivious because it was the first dance that allowed a man to put his arms around a woman in public! In fact, the clergy called it "the rhythmic incantation of the devil." {From an *Ann Landers* column . . . a great source of romantic ideas and other interesting tidbits.}

Touch, Love—Cha-cha-cha. Work, Play—Cha-cha-cha.
Laugh, Cry—Cha-cha-cha. Live, Learn—Cha-cha-cha.
Give, Take—Cha-cha-cha.

There is, of course, no answer to the Great Mystery of why women who *love* to dance always marry men who *hate* to dance. Nevertheless, here are a few observations about dancing. ✦ Men who are glad to play tennis with you often balk at dancing. Why? Partly because we are more comfortable in a *competitive* situation than we are in one that calls for *cooperation*. ✦ Some women who are normally graceful become awkward when close-dancing. Why? Because after thirty-some years of liberation, they find it difficult to follow a man's lead.

Tip: Customized Dance Tapes

You don't have to invest a fortune in albums or CDs in order to get a great dance tape (or a tape of favorite love songs). Personics will create a custom cassette tape and even print your two-line message on the cover (great as a gift!). ✦ *Personics* is a catalog of over 2,000 of the latest and greatest music in rock, soul, pop, dance, country, and rap hits. You choose the hits you want, and they're assembled on a single tape for your convenience. Each tape is recorded from a super-high quality CD-ROM master disk licensed from the original recording company. (Eliminating the guilt over illegally re-taping songs.) The cost is only $1.10 per song! ✦ Call for a free catalog: 415-592-1700, or write to Personics, 891 Bing Street, San Carlos, California 94070.

Here's another dance familiar to you all. It's called *Two Steps Forward, One Step Back.* ✦ First, it helps to remember that *all of us* dance this dance. Second, you still have lots of room to dance these steps in your own unique way. Some couples just seem to "get it," and dance fairly smoothly through life together. Some of us glide effortlessly *forward*, and resist the *backward* step, as if it were somehow not really a part of the dance. Some of us get out of phase with our partners: She's still moving *forward* while I'm stepping *back*. This makes for a lot of jostling and arguing on the dance floor of life! ✦ The important thing to remember about *Two Steps Forward, One Step Back* is that, unlike the other dances in your life, you have *no choice* but to dance it sometimes. But you *can* choose whether or not to dance it *gracefully*.

Ideas: Celebrate! Celebrate! Dance to the Music!

✣ Do you believe, as some folks do, that dancing is a form of foreplay? Why don't you try it and see?!

✣ What song makes you lose control, and want to dance like a wild savage? . . . *Well?!*

✣ Don't think about this—*just do it:* Pick up the phone, call the nearest Arthur Murray Dance Studio and sign-up for a dance class.

✣ Do you remember what song you first danced to at your wedding? (If not, ask someone in your family who will know.) Find a recording of that song. Create a personal "Couple's Ritual" using it. (See the Rituals chapter for some tips.)

Resources

☆ *The Wellness Workbook*, by John W. Travis & Regina Sara Ryan

☆ *The Dance of Intimacy: A Woman's Guide to Courageous Acts of Change in Key Relationships*, by Harriet Goldhor Lerner

☆ *Inner Joy*, by Harold H. Bloomfield

☆ *The Dance of Life*, by Edward T. Hall

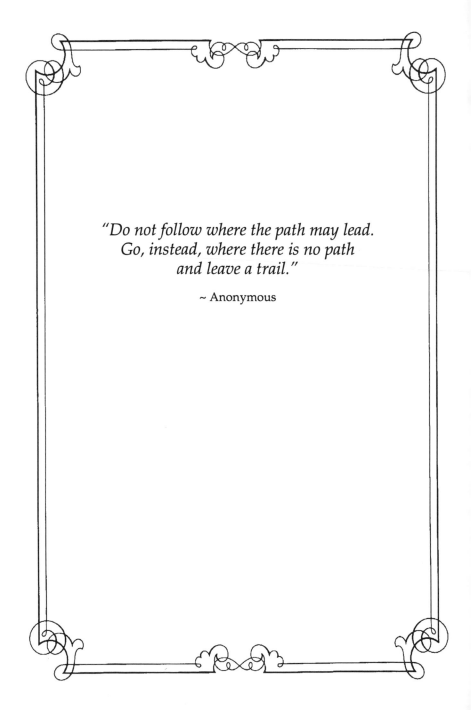

*"Do not follow where the path may lead.
Go, instead, where there is no path
and leave a trail."*

~ Anonymous

Eccentricity

This chapter is about expressing, exploring, *reveling* in your unique strangeness, your quirkiness—your **eccentricity**. And more than *that*, this chapter will help you become an *eccentric couple*—one of the greatest accomplishments you could aspire to [in my humble yet twisted opinion].

Being eccentric is *not* the same as being *unique*. You're *unique* if you're the only person on your block who collects stamps; you're *eccentric* if you wallpaper your bedroom with Elvis stamps. You're *unique* if you have one brown eye and one blue eye; you're *eccentric* if you wear sneakers with a tuxedo.

Homework: Daily Eccentricity

Eccentrics look at the world *just a little differently* from the rest of us. Let's use our creativity to practice being eccentric. ✦ This idea comes from Sandra, who attended the Romance Class last year: Assign each day of the week a flavor. Here's how Sandra's week tastes:

- ♣ Sunday—*Apple*
- ♣ Monday—*Coffee*
- ♣ Tuesday—*French fries*
- ♣ Wednesday—*Strawberry*
- ♣ Thursday—*Mint*
- ♣ Friday—*Beer*
- ♣ Saturday—*Chocolate*

If this were your lover's week, what kinds of romantic gestures could you come up with for each day? What kinds of gifts could you buy? What kind of day-trips could you arrange? ✦ What *other* attributes might you assign to the days of the week? How about . . . Colors?—Is Monday blue or black? . . . Sounds or songs?—Does Tuesday sound like Frank Sinatra; does Friday rock like the Rolling Stones? . . . Aromas?—Does Sunday smell like incense; does Thursday smell like an ocean breeze? ✦ What about the months of the year? What about the hours of the day? What about people? Animals? Cities? States? Seasons? Holidays? How could you assign each of these things an eccentric descriptor to make them interesting and unusual?

I love people who have eccentric ways of viewing the world or understanding themselves. Craig S., a good friend of mine who's a great actor-singer once told me that he taps into his "Inner Characters" as a way to help him portray various characters on stage. He says we *all* have a cast of inner characters, but that most people are out of touch with them. We're scared of some of them; embarrassed by others; we've forgotten about some of them; and censored others. I'll let him speak... ✦ "I've named my characters in a sort-of generic but descriptive way. There's the Intellectual, the Playboy, and the Asshole. There's the Explorer, the Fool, and the Bum. There's the Macho Man, the Little Kid, and the Captain. I'll even admit that some of my inner characters include the Mother, the Little Girl, and the Slut. We all have both masculine and feminine sides to our psyches, and if you can tap into them when you need to, it makes you a better actor—and perhaps a healthier, more well-balanced human being." ✦ "I have a friend who has all of her inner characters *named*. There's Mae West, Superman, Mother Teresa, Albert Einstein, Richard Nixon, Madonna, John Wayne, Ross Perot, Betty Friedan, Rosanne, Mr. Spock, Blondie, Brenda Starr, Donna Reed, and the Wicked Witch of the West!" ✦ This lighthearted approach to our inner lives can cast some serious light on our personalities. It can also help us understand our partners better.

Homework: Identifying Your "Inner Characters"

▲ List your *own* cast of inner characters. (See the description above.) You can name them or describe them. Be *wacky*. Go for it!

▲ Read your list to your lover. Describe each character.
- Which are your favorite characters? Which do you identify with?
- Which characters do you *loathe*?
- Do you have a "love/hate" relationship with any of them?

▲ Can your partner add any characters to your list?! (Those characters that you'd rather forget, or that you're blind to, for some reason.)

▲ Discuss these issues:
- Which of your characters are your friends?
- Which characters sabotage you?
- Which characters does your partner love? Hate? Tolerate? Fear?

You've been to "black tie" affairs, right? But I'll bet you've never experienced one like Trudy M. created for her husband last year for their anniversary... ✦ She sent him a formal invitation to an "Elegant Dinner for Two at Home. Attire: Black Tie." Enclosed in the envelope was a black bow tie—and instructions saying that the tie was the *entire* outfit! ("When I say 'Black Tie,' I *mean* black tie!") ✦ Husband Jack, being an open-minded kind of guy, played along, showing-up in the dining room at the proper time in the proper attire. Trudy, dressed in a black bow tie and matching garter belt and stockings, greeted him with a glass of champagne. Needless to say, they had a most memorable evening.

And then there was the guy who astonished his girlfriend by wall-papering his bedroom with the sheet music to her favorite song: "You Are So Beautiful (To Me)," by Joe Cocker.

Louise J. once called her husband's secretary, saying there was a "family emergency," and that he was needed at home immediately. When he arrived at home he found Louise upstairs in bed—dressed in her sexiest lingerie, anxiously waiting for him. "You call *this* a 'family emergency' ?!" he bellowed. "Yes," Louise replied, "If you don't make love to me right now, I'll *die!*" Her husband stood there in stunned silence for a moment—then burst into laughter and proceeded to save her life.

Congratulate yourself—you're a totally unique person. There was a one-in-ten-billion-quadrillion-mega-zillion chance that you would exist in the universe. You have the right to be as unique, eccentric and quirky as you like!

Resources

☆ *Drawing on the Right Side of the Brain*, by B. Edwards
☆ *Left Handed Teaching*, by G. Castillo
☆ *Psycho-Cybernetics*, by M. Maltz
☆ *Living from the Inside Out*, by Teresa McAlister Adams
☆ *The Courage to Love*, by Edith Weigert
☆ *Wishcraft: How To Get What You Really Want*, by Barbara Sher

---

Passion

Wanting to jump out of bed in the morning.
Wanting the night to never end.
Wanting the moonlight to last forever.
Wanting to reach and touch the sky.
Wanting forever to be longer.

~ Veronica M. Hay
From *In A Dream, You Can Do Anything, A Collection of Words*

Emotions

Mr. Spock fought to control his. The Tin Man wished he had some. *Emotions.* They drive us crazy. They confuse us. They delight us. Women tend to be more in touch with them. *Emotions.* Some people say that love is the prime emotion. Others claim that love isn't a feeling at all: They say love is a decision we make.

Emotional generosity may be the single most important characteristic of healthy, loving, long-term relationships. Are you generous with your feelings? Do you express your love for your partner often enough? Do you share your joys, accomplishments and dreams with him? And conversely, do you share your concerns, pains and insecurities with her? Emotional generosity includes the negative feelings as well as the positive ones!

Homework: Exploring Emotions

➤ Which emotions are your *favorites*? Which do you *express* most often?
➤ How many different emotions can you list in 10 minutes? Ready, set, *go!* (Those who study such things say there are several hundred emotions!)
➤ Why do you think you're more comfortable with some emotions than with others? Are you following patterns set down by your family?
➤ Are you and your partner comfortable expressing the same kinds of emotions?

Emotions are signals. They contain *valuable information.* They're messages from deep inside your psyche that could help you *in every area of your life* if you'd only pay more attention to them! Not only will your intimate relationship benefit if you "tune-in" to your emotions, your *business life* will improve, too. ✦ If you study the lives of successful businesspeople, you'll find that most of them combined their logic and intellect with the power of intuition and the energy of emotion. What *drives* the most successful people? What motivates them to achieve greatness? It's not numbers on a balance sheet, I'll tell you that! It's the challenge, the *thrill* of accomplishment; it's commitment to a cause; it's the pursuit of a vision. They're all driven by *emotion.*

"Better relationships through biology." Here's what the experts say: Our intelligence and logic are located in the most recently evolved part of our brains. Whereas our *emotions* are located in the older, more instinctive, more animalistic part of our brains. What this means is that our emotions often seem to have "a mind of their own." We simply don't have as much control over our emotions as we would like to have. ✦ This wreaks havoc in a society that values intellect and logic over emotion and intuition. Think about it: Most of our learning and all of our schooling is focused on training our intellectual abilities. Very little time is devoted to observing, understanding or controlling our emotions. ✦ Is it any wonder, then, that we have over-developed the skills that ensure our success in the "outside"/material/practical world, and under-developed the skills that enhance our "inner"/emotional/relationship world? We learn competition instead of cooperation. We practice caution instead of trust. We're serious instead of playful. We reward confidence over questioning. We value logic instead of emotion. We expect obedience instead of curiosity. We practice manipulating instead of trusting. We give orders instead of listening. ✦ No *wonder* it's so difficult to create intimate relationships! Maybe it's time we start respecting and practicing some of our under-utilized/emotional/intuitive skills.

People used to believe that feelings of love actually emanated from the heart. We now know that our emotions are a phenomenon of the mind. Right? *Wrong!* The most current thinking is that our minds and bodies are so inextricably linked that emotions exist throughout us—both mind and body. The exciting insight here is that the creation of emotions can be a two-way street. Many of us have been aware that our state of mind greatly affects our moods and emotions. Well, it's also true that you can use your body to affect your state of mind and your emotional states. Your breathing patterns, posture, and facial expressions all affect your emotional state. ✦ This concept is fairly new and in the infancy of its development. Stay tuned for further studies! The thing to remember and respect is that the physical body is a remarkable and powerful tool for enhancing our lives on *all* levels—intellectual, emotional and spiritual. The three are inextricably intertwined, and we do ourselves a disservice when we separate them too much.

Homework: Saturday Night at the Movies

There's no better way to tug on the old heartstrings than by watching a great romantic film together.   ✦   This coming weekend is hereby declared "Romantic Movie Weekend." Rent at least three of these movies: One for Friday night, one for Saturday night, and one for Sunday afternoon.

➤ *Sleepless In Seattle*
➤ *Last of the Mohicans*
➤ *Somewhere In Time*
➤ *Beaches*
➤ *Love Story*
➤ *Camelot*
➤ *Breakfast at Tiffany's*
➤ *The Ghost and Mrs. Muir*
➤ *Dirty Dancing*
➤ *Ghost*
➤ *Doctor Zhivago*
➤ *When Harry Met Sally*
➤ *The Way We Were*
➤ *Love With a Proper Stranger*

➤ *Fried Green Tomatoes*
➤ *Casablanca*
➤ *A Man and a Woman*
➤ *Laura*
➤ *Where the Boys Are (1960 version)*
➤ *Bull Durham*
➤ *Annie Hall*
➤ *The Desert Song*
➤ *Gone With the Wind*
➤ *Lawrence of Arabia*
➤ *Same Time Next Year*
➤ *Brian's Song*
➤ *Wuthering Heights*
➤ *Long Hot Summer (1958 version)*

These are the movies that get the most votes among Romance Class attendees and people who write to me, describing in *detail* why their particular favorite romantic movie is The Greatest Movie Ever Made.

What happens to emotions when they're not acknowledged or acted-on? No, they don't disappear. They go *underground*, build-up pressure, and leak out unexpectedly and uncontrollably. Or they suddenly explode. Better to deal with them upfront, don't you think?

Resources

☆ *Awakening the Heart: East/West Approaches to Psychotherapy and the Healing Relationship*, by John Welwood
☆ *The Art of Loving*, by Erich Fromm
☆ *The Passionate Life*, by Sam Keen
☆ *The Human Connection*, by Ashley Montagu

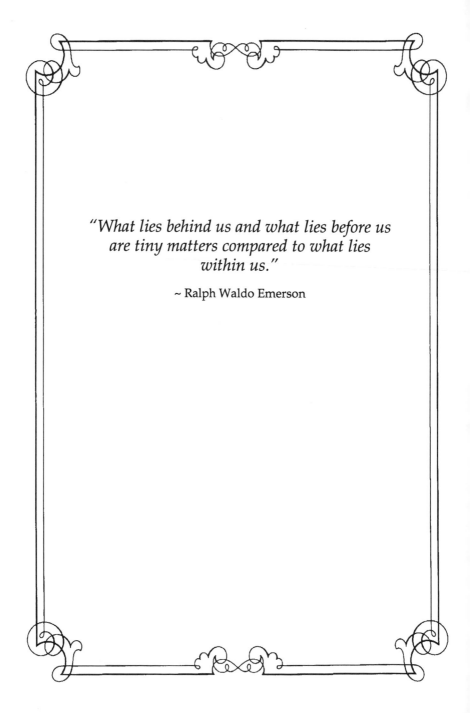

*"What lies behind us and what lies before us
are tiny matters compared to what lies
within us."*

~ Ralph Waldo Emerson

Empowerment

Love is subtle,
and therefore often overlooked.
Love is quiet, and therefore sometimes lost amid the noise.
Love is gentle, and therefore thought to lack strength.
But love powers the universe
and every heart in it.

Love is the most powerful force in your life. This is *not* a theory. It is *not* just a religious platitude. Love is *empowering*. It can change your mindset, your outlook on life, your self-esteem and confidence. It can and does affect every aspect of your life.

FYI: Empowerment & Emotions

Your emotions have a direct impact on your ability to get things done, on your self-esteem, and on whether or not you feel empowered.

Negative/Paralyzing States

▼ Fear
▼ Confusion
▼ Sadness
▼ Anger
▼ Doubt
▼ Depression
▼ Frustration
▼ Anxiety
▼ Pity

Positive/Enabling States

▲ Love
▲ Confidence
▲ Joy
▲ Faith/belief
▲ Inner peace/centeredness
▲ Curiosity
▲ Creativity
▲ Good health
▲ Understanding & empathy

Do you believe that you have much—or any—control over your emotions, your thoughts, and your state of mind? You do!

Are you ready for a little paradox? *Giving* is more empowering than *taking*. The more you give of yourself, the more you *have* to give. This is a secret of tireless individuals. They're energized by giving, helping, loving other people. Why? Because giving creates abundance, whereas taking promotes scarcity. Why? I don't know . . . It's a Law of the Universe.

Many people overlook the link between forgiveness and empowerment. Why is forgiveness important? Because it frees you. It frees emotional, psychic and physical energy. Forgiveness *empowers* you. ✦ Many people misunderstand the true meaning and power of forgiveness, thinking that it's just a nice way of "letting someone off the hook." Forgivensss has more to do with *you* than it does with the person you're forgiving. ✦ When you remain in anger, wallow in self-pity, stand on principle, blame others for your troubles, simmer in rage, or withhold forgiveness, you are a prisoner of your own negative emotions. ✦ Regardless of whether you view forgiveness from a practical/psychological point-of-view, or from a spiritual point-of-view, forgiveness is a key to happiness and fulfillment. Forgiveness is good for your mental health. It certainly empowers you. And it sure plays quite a role in every spiritual Path I've ever encountered. Maybe they're on to something!

"If you could only love enough,
you could be the most powerful person in the world."

~Emmett Fox

Words are *powerful*. Please use them with caution. ✦ You can either empower or disempower your partner with the words you use. Used well and compassionately, language conveys our love eloquently. Language can also mislead, confuse and hurt us when used carelessly or cruelly. ✦ One of the biggest untruths we tell children is in the rhyme "Sticks and stones may break my bones, but words will never hurt me!" Do you remember how it hurt to be called a sissy? Or ugly? —And we don't "grow out of it"! ✦ Words can inspire us—they can also incite riots! Words. They're powerful tools. Use them with care. ✦ Do you remember the movie *Roxanne*? Do you remember why Daryl Hannah's character falls in love with Steve Martin's character? She falls in love with his *words* long before she falls in love with *him*. (Go rent it this weekend.)

Question: What Empowers You?

These are some of the things that empower Romance Class participants:

➢ "My belief in myself."
➢ "The support of my wife."
➢ "Exercise."
➢ "My relationship. Knowing I have a safe haven."
➢ "Knowing that my friends are with me all the way."
➢ "My faith in God."
➢ "Realizing that my emotions don't control my actions."
➢ "Knowledge."
➢ "My vision of the future. My dreams."

Question: What Empowers *You?*

■ When was the last time you experienced the feeling of empowerment?
● What conditions (internal and external) were present?
■ What can you do *today* to re-create empowerment in your life?
● What blocks your empowerment? What can you do about it?
■ How can your partner help you?

"The meeting of preparation with opportunity generates the offspring we call luck."

~ Anthony Robbins

Resources

☆ *The Artist's Way: A Spiritual Path to Higher Creativity*, by Julia Cameron
☆ *Awaken the Giant Within*, by Anthony Robbins
☆ *Unlimited Power*, by Anthony Robbins
☆ *Wishcraft: How to Get What You Really Want*, by Barbara Sher
☆ *The Power Is Within You*, by Louise Hay
☆ *In The Company of Men: Freeing the Masculine Heart*, by Marvin Allen and Jo Robinson
☆ *The Inner Lover: Using Passion as a Way to Self-Empowerment*, by Valerie Harms
☆ *Peak Performance: Mental Training Techniques of the World's Greatest Athletes*, by Charles A. Garfield
☆ *Flow: The Psychology of Optimal Experience*, by Mihaly Csikszentmihalyi

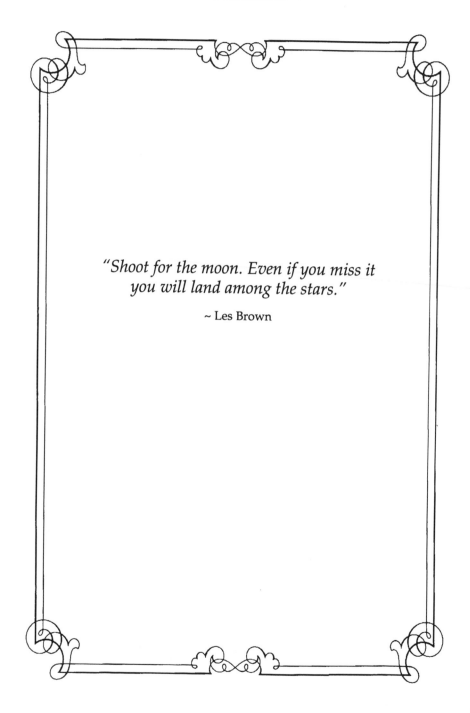

"Shoot for the moon. Even if you miss it you will land among the stars."

~ Les Brown

Expectations

One of the surest ways to destroy a relationship is to enter it with a lot of expectations. ✦ Here's where some folks get confused with this expectation-thing: They confuse *value* expectations with *behavior* expectations. It's *okay* to have *value expectations*, but it's *not* okay to have *behavior expectations*. (It's okay to expect your partner to be honest, compassionate and loving with you. But it's *not* okay to expect her to wash all the dishes/him to earn $100,000 per year/her to have sex whenever you feel like it/him to express emotion as easily as you do.) ✦ Let me clarify one thing: When I use the word "okay" above, it's not from a *judgmental* point-of-view, but from a *practical*, real-world point-of-view. In other words, people's lives and experiences prove over and over again that those who have *value expectations* have happier and more fulfilling relationships; while those with *behavior expectations* have rocky relationships that often break-up.

Homework: Expectations, Preferences & Wishes

Not all expectations are bad. It is appropriate for you to expect your lover to live up to your wedding vows, to be financially responsible, to be a good parent to your children. These may be viewed as "core expectations." Core expectations are reasonable and generally non-negotiable. ✦ Any expectations you have of your partner that are not core expectations are likely to cause you problems. Here's a way out:

✓ Clearly identify your core expectations and differentiate them from the rest of your expectations.
✓ Transform your *expectations* into *preferences*.
✓ List 10 expectations that you have of your partner.
✓ List 10 expectations that you feel your partner has of *you*.
✓ Trade lists with your lover.
✓ Discuss these *expectations* as *preferences* or *wishes*.

How *hard* do you expect to have to work on your relationship? If your answer is anything other than *"Damn hard,"* you have unrealistic expectations. ✦ How *long* do you expect to have to work on your relationship? If your answer is anything other than *"For the rest of my life,"* you're off by several decades!

Exercise: Fill-In-The-Blanks

▼ "I feel sad when you _____."
▼ "I feel mad when you _____."
▼ "I feel ignored when you _____."

▲ "I feel loved when you _____."
▲ "I feel cherished when you _____."
▲ "I feel sexy when you _____."

Complete each sentence with at *least* five different phrases. Trade lists with your lover. Which expectations are realistic? Which do you need to modify? Where can you compromise to make things work better?

Questions: About Marriage

Regardless of whether you're single, newlyweds or old timers, answering these questions will shed some light on your expectations for your intimate relationship. (Adjust the questions to fit your marital status.)

✳ What did you expect marriage to be like?
✳ What's *better* than you expected? What's *worse* than you expected?
✳ How is your marriage *just like* your parents' marriage? How is it *different?*
✳ Which of your expectations aren't being met?
   ☞ Do you believe that they're reasonable expectations?
   ☞ Does your partner agree?
✳ Do you feel put under pressure by any of your partner's expectations?
✳ How much compromising did you expect to have to do in your marriage?

Did you expect love to *stay*, once you found it? Did you expect love to be easier, more "natural"? Did you expect love to find you? Did you expect your lover to view love exactly as you do?

From George's shoebox (see explanation in the Gifts chapter):

> *"I fell in love with what I expected you to be—*
> *I love what I've discovered you are."*
>
> ~ Dale F. Mead

Don't expect your relationship to work on Automatic Pilot.
You'll eventually crash.

Lest the word "expectation" be cast in a totally negative light, here are some expectations that all healthy couples have: You assume that your partner is a loving and lovable person; that he/she has your best interests at heart; that anything other than loving behavior is *a call for love.* In other words, you give your lover the "benefit of the doubt." ✦ The minute you start doubting your partner's motives and goodwill, you've got some serious problems that you'd better deal with quickly.

"At the beginning of marriage, you're thrilled—believing that you've reached a triumphant height . . . when actually you've just made a precarious takeoff." {Jan R., writing from Cleveland.}

Resources

☆ *You're Not What I Expected: Learning To Love the Opposite Sex,* by Polly Young-Eisendrath

☆ *After the Honeymoon: How Conflict Can Improve Your Relationship,* by Daniel B. Wile

☆ *Marital Myths,* by Arnold Lazarus

☆ *Training in Marriage Enrichment,* by Don Kinkmeyer & Jon Carlsen

---

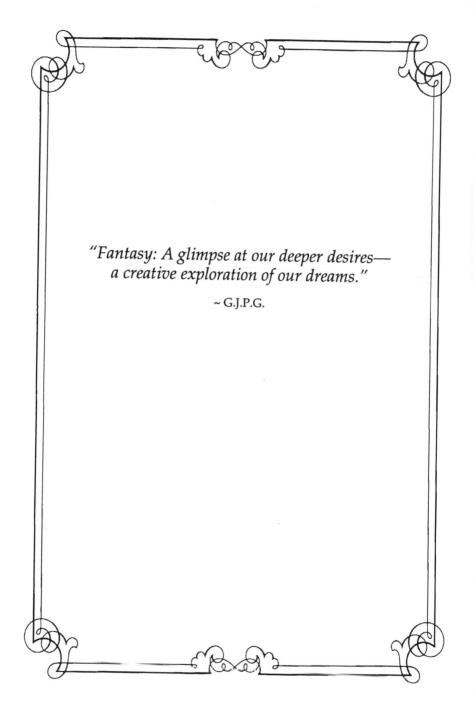

"Fantasy: A glimpse at our deeper desires—
a creative exploration of our dreams."

~ G.J.P.G.

Fantasy

A romp with a playmate. A romantic interlude with a Chippendale dancer. A date with that high school cheerleader who wouldn't give you a second glance. An intimate dinner with a millionaire bachelor on his yacht. ✦ All of this can be yours—all without leaving your spouse of 40 years! If you harness the creative potential of your imagination, there's no telling where your fantasies may lead you!

Let's get one thing straight: We're not talking about *living* a fantasy, but about incorporating fantasy into your life.

FYI: Fantasy Baseball

This probably isn't what you imagined when your guy said he's had a "Lifelong fantasy that he's too embarrassed to admit" . . . but it's true that many men harbor a secret fantasy to play major league baseball. Well, you could help him fulfill that fantasy! ✦ About two-thirds of all major league baseball teams offer "Fantasy Camps." They're held in January and February, right before spring training starts. The cost is around $3,000 to $4,000 for a week of "eating, sleeping and breathing baseball." Participants rub shoulders with baseball stars; get serious coaching, practice ball and play at least one baseball game per day. They even get to wear official team uniforms—with their names stitched on the back! ✦ For the fantasy of a lifetime for the serious fan, call his favorite team and ask about their "Fantasy Baseball Camp" program. (And, yes, *women* are invited to participate in most of the programs.) *Play ball!*

Suggestions: Inspiring Sexual Fantasy

How do you inspire your imagination for fantasy?

➤ Read some good erotic fiction.
➤ Tap into your "Inner Characters." (See the Eccentricity Chapter.)
➤ Ask your lover to describe his/her favorite fantasy. See if you can build on that concept.
➤ Read *Cosmo*. Are those advice articles fact or fantasy. (Who *cares*?!)
➤ Discuss your erotic dreams.
➤ Act out some of your favorite love songs!

Homework: X-Rated Fantasies

Sharing your sexual fantasies with your partner will enhance your sexual communication, and—once you overcome the awkwardness—will build intimacy. Guaranteed.

First, here are a few facts about sexual fantasies:

✣ *Everyone* has them—whether they admit to it or *not!*
✣ Fantasizing about people other than your partner is *not* a betrayal of him or her.
✣ It's the *suppression* of fantasies that causes psychological problems. Expression and exploration of them leads to good mental health . . . not to mention good sex!

Now, let's try an exercise . . .

✳ Note: One Romance Class participant calls sex fantasies "Fairy Tales for Adults." I *like* that.
✳ Sit down with your partner, two pads of paper and two pens.
✳ Each of you writes-down one of your favorite sexual fantasies. (Writing works better than talking at this stage because writing is a private, personal thing. There's no embarrassment.)
✳ Trade stories and read them quietly.
✳ Ask each other questions to clarify and explore the fantasy more deeply. (Once we overcome a little embarrassment, most of us are more expressive when we talk than when we write.)

You need to understand upfront that this exercise will definitely produce some anxiety. (But if you can't risk a little anxiety with your life partner, you'd better just hang it up altogether!) How do you get past the anxiety? Talk! And then choose a time within the next week to "experiment." (Only one fantasy per night, *please!*)

Note: Do's & Don'ts of Sexual Fantasies

☞ *Do* go all out—costumes, props, settings.
☛ *Don't* take it too seriously!
☞ *Do* stay in character!
☛ *Don't* share your fantasy escapades with anyone!
☞ *Do* go along with your partner's creativity.
☛ *Don't* break the mood.
☞ *Do* plan your story line with your partner, at least until you get really good at this!

The story: Linda's husband Paulspends more time in their garage than he does in their bedroom. One day Linda was inspired by the Snap-on Tools "girlie" calendar Paul has on the wall of the garage . . . In preparation she covered all the garage windows and locked the outside doors. Then, one evening when Paul was adjusting a carburetor, she donned her sexiest lingerie and pranced into the garage. Before her astonished hubby could say a word, she took the calendar from the wall, and struck matching poses—draping herself over the Chevy. Needless to say, they made love in the back seat of the car—something they hadn't done in 27 years. ✦ The happy ending: Inspired by Linda's brazen display of creativity and passion, Paul took Linda on a surprise weekend to a romantic inn she'd always dreamed of visiting—where they stayed in the honeymoon suite—complete with canopy bed and Jacuzzi. ✦ They now have a monthly "Changing of the Calendar" ceremony. —Use your imagination! ✦ You, too, can get a Snap-on calendar for just $12. Write to Snap-on Tools Corp., 2801 80th Street, Kenosha, Wisconsin 53141.

Romance is the environment in which love flourishes.

Resources

☆ *Fantasex*, by Rolf Milonas
☆ *Yellow Silk: Erotic Arts and Letters*, (the *book*) edited by Lily Pond & Richard Russo
☆ *Yellow Silk: Journal of the Erotic Arts*, (the *magazine*). Visit a good bookstore or write to P.O. Box 6374, Albany, California 94706.
☆ *For Love*, by Sue Miller
☆ *Pleasures*—Erotica for women *by* women, edited by Lonnie Barbach
☆ *My Secret Garden*, by Nancy Friday
☆ *Intimate Play: Playful Secrets for Falling and Staying in Love*, by William Betcher
☆ *Forbidden Journeys: Fairy Tales & Fantasies by Victorian Women Writers*, ed. Nina Auerbach

"Love is letting go of fear."

~ Gerald Jampolsky

Fear

This is going to be the least-read chapter in the book . . . I just *know* it. They'll say, "Who wants to read about *fear* in a book about *love*?" It's important to talk about fear because, as I see it, *fear is simply a call for love.* ✦ Fear (and the hundreds of forms it takes) seems to block love from our lives. Fear paralyzes us and diminishes us. Fear keeps us from getting closer to those whom we love the most. Fear makes us suspicious, defensive and judgmental. Fear seems to be a big thing. ✦ But if you re-interpret fear as *a call for love*, look what happens: You treat your *own* fears with understanding rather than self-recrimination. And you treat your *partner* with compassion rather than criticism. ✦ Here's the mechanism: Fear begets fear, and love begets love. If you see fear as a "real thing," you're going to *react* to it with fear, and actually generate *more* fear. But if you see fear simply as a lack of love, it's a rather simple matter to see that the appropriate response is *love.*

Many people experience what I call the "Great Fears": That long-term relationships smother passion. That commitment kills romance. That marriage ends excitement. ✦ If you believe these things, then it's perfectly understandable that you'll resist committing and settling-down with one person. You see, people *love* romance/passion/excitement in their lives. These things energize us and give meaning to our lives. We fear losing them. *But it's a misplaced fear.* It's upside-down and backwards thinking, which is a typical trap of the modern world. It's the same kind of thinking that leads you to believe that love is weak and hate is strong. ✦ Here are some Truths: Love is the strongest force in the universe. Romance blossoms in *intimate* long-term relationships. Commitment fosters passion. Great marriages are hotbeds of excitement.

Are you angry? Are you sad? Depressed? Bitter? Lonely? Frustrated? Confused? Underneath all of these feelings is a layer of fear. If you deal with the *fear* instead of its surface expression, you'll solve the cause of the problem, and not merely its symptoms.

Where does our fear of intimacy come from? Why are we so reluctant to risk ourselves for the sake of love? ✦ In part because we received mixed messages about love from our parents. Few of us experienced unconditional love. ✦ Also in part because fear just naturally fills-in any spaces left open when there's a lack of love. [In fact, that's the true essence of fear: It's not really a thing or concept unto itself, it's simply a lack of love. Read *A Course In Miracles* if you'd like to explore this concept further.]

Fear can actually be a helpful emotion, *if* you know how to use it. Fear, pain and anger are signals that something is wrong. If you take the time to *explore* these difficult feelings, instead of sweeping them under the rug, you'll learn something about yourself, and possibly gain some control over your response to your feelings. ✦ What you need to do is dig *into* the fear to find out what's causing it. You see, fear is kind-of a *generic* emotion that masks other, more specific feelings. For example, you may be feeling angry, and expressing that anger at your hapless lover, when in reality you may be feeling incompetent, unloved or threatened in some way. In fact, we're rarely angry for the reasons we think we are.

FYI: Identifying Fears

* Fear of rejection. ("I'm afraid he won't accept me for who I am.")
* Fear of abandonment. ("If she knew this about me, she'd leave.")
* Fear of your own anger. ("My rage might be uncontrollable.")
* Fear of inadequacy. ("What if I'm not good enough?")
* What *other* fears can you identify?

Tips: Overcoming Fear

* People rarely overcome major fears by themselves. It seems to be the nature of fears that they overwhelm us and short-circuit our coping mechanisms. Outside help is often required.
* This sets-up a particularly nasty Catch-22 when the fear involves another person—your significant other, lover, spouse.
* This is why counselors and therapists can be so helpful.

Suggestion: Pop the Cork!

❑ "Bottled-up anger/guilt/frustration/fear." We've all got a supply, right?

❑ You'd like to simply dispose of the bottles, but we always seem to have a basement full of them.

❑ Like bottles of champagne under pressure, we keep them corked with logic or indifference.

❑ We're afraid of the explosion that our fear, pain and anger would cause, if we ever loosened the cork.

❑ So why don't we simply toss these bottles away? Because these bottles contain a *mixture* of positive and negative emotions. The bottom of every bottle contains our most *valuable possessions*: Our feelings of love, tenderness, childlike innocence, creativity and joy.

❑ We've forgotten that the sweet-tasting wine of our love is also bottled-up inside there!

❑ Popping the cork is *scary*. Dealing with your fears is never easy or fun. But it's necessary if you want to drink fully of everything life has to offer you.

Love is letting go of fear. ✦ It's not only the Truth, it's also the name of a great book by Gerald Jampolsky. Based on principles of forgiveness, the lessons in the book will teach you to let go of fear and remember that our very *essence* is love.

Resources

☆ *A Course In Miracles*, Foundation For Inner Peace

☆ *Guilt Is the Teacher, Love Is the Lesson*, by J. Borysenko

☆ *Love Is Letting Go of Fear*, by Gerald Jampolsky

☆ *A Book for Couples*, by Hugh & Gayle Prather

☆ *The Courage to Create*, by Rollo May

*"Relationships are built on feelings,
not on facts."*

~ G.J.P.G.

Feelings

"You wanna know the problem with this 'feeling-thing'?—It's too out- of-control. You *never* know what's going to come up. I hate being at the mercy of my feelings. I *know* they're in there—I'm no dummy! But frankly, things are fine now . . . Why rock the boat?" [Compiled from hundreds of Romance Class conversations with Real Guys.] ✦ There's an underlying assumption here that *our feelings control us*. **This is not true!** It *is* true that *what* you feel is largely out of your control. Feelings just pop-up of their own accord. But it is *also* true that **you are in control of how you respond to those feelings** . ✦ You have immense power! What often happens, however, is that we *abandon* this power—we deny our own responsibility for our actions. When this happens, our feelings *do* control us—but with our permission! [I always have to go over this point at least twice in the Romance Class. You may want to read this paragraph again.] ✦ This is not just *my* opinion. It's not just more self-help bullshit. Many psychologists, philosophers, spiritual paths and many, many people's experiences are in agreement on this point.

Tip: Playing With Blocks . . .

- ■ . . . *emotional* blocks, that is. What are your favorite types of blocks?
- ■ We *all* have blocks. So instead of keeping them to ourselves, and pretending we're the only ones who have them, let's take 'em out and play with 'em!
- ■ How do you block your feelings?
  - ❒ Do you freeze them? Do you go numb? Do you feel nothing at all?
  - ❒ Do you submerge them? Do you cover them up with busyness?
  - ❒ Do you ignore them? Pretend they're not there at all?
- ■ Here are the problems that develop with each type of block:
  - ❏ When you go numb, you block not only fear and anger, you also block your feelings of love and joy.
  - ❏ If you submerge your feelings, they eventually leak out. And they have a tendency to do so in unexpected and unpleasant ways.
  - ❏ If you simply ignore your feelings, you turn into a logical zombie.
- ■ Blocks *are* functional—they allow us to move forward in our day-to-day lives. But the long-term price we pay is phenomenally high.

Earlier in this chapter I said that what we feel is largely out of our control. This is true . . . but let's take a second look at the statement with a focus on the phrase *"largely* out of our control." If you choose to be conscious of your "Self-Talk," and exercise more of your personal power, you'll find that you can actually *create* feelings. If you adopt the mindset, attitude and affect that go along with any particular emotion, you can experience that emotion. ✦ Why should this be so surprising? Our minds are incredibly powerful instruments that we barely understand and rarely tap into very deeply.

A brief note about "Self-Talk." Self-Talk is that constant chatter that goes on inside our heads. I don't mean "hearing voices," but that internal dialogue that's a natural part of our conscious minds. It's often a *critical* voice ("Why did you say *that,* you fool!"). We can, however, gain a great deal of control over our Self-Talk, and give ourselves much more positive messages. Through the use of affirmations, for example, we can affect our beliefs about ourselves and our relationships.

Homework: Lists

▶ Make a list of 10 things that you have to be happy/thankful for.
▶ Make a list of 10 things that you have to be sad/worried/depressed about.
▶ Keep these two lists with you for the next month. Add 10 more items to each list each day. [Yes, for 30 days!]
▶ (Nearly everyone can keep the "happy" list going for much longer than a month. But the "sad" list seems to fill-up in about a week. Think about it.)

What's the difference between *joy* and *happiness*? What's the dividing line between *anger* and *fury*? What's the difference between *sexual* and *sensual*? How do you know if it's *love* or *lust*?

Respond to *feelings,* not just to information. ✦ Much of our communication in the "outside world" involves the relaying of *information.* But we need to change gears when we go home . . . Because much of our communication in our intimate relationship is (or should be) about *feelings,* not information. If your partner is trying to express feelings, and you respond on an informational level, he or she has not really been "heard." ✦ Why is this important? Because relationships are built on feelings, not on facts.

Idea: Practice Makes Perfect

Let's practice getting in touch with a variety of emotions. Each day this week, focus on one specific emotion. Here's one possible week:

- ✳ Sunday: *Tenderness*
- ✳ Monday: *Joy*
- ✳ Tuesday: *Nostalgia*
- ✳ Wednesday: *Sadness*
- ✳ Thursday: *Peace*
- ✳ Friday: *Passion*
- ✳ Saturday: *Love*

Which emotions are you most in touch with? What are the benefits of experiencing each of these feelings? Did you include your partner in any or all of these feelings?   ✦   Plan a *second* week of *different* feelings.   ✦   Plan a *third* week of feelings in which you and your partner focus on the same feelings on the same days. Was it more enjoyable? Did you gain any additional insights?

Suppressing your feelings requires a lot of energy—both *emotional* energy and *physical* energy. When you fail to talk about your feelings they build up and drain energy from your relationship. *Passion* is the first casualty; then goes the *fun*; then your *interest* fades; and finally, even your *respect* for the other person dwindles.   ✦   You liberate *tremendous* amounts of energy when you express your feelings. Energy that you can channel into your relationship, your career, your family, your *life!*

"How To Make Friends With Your Feelings" is the sub-title of a great book by psychologist and speaker Jay Uhler. *Uniquely Human* is a guide through the maze of your emotions to the security and confidence of self-control. If your bookstore is out of stock, you can get a copy directly from the publisher by writing to Ambassador Press International, P.O. Box 1661, Andover, Massachusetts 01810.

Resources

- ☆ *Focusing*, by E. Gendlin
- ☆ *How Men Feel*, by Anthony Astrachan
- ☆ *What You Feel, You Can Heal!* by John Gray
- ☆ *Why Can't Men Open Up?* by Steven Naifeh & Gregory White Smith

---

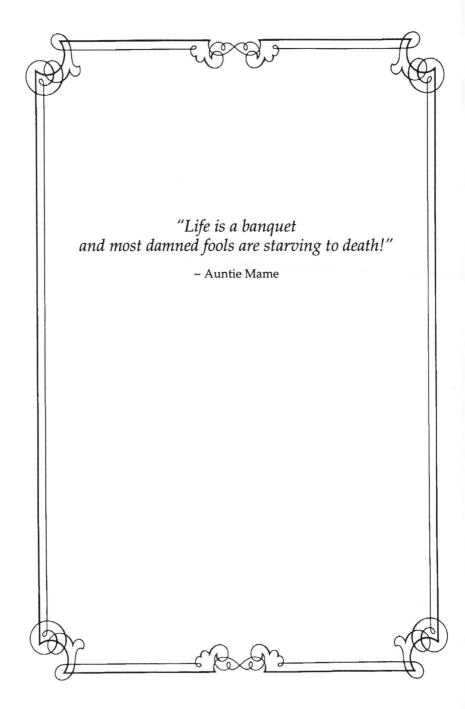

*"Life is a banquet
and most damned fools are starving to death!"*

~ Auntie Mame

Food

FYI: Popsicles for Grownups

- ❒ Fill a blender 3/4 full with frozen strawberries
- ❒ Add 3 to 4 teaspoons of sugar
- ❒ Throw-in 1 shot of Rose's lime juice
- ❒ Add 4 shots of Tequila
- ❒ Add 2 shots of Cointreau
- ❒ Add ice
- ❒ Blend 'em
- ❒ You're aiming for a smooth, pudding-like consistency
- ❒ Pour into paper cups
- ❒ Add a wooden handle/Popsicle stick/or spoon
- ❒ Stick 'em in the freezer

Have you read the book *Like Water For Chocolate*, by Laura Esquivel? It's wonderful, romantic and erotic. And it's got one of the best sub-titles I've ever seen: "A Novel in Monthly Installments with Recipes, Romances and Home Remedies." The book will put you back in touch with the sensuous nature of food. ✦ One creative woman in the Romance Class told us that she's been cooking the recipes from the book. And, she occasionally reads relevant passages out loud to her husband before serving a meal.

Tip: Wining & Dining

Trains have a 19th Century romance about them. And wine is the ultimate sensory complement to a romantic experience. Put them together and you get . . . the Napa Valley Wine Train! ✦ A scenic, leisurely-paced 36-mile ride aboard elegant Pullman cars awaits you! You'll sample wines from throughout the Napa Valley. You'll enjoy a three-course lunch or a five-course dinner. You'll experience a great, romantic time. ✦ Call 800-522-4142 or 800-427-4124 in California, or write to the Napa Valley Wine Train, 1275 McKinstry Street, Napa, California 94549.

You may be surprised to discover how many different types of foods can be shaped, formed, cut or squeezed into hearts! Pancakes, pizzas, salads, breads, quiches, tarts, vegetables, cookies and cakes!

Recipe: Heart-Shaped Pizza!

Here's my favorite recipe for home-made, heart-shaped pizza:

Dough

1 package powdered yeast
1/3 cup plus 2 tablespoons warm water
1 tablespoon honey
1-1/2 cups flour
1/4 cup olive oil
1/2 teaspoon salt

In a small bowl, dissolve the honey in warm water. Gently stir in the yeast until it dissolves. Let it stand for 5 minutes. ✦ Mix the flour and salt in a bowl. Make a well in the center of the flour, and pour in the oil and yeast. Mix well. Then take the dough out and knead it for 5 minutes. Put it in a lightly oiled bowl and cover. Let rise until doubled (about 1 hour).

Topping

2 tablespoons olive oil
1 small onion, chopped fine
1 green pepper, chopped fine
2 cloves garlic
1-1/2 cup tomato puree (15 ounce can)
1/2 teaspoon salt
3/4 teaspoon sugar
1/2 teaspoon pepper
1/2 teaspoon basil
1 pinch of love
1-1/4 teaspoon oregano
4 cups shredded Mozzarella cheese
Lots of sliced pepperoni

Saute onion, garlic and green pepper in olive oil for 5 minutes. Add tomato puree and seasonings. Simmer for 10 minutes. ✦ Preheat oven to 400° F. Roll out dough and shape into a heart. Place it on a lightly greased pizza crisper or cookie sheet. Spread the tomato mixture on top. Cover with shredded cheese, then pepperoni. ✦ Bake 15-20 minutes on lowest rack in the oven. Serve with love.

FYI: A Gardener's Love Notes

Some people have good imaginations . . . And *then* there are some people who are *truly crazed*. The following are representations of several "Food Notes" that John Z. has sent to his wife Susan over the past 10 years. She sent me photos of these things, and let me tell you, they're *really* cool. John uses actual food in these notes. Sometimes the food items are pasted to paper, and sometimes the notes are attached to the food. ✦ Imagine, in the following lines, that the bracketed food words are the actual items.

✤ Please go out on a [*date*] with me!
✤ You're the [*apple*] of my eye.
✤ [*Honey*], where have you been [*olive*] my life?
✤ If we [*cantaloupe*], [*lettuce*] live together!
✤ Please don't [*squash*] my hopes!
✤ We're quite a [*pear*].
✤ Sweetheart, you're a [*peach*].
✤ [*Peas*] be mine!
✤ [*Olive*] you.

What *other* food-puns can you think of? (Using Cheerios or Hershey's Kisses or . . .) You could *also* create puns using *other* objects. Hmmmm . . . Bolts and screws, cars, body parts (!), household items, computers, etc.

From George's shoebox (see the Gifts chapter for an explanation):

"The three words that, said regularly, can save your marriage.
No, it's not 'I love you'—It's 'Let's eat out'."

~ Anonymous

Resources

☆ *Fit or Fat*, by Covert Bailey
☆ *Wines, Cordials and Brandies: How to Make Them*, Vanguard Press
☆ *Feeding the Hungry Heart*, by G. Roth
☆ *Love Potions: A Guide to Aphrodisiacs and Sexual Pleasures*, by Cynthia Merris Watson
☆ *The Foods of Love*, by Max de Roche

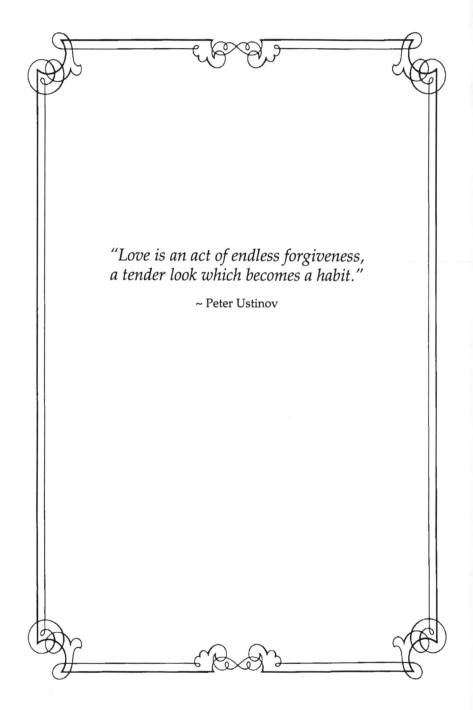

*"Love is an act of endless forgiveness,
a tender look which becomes a habit."*

~ Peter Ustinov

Forgiveness

Forgiveness certainly has an important role to play in our intimate relationships. Long-term intimate realtionships are the perfect forum for practicing forgiveness. ✦ Why? Well, every married person *I* know, believes heartily that his or her spouse is in *great* need of forgiveness! And if their honesty matches their wry humor, they'll admit that they themselves do boneheaded things on a regular basis that require forgiveness! ✦ One woman in the Romance Class suggested that the very *purpose* of marriage was to give us a place to practice forgiveness!

Homework: Forgiveness Discussions

✤ This is a couples exercise, and it's not an easy one. So set aside an entire morning, afternoon or evening when you won't be interrupted.

✤ Make sure you're both in a positive, loving mood to begin with. Otherwise, schedule a different time for this exercise.

✤ Each of you begins by writing two lists.
   1) "Resentments and angers that I'm harboring against my partner." ("Things I need to forgive him/her for.")
   2) "Things I've done that I know have upset or angered my partner." ("Things that I need to be forgiven for.")

✤ Discuss the items on your lists one by one. Give each item the time and attention it deserves. If you have to add a second, third and fourth session to this one, do so.

✤ Proceed through your lists in pairs: One item from List #1, and one item from List #2. This helps keep you balanced. It's a reminder that we all play *both* roles in our relationship; that we all need to forgive and to *be* forgiven.

✤ You may want to review some of the items in the Communication chapter and the Arguing chapter for tips on keeping your communication on track.

✤ And last but not least, forgive *yourself* for being angry/nasty/unforgiving in the first place. True forgiveness does not engender guilt.

✤ The purpose here is to clear the air, to lighten your load. If either of you is still feeling guilty, it's a signal that you still need to work through some issues. (These things take *time!*)

✤ Create a ritual for ending these Forgiveness Discussions. (See the Rituals chapter.) Re-affirm your love for your partner.

I was originally planning to write chapters on *Heartbreak* and *Pain*. But Karen R., in a recent Romance Class, pointed out to me that focusing on the *solution* would be much more productive than focusing on the *problem*. So here it is, the solution: *Forgiveness*. ✦ I've talked with thousands of people over the years, and I've done a lot of research on heartbreak, pain and healing. And as far as I can see, it all boils down to *forgiveness*. Let me clarify: I do *not* mean a simple, childlike "I forgive you," or a simplistic (and unrealistic) philosophy of "Forgive and forget!" I mean a deep, genuine, well analyzed forgiveness that follows some type of psychological and/or spiritual process. ✦ What does *forgiveness* have to do with *romance*? Just this: You cannot love fully if you're full of rage or guilt or anger or resentment. These emotional wounds need to be healed before you can come anywhere *near* fulfilling your potential as a partner, lover or spouse. ✦ Forgiveness is the goal or the result of many techniques and processes. Many of them do not use the *word* "forgiveness," but it is nevertheless an integral part of what transpires. From Tony Robbins' empowerment seminars to psychotherapy; from Christianity to Buddhism; from 12-step programs to Marriage Encounter— they all teach forgiveness in a variety of ways. ✦ Most emotional and psychological breakthroughs that people make come about after true forgiveness is achieved.

"Love means never having to say you're sorry." Some people actually *believe* that crap! In this imperfect world of ours, the very *essence* of love is forgiveness. Love involves the continual renewal of commitment amid adversity. Love confronts disagreements and mistakes and faults and omissions and hurts—and forgives them all.

Homework: The "Forgiveness Letter"

Unexpressed resentments and grudges will drain your loving energy. But sometimes you simply *can't* talk directly to your partner—or you're not quite ready to deal with it head-on. That's okay. A "Forgiveness Letter" will help you express your feelings, focus your thoughts, and move toward true forgiveness.

✛ This is a *personal* exercise, not to be shared with anyone. You're *not* going to send this letter or share it with *anyone.*

✛ Choose one issue that's upsetting you in your relationship.

✛ Start writing—and don't stop for half an hour, or when you've fully expressed yourself, whichever is longer.

✛ Don't worry about grammar, logic, reasonableness or politeness.

✛ Write what you feel. Write what you think. Write what you suspect. Write what you fantasize.

✛ Consider exploring these feelings: Hurt, sadness, fear, insecurity, anger, blame, guilt, resentment, jealousy, self-righteousness.

✛ Make this letter as negative and as strongly-worded as possible.

✛ Make no effort to solve problems or be reasonable.

✛ Then, when you've exhausted all of the negative emotions you can possibly think of . . .

✛ Write a P.S.

✛ Begin to add a little balance here. Introduce the concepts of understanding, forgiveness, kindness, compassion and love.

   ✧ If you can't bring yourself to feel much forgiveness right now, don't worry about it.

   ✧ Set the letter aside (in a safe place!) and come back to it tomorrow.

   ✧ Take as long as you like—days or weeks, if you desire—but continue working until your P.S. brings your letter full-circle, and helps you come to terms with the negative feelings inside you.

✛ Some people write a whole *series* of letters.

✛ Some of them even write responses back to themselves, taking on the role of the person the letter is addressed to. A wonderfully creative approach, don't you think?

Resources

☆ *A Course In Miracles*, Foundations For Inner Peace
☆ *A Return to Love*, by Marianne Williamson
☆ *Healing the Shame that Binds You*, by John Bradshaw
☆ *Making Peace With Your Parents*, by Harold H. Bloomfield

*"In our play
we reveal what kind of people we are."*

~ Ovid

Games

Here's a chapter that doesn't get too serious. View it as a recess from the other lessons. ✦ Several of these games come from creative and fun-loving readers or class participants. Thanks to all!

FYI: "The Game"

How would you like to experience sex with the passion and excitement that was there when you first started playing the sport? Regardless of how long you've been together with your partner, this game will re-ignite some of that lost passion. ✦ Simply called "The Game" by inventors J. and H. Roberts, this game is essentially a "sexual fast." J. says, "It's *amazing* how *badly* you want something that you know you can't have!" ✦ Here's how The Game is played . . .

❏ One of you begins by simply asking your partner if he or she wants to play "The Game."
❏ Your partner must accept your offer, in order for you to continue.
❏ The general rules of the game are:
   ✗ Neither of you can have *any* sexual contact . . .
   ✗ . . . Until a specific date.
   ✗ (The originator of The Game gets to set the date.)
   ✗ The originator also gets to customize The Game in creative ways to make it more interesting—and *tantalizing*.
❏ Some variations for you to consider:
   ✗ Instead of a specific *date* to aim for, you may define a set of conditions that must be met before you can have sex.
   ✗ Is teasing allowed? Verbal or visual?
   ✗ Is touching allowed? Excluding certain parts of the body?

J. tells me that he and his wife have been playing The Game for about 15 years of their 20-year marriage. They tend to play it once or twice a year. (It loses its *punch* if you play it too often!) "The Game makes us feel like a couple of horny teenagers!" ✦ [Not available from Milton-Bradley or Parker Brothers!]

Games can be used as metaphors to help you understand yourself, your partner and your relationship. ✦ Are you playing *with* one another or *against* one another. Is it a friendly competition or a fierce battle? Are you a good loser? A gracious winner? ✦ Do you tend to get stuck in stalemates? Is your relationship as much fun as *Twister*? Is your relationship a *Risk*? Did you marry him for the *Easy Money*? Is your relationship in *Jeopardy*? ✦ Are you both playing the same game at the same time? Do you both understand the rules? Are you playing fair?

FYI: The "Glad Game"

I'm almost embarrassed to suggest this game . . . but *several* Romance Class participants have mentioned this game to me over the years, so there *must* be something to it. ✦ Playing The Glad Game is deceptively simple. Its one rule: Find *something* to be **glad** about *in any situation*. This game has helped many couples see a spark of hope in their darkest moments. Part of this game's magic comes from the phenomenon that the happiness of *your* spirit affects those around you. You see, it's effective because it puts us in touch with our real Self, the true source of who we really are. It empowers us because it makes us aware of who we really are. It reminds us that external events and other people have no real power over us; they don't make us happy or unhappy. ✦ {Those of you with long memories may remember where the Glad Game comes from: It was taught to Polyanna by her father, in the classic book by Eleanor Porter!}

During a group brainstorming session in the Romance Class, one couple decided to create a board game based on their relationship. They outlined the entire concept during a coffee break. They're not planning to sell the game to Milton Bradley, they're doing it as an exercise in creativity and closeness. ✦ They call it The Togetherness Game, and it's become a metaphor for their relationship. Every year or two they send me a photo of the most recent version of the game. It's truly a fascinating project. There's a game board (that keeps getting bigger); there are pieces that represent them, their families, friends and colleagues; there are cards and money and dice and spinners. It's wonderfully complex and totally intriguing. The Rules keep changing, too. ✦ "We work on the game, create and modify the game much more than we ever play it," M.R. says. "We figure that we're *living* the game every day, so why do we need to *play* it? The game is like therapy for us. It helps us understand ourselves better, it keeps us in communication, and it's tons of fun!" ✦ *Cool*, huh?

FYI: Adolescence—The Game

I think it's great that people are getting in touch with their "Inner Child." But a thought just occurred to me: If I've got an Inner Child in there, I must have an "Inner Teenager," too! Now, aside from the pimples and cracking voice and a little insecurity, I had a *great* time during my adolescence. Many of the things that defined that period of our lives are wonderful, creative and passionate characteristics. ✦ Think about your teenage years. Imagine all the romantic concepts you could generate by *thinking* like a teenager and maybe even *acting* like a teenager. Do you remember . . .

✔ "Parking"!
✔ Going a little *overboard*. "All things in moderation—*including* moderation!"
✔ Infatuation
✔ Questioning authority
✔ "Making-out"
✔ Going steady
✔ Pulling "all-nighters"
✔ Sitting on his lap
✔ Holding hands

{*Special* thanks to Diane C., Wendy W. & Laurie H.}

Resources

☆ *World Wide Games* catalog—Games, puzzles, brain teasers, posters, fun gifts n' stuff! Call 800-243-9232, or write P.O. Box 517, Colchester, Connecticut 06415.

☆ The "Getting To Know You Better" board game. A two-person game for lovers that helps you learn more about each other. Just $25, from the *Seasons* catalog. Call 800-776-9677, or write P.O. Box 64545, Saint Paul, Minnesota 55164.

☆ *Games People Play: The Psychology of Human Relationships*, by Eric Berne

☆ *A Whack on the Side of the Head: How You Can Be More Creative*, by Roger von Oech

☆ *Beyond Games and Scripts*, by Eric Berne

☆ *Intimate Play*, by William Betcher

☆ *More Games For The Superintelligent*, by James Fixx

☆ *New Games Books*, ed. by A Fluegelman

☆ *The Well-Played Game: A Player's Philosophy*, by B. DeKoven

---

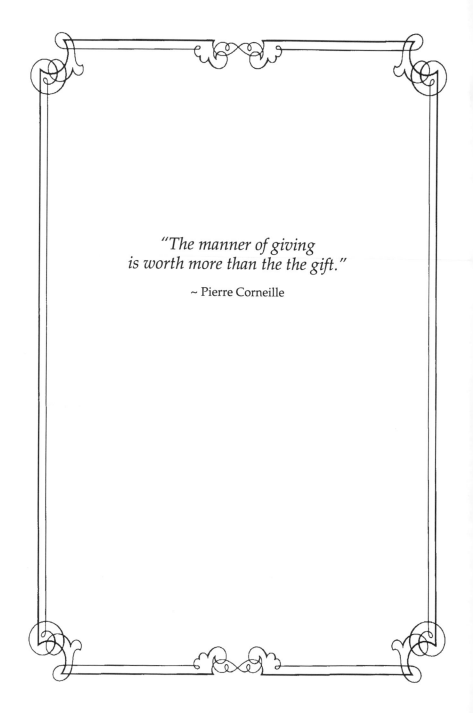

*"The manner of giving
is worth more than the the gift."*

~ Pierre Corneille

Gifts

In the Romance Class we make a distinction between *gifts* and *presents*. A *gift* is something that the *receiver* wants. A *present* is something that the *giver* wants the receiver to have. ✦ One is *not* better than the other. Gifts say more about the *receiver*—you've listened to her, and are responding with an appropriate gift. Presents say more about the *giver*—they express your feelings.

FYI: A Puzzling Proposition

Is your partner a puzzle to you? Then you should have him made into a jigsaw puzzle! You can get a high-quality, 14" x 19", 494-piece jigsaw puzzle made from a color snapshot (3-1/2" x 5" to 5" x 7"). ✦ Just $38.95 from *World Wide Games*. Call 800-243-9232, or write to P.O. Box 517, Colchester, Connecticut 06415. (And, they have a great catalog of other puzzles and games n' stuff!)

Tip: Beam me up, Scotty!

If your lover is a true Star Trek fan, you're *certain* to find the perfect gift in the *Star Trek* catalog! Scripts, pins, poster, patches, jewelry, clothing and more— from the Classic Trek, The Next Generation, and Deep Space Nine. Only $2 in this quadrant of the galaxy. Write to Shop At Home, 2080 South Holly Street, P.O. Box 221050, Denver, Colorado 80222.

FYI: "Techno-Romance"

New on the scene is "Techno-Romantic" jewelry. Designer Thomas Mann's technique juxtaposes high-tech materials with romantic images. Hearts and victorian photographs somehow co-exist within a context of metal, lucite, mathematical symbols and pieces of industry/technology. [Hard to describe, intriguing to experience.] For the offbeat and artistic! For more info, call Thomas Mann Design in New Orleans, Louisiana, at 504-581-2111.

Do you always rush out and buy gifts at the last minute? —Buy a few gifts *now, and stash them away* for future gift-giving. ✦ Do you hate the hassle of shopping? —Do your shopping by catalog. There are millions of them.

FYI: How to Save $100,000 in Gifts Over theCourse of Your Life

* Give your lover the gift of your *undivided* attention . . . *often.*
* That's all!
* {"Nah! That's too easy."}
* ["*Hah*! Try it!"]

Suggestion: Get Stoned

*Gem*stoned, that is! Jewelry is one of the best gifts because it can be very symbolic, it's available in every price range, and it lasts forever. Diamonds are, of course, wonderful. But don't forget about all the different gemstones that come in a rainbow of colors. ✦ You could choose a color to express your feelings; to match your lover's eyes; to accompany a poem you've written for a special occasion. Be creative!

* *Red:* Ruby, garnet, tourmaline, spinel, red beryl, coral
* *Blue:* Sapphire, tanzanite, topaz, zircon, tourmaline, spinel, aquamarine
* *Green:* Emerald, garnet, peridot, sapphire, jade, andalusite
* *Purple:* Amethyst, sapphire, tanzanite, spinel, garnet
* *Pink:* Tourmaline, sapphire, spinel, kunzite, morganite, pearl, coral
* *Yellow:* Citrine, sapphire, topaz, fire opal, garnet, tourmaline
* *Brown:* Topaz, andalusite, smoky quartz, tourmaline
* *White:* Moonstone, pearl, jade

For more info:

* The Jewelers of America offer a free pamphlet called "What You Should Know About Colored Gemstones." Write to them at 1185 Avenue of the Americas, 30th Floor, New York City 10036.
* The American Gem Society offers a jewelers' directory and access to its member retailers. Call 213-936-4367.

FYI: Gifts for Sports Fans

If your lover loves football (or baseball or hockey) *almost* as much as he loves *you* . . . then you *really* ought to get him an official Team Ring. Licensed by the NFL, NHL and Major League Baseball, the rings are made by L.G. Balfour, makers of rings for numerous Super Bowl, Stanley Cup and World Series championship events. ✦ The cost? Just $95. Call 800-235-6533, or write to L.G. Balfour, 301 Oxford Valley Road, P.O. Box 374, Yardley, Pennsylvania 19067.

George B. came to the Romance Class one evening with a shoebox under his arm and a big smile on his face. I'll let George speak, because he can tell his story better than I. ✦ "I ain't college-educated like a lot of you in this room, but my love for my wife is deep n' intense. And I don't have lots of money to buy fancy gifts. But I manage to bring my wife one flower a week—*every* week—no matter *what*. And I figured-out a way to make each flower different and special: Each one has a note attached. But I ain't a writer like you—as you can probably tell—but I figured-out a way to be as eloquent as a poet. I borrow other people's words and I save 'em in this box. I been savin' quotes for 'bout 32 years now, I think. My system is better than a fancy file or a dang computer. I can pull out a great quote for a note—in fact, my wife calls 'em my 'Love Quote Notes'—in a flash. Here's one:

> *'I am, in every thought of my heart, yours.'*

Y'know who said that? Woodrow Wilson! Bet ya didn't know he was romantic, eh? See, the way I figure it, we all feel the same stuff. It's just that some people can get it out—express it—better 'n others. What I do is just kinda keep my eyes open. I don't really search for this stuff. It kinda finds *me*, if that makes any sense. Here's another one:

> *'Thank you for your presence in my life . . . you encourage me*
> *to go beyond myself.'*

That's by Linda DuPuy Moore. To tell you the truth, I don't know who half these people are, but that ain't what's really important, is it? 'Cause when I use 'em, their words become *mine*, too!"

Resources

☆ *A Gift to Myself*, by Charles Whitfield
☆ *Try Giving Yourself Away*, by David Dunn
☆ *Creative Gift Packagings*, by Yoko Kondo

"One does not fall 'in' or 'out' of love.
One grows in love."

~ Leo Buscaglia

Growth

Donna Sommerfield set me straight one evening in the Romance Class. "You use the words *change* and *growth* interchangeably—and they're *not* the same! *Change* is inevitable, but *growth* is not! The weather changes, but it doesn't grow. Growth implies *positive, directed* change. Growth requires purpose and commitment and action." I stand corrected!

If your relationship is to grow and change for the better, *both of you must participate*. One person alone cannot do it! Here's why: We're talking about the *relationship*—not about either of you as individuals. Sure, you can change and grow as an individual, but if only *one* of you is doing the changing, it unbalances the relationship, making it wobbly and weak. If one of you changes a great deal while the other remains stagnant and "happy" with the status quo, the relationship will wither and die. Both of you must work (and play) at the relationship together. ✦ You can't *force* change in a relationship—it simply doesn't work that way. And you can't coerce your partner—it will always backfire on you. Either you work (and play) together or it doesn't work at all!

Like all living things, relationships either grow or they die.
They change or they stagnate.
They're either getting better
or they're getting worse.

Some people see growth as a threat to their relationships. They *like* things the way they are! Rest assured that change and growth are *not* enemies of relationships—they enhance and deepen relationships. The *real* enemies are a lack of intimacy and a failure to communicate. ✦ Growing does *not* mean "growing apart"—unless there's little trust, intimacy or communication in your relationship. "Growing apart" also happens when one partner grows and the other one refuses, or is stuck, or is scared. But you must realize that these problems are not caused by the growth, but by lack of self-esteem, lack of knowledge, lack of love, and/or lots of fear.

Tip: Lessons from Childhood

One evening during a break in the Romance Class, I noticed that a "Parenting Skills" class was going on across the hall. I stood in the doorway and was fascinated to learn that the 10 key skills they said children needed to learn applied so well to the skills adults need in our intimate relationships. I borrowed a copy of their textbook, and used it to conduct the next hour of the Romance Class. The structure suited my material so well that no one suspected that I was teaching them a *children's* curriculum!   ✦   I suggest that you grab a copy of *MegaSkills*, by Dorothy Rich. It will help you care for the child within yourself, and it will provide surprising insights about your adult relationships.   ✦   Here are the 10 MegaSkills . . .

1. *Confidence:* Feeling able to do it
2. *Motivation:* Wanting to do it
3. *Effort:* Being willing to work hard
4. *Responsibility:* Doing what's right
5. *Initiative:* Moving into action
6. *Perseverance:* Completing what you start
7. *Caring:* Showing concern for others
8. *Teamwork:* Working with others
9. *Common Sense:* Using good judgment
10. *Problem Solving:* Putting what you know and what you can do into action

Which skills come naturally to you? Which do you need to work on? Does your partner agree with your evaluation of yourself?

Many people have a skewed view of growing up. They think that being an adult means leaving behind many of the (best) attributes of being young: Playfulness, leisure and adventure. They are wrong, *wrong, wrong!* "Maturing is a process of adding things/experiences/knowledge/people to your life," said Joe B., a retiree who attended the Romance Class with his wife of 46 years. "It's about *adding* things—not *subtracting* things. Too many young folks who are are in a rush to 'grow up' leave behind the very things that give life its spark."   ✦   Do you think that *adventure* is a thing of adolescence? If so, then chances are good that you have no adventure in your relationship. Do you think that *playing* is for kids? If so, you probably have little fun in your relationship.   ✦   In study after study, people who have extramarital affairs reaffirm that it's not sex they're after, but adventure, passion and excitement. *Think* about it.

This word *paradigm* seems to have taken over the English language lately. Well, as over-used as it may be, it's *still* a useful concept to help us survive and thrive in our long-term relationships. You see, if we are to make it through several decades together, we must not merely grow and change, but we must undergo several paradigm shifts throughout the course of our lives. ✦ A paradigm is a model, a way to understand the world, a set of rules and assumptions that accurately describe our experience or expectations. ✦ Our society is currently undergoing a paradigm shift in the concept of marriage and long-term relationships. The previous model has been a "Dominant-Submissive" model, with the man as the undisputed master of the house. We are now in a transition, as we attempt to create a relationship paradigm based on equality and true love, instead of on prescribed roles and obedience. ✦ Other paradigm shifts that we'll all be dealing with in the coming decades include: Our *work environments*, as corporations re-create themselves to survive in the modern world; our concept of *communication*, as telephones, computers and TVs merge; the concept of *family*, as two-career couples, single parents and other non-traditional family models are explored; and the way we view *aging*, as we Baby Boomers get older and refuse to "grow up" properly!

Homework: Let's Get Specific

Grab your pad and pen . . .

☞ How do you—personally—want to grow?
   ○ What *existing* characteristics do you want to nurture and expand?
   ○ What *new* skills/abilities/traits do you want to acquire?
☞ How do you want your relationship to grow?
   ○ What characteristics do you want to retain from your dating years?
   ○ How do you want your relationship to change and grow?
   ○ How will you have to grow in order to bring this about? How will your partner have to grow?
☞ Brainstorm two strategies for achieving each goal that you've listed.

Resources

☆ *Passages: Predictable Crises in Adult Life*, by Gail Sheehy
☆ *Transformations: Growth and Change in Adult Life*, by Roger Gould
☆ *Creating Love: The Next Stage of Growth*, by John Bradshaw

---

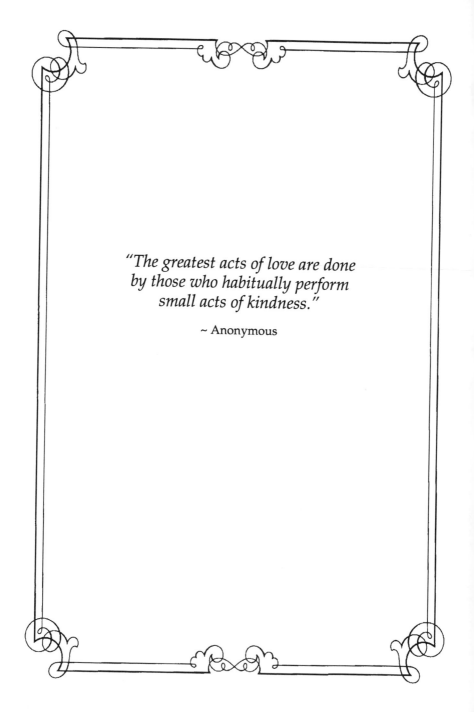

"The greatest acts of love are done by those who habitually perform small acts of kindness."

~ Anonymous

Habits

Name some habits . . . Smoking. Overeating. Biting your fingernails. Loving. *Loving*? ✦ Yes, love is a habit. A *good* habit. Thinking about love as a *habit* instead of some larger-than-life concept helps many people understand and live their love much more effectively.

Bad habits have a way of sneaking into our lives, don't they? All loving couples start out together with the best of intentions. But we eventually fall into hurtful habits, both large and small, that eat away at our relationship. What can we do about it? ✦ First of all, we can give habits the respect they deserve. What I mean is to respect the *power* that habits have. We need to acknowledge that *habits are hard to change*! They require *us* to change. And a lot of us are pretty darn stubborn. [Just ask Tracey about me!] ✦ Secondly, you must put forth a lot of effort, energy and emotional commitment in order to change the hurtful "habits of the heart" that damage our relationships. ✦ You also need to be patient with yourself. Don't expect to change lifelong habits overnight.

Homework: Lying, Cheating & Stealing

I highly recommend the habits of *lying*, *cheating* and *stealing*. The goal, of course, is *divorce*. When practiced properly, all of these things can lead to a wonderfully romantic relationship!

✗ **Lie**—Lie in bed together more often.
✗ **Cheat**—Cheat on your budget: Take your honey on a surprise three-day vacation somewhere exotic. Cheat on your diet: Order champagne cocktails with dinner.
✗ **Steal**—Steal time away from your job and your other responsibilities, and give it to your relationship.
✗ **Divorce**—Divorce yourself from your worries. Divorce yourself from the thousand-and-one distractions and responsibilities and "shoulds" in your life.

Did you know that we all have "emotional habits"?—Patterns of reacting, habits of feeling that become roads we travel without even thinking about it. Here's what happens . . . Early in our relationships we're open and receptive to new feelings and experiences with our new lover. We're alive, passionate, communicative. As time goes on, we inevitably fall into various emotional habits. One partner sulks when unhappy, and the other learns to tiptoe around touchy issues. One partner's sex drive is lower than the other's, and because they never discuss their differences, they argue about *other* things like money or kids or work. ✦ These kinds of emotional habits squeeze the joy out of life, and they drain the passion from your relationship. If you say or think any of these phrases frequently, you're probably stuck in negative emotional habits:

▲ "We never really *talk* anymore."
▲ "Sex life? *What* sex life?"
▲ "Yeah, I love her, but there's no *passion* anymore."
▲ "Look, you just gotta accept that two people aren't going to be infatuated with each other forever. It's realistic to lower your expectations."

Can you avoid falling into these bad habits? Probably not. But I think it's best to make the mistakes. Then you can learn from them. Otherwise, you're living your life too cautiously, and you're tip-toeing around your partner, forever afraid of making a mistake or hurting his feelings.

Exercises: Practicing Good Habits

Taking your lover for granted is one of the worst habits you can fall into. Here are some exercises to help you develop more loving habits:

✳ Show appreciation more often. (Healthy couples tend to express appreciation for their partners at least three times a day.)
✳ Focus on your good memories instead of the bad.
✳ Focus on your partner's good qualities instead of the bad.
✳ Don't forget that we all need to feel appreciated for a *variety* of our qualities. (She needs to be appreciated for more than her looks. He needs to be appreciated for more than his earning potential.)
✳ Begin your day by telling your lover one specific thing you love about her.
✳ End your day by telling your love one specific thing you appreciate that he did today.

FYI: "The 7 Habits of Highly Effective Lovers"

The fastest learners know how to take the lessons and habits from *one* area of life and apply them to *another.* ✦ When I read books, I often "re-title" them in my head. Anthony Robbins' *Unlimited Power* becomes *Unlimited Love.* And Stephen Covey's bestseller *The 7 Habits of Highly Effective People* becomes *The 7 Habits of Highly Effective Lovers.* To illustrate how well this translation works, here are the seven habits (think about them with your *relationship* in mind):

Habit 1 *Be proactive*—Principles of personal vision
Habit 2 *Begin with the end in mind*—Principles of personal leadership
Habit 3 *Put first things first*—Principles of personal management
Habit 4 *Think Win/Win*—Principles of interpersonal leadership
Habit 5 *Seek first to understand, then to be understood*—Principles of empathic communication
Habit 6 *Synergize*—Principles of creative cooperation
Habit 7 *Sharpen the saw*—Principles of balanced self-renewal

Sometimes it's helpful to have a list or a structure to help us conceptualize certain ideas. This book does a great job of organizing a system of thought into seven identifiable and memorable categories. ✦ Romantics naturally practice these habits, but we can all use some reminders and a broadening of our point-of-view. Personally, I was greatly inspired by Habit #1. I've always had a certain Vision about relationships and the way love functions in our lives, which my books express—but Stephen Covey's book helped me to clarify my thoughts. I think it will help you clarify your thoughts and values, too.

"Creative thinking may mean simply the realization that there's no particular virtue in doing things the way they have always been done."

~ Rudolf Flesch

Resources

☆ *Habits of the Heart*, by Robert Bellah
☆ *The 7 Habits of Highly Effective People*, by Stephen R. Covey
☆ *Intimate Partners: Patterns in Love and Marriage*, by Maggie Scarf
☆ *Unlimited Power*, by Anthony Robbins

"Most of us go through life
not knowing what we want,
but feeling darned sure this isn't it."

~ Anonymous

Help!

"He who never asks for help
never gives the gift of allowing others to share their love."

~ Anonymous

Resources: Spiritual

✴ **A Course In Miracles**—is a three volume book presenting a spiritual Path that combines modern psychological principles with Christianity and Eastern thought. ✦ The Miracle Distribution Center offers a variety of related books, tapes and games. Write to 1141 East Ash Avenue, Fullerton, California 92631; or call 714-738-8380 or 800-359-2246.

✴ **Marriage Magazine**—*"Celebrating the Potential of Marriage"*—shares the vision of the infinite potential of marriage. It celebrates the ideal of a long-term, intimate, forever growing union, while accepting the reality of our imperfect selves and relationships as they are now. A subscription is just $15. Write to *Marriage*, 955 Lake Drive, St. Paul, Minnesota 55120; or call 612-454-6434.

Resources: Sex

➤ **Sex Question Hotline**: A 24-hour hotline for sex questions was recently created by the Masters and Johnson Institute. Call 900-933-6868. (The Institute, located in St. Louis, Missouri, can be reached at 314-781-2224.)

➤ **Yellow Silk**—*Journal of Erotic Arts*. This well-written and beautifully illustrated magazine presents erotica in fictional, poetic and graphic form. Elegant, sexual and sensual. A subscription is just $30. Write to Yellow Silk, P.O. Box 6374, Albany, California 94706.

One of the best places to look for help is *inside yourself*. I truly believe that we all have a Wisdom inside ourselves that knows what's Right for each of us. ✦ When you go to others for help, you've got to be careful that they don't put their own agenda ahead of your best interests. ✦ Learning to "tune-in" to your Inner Voice is not an easy thing to do. But finding that Companion is like finding a long-lost friend.

Resources: Holistic Workshops

These centers for holistic studies offer a wide variety of classes and workshops that tend to focus on improving human potential, increaseing self-esteem, promoting natural health, and teaching physical and mental fitness.

❖ **California Institute of Integral Studies**: 765 Ashbury Street, San Francisco, California 94117; 415-753-6100.

❖ **Interface**: 55 Wheeler Street, Cambridge, Massachusetts 02138; 617-876-4600.

❖ **The Naropa Institute**: 2130 Arapahoe Avenue, Boulder, Colorado 80302; 303-444-0202.

❖ **The New York Open Center**: 83 Spring Street, New York, New York 10012; 212-219-2527.

❖ **Oasis Center**: 7463 Sheridan Road, Chicago, Illinois 60626; 312-274-6777.

Time does *not* heal all wounds! Time is a *component* in the healing process, but I sure want a doctor's help when I break my leg! In the same way, *heart*breaks don't heal by themselves either. ✦ How *do* heartbreaks heal? With understanding, growth and forgiveness. With the help and support of friends, family, therapists and/or spiritual counselors.

Resources: Couple-Oriented

💗 **Marriage Encounter** is an international organization that focuses on the spiritual as well as practical needs of couples dedicated to their long-term, monogamous relationships. "Marriage Encounter Weekends" help couples re-experience their love and refresh their relationship. Many couples also gather in self-directed groups in hundreds of cities and towns. Call for more information: 800-795-5683.

💗 **The PAIRS Foundation** (Practical Application of Intimate Relationship Skills): PAIRS is a 120-hour course for couples, offered by trained leaders. It provides a carefully sequenced, guided series of lectures and experiences that teach new perceptions and skills. Contact: 3705 South George Mason Drive, Suite C-8, Falls Church, Virginia 22041; or call 703-998-5550 or 800-842-7470.

Resources: Romance

❦ **"Romantic Traveling" newsletter**—is for lovers with wanderlust. This quarterly newsletter gives you specific recommendations and reviews of romantic destinations, elegant restaurants, and lovely hotels, inns and B&Bs. Just $15 per year. Write to Winterbourne Press, 236 West Portal, Suite 237, San Francisco, California 94127; or call 415-731-8239.

❦ **"The LoveLetter" newsletter**—presents more romantic ideas, strategies and tips—from the author of *1001 Ways To Be Romantic*. The first year's subscription is *free* (a $25 value). Write to LoveLetter, P.O. Box 226, Weymouth, Massachusetts 02188.

Resources: Personal Growth

☞ **Feldenkrais**: "Awareness Through Movement" is a unique method that uses gentle, guided body movements to put you in touch with your psychological self as well as your physical self. Contact the Feldenkrais Guild, 524 Ellsworth Street, P.O. Box 489, Albany, Oregon 97321; 503-926-0981.

☞ **Robbins Research Institute**: Founded by powerhouse motivator Anthony Robbins, the Institute offers a variety of day-long, weekend, and week-long seminars. Write to: Torrey Pines Business & Research Park, 3366 North Torrey Pines Court, Suite 100, La Jolla, California 92037.

Resources: Self-Esteem

✛ **Louise L. Hay Educational Institute** helps people restructure their lives through self-esteem and self-love. For information on books, workshops and lectures, write to: Hay House, Inc., P.O. Box 2212, Santa Monica, California 90406.

✛ **Esalen Institute**: This well-known residential center hosts a wide variety of workshops and classes that develop self-esteem and promote holistic health. Write to: Esalen Institute, Big Sur, California 93920; or call 408-667-3000

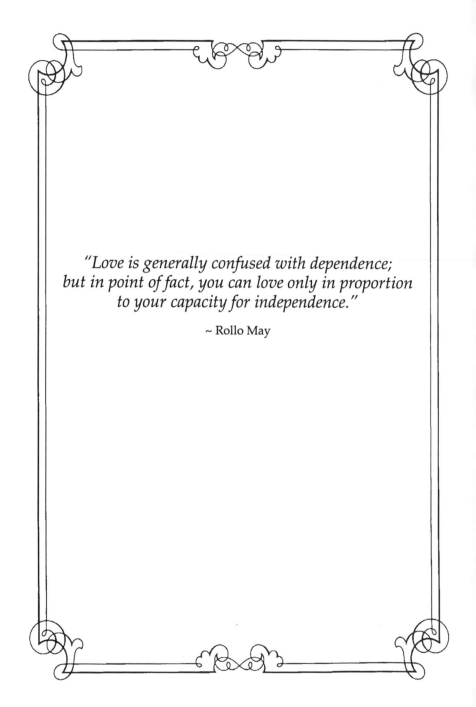

*"Love is generally confused with dependence;
but in point of fact, you can love only in proportion
to your capacity for independence."*

~ Rollo May

Interdependence

While issues of independence are important in everyone's life, it seems that it's the issues of *inter*dependence that give most couples a hard time. We're all faced with the question of how to balance our lives as healthy, independent individuals with our need for companionship and true love, i.e., interdependence with another. ✦ Don't look for any easy answers here, because there are none! This is one of the issues that Tracey and I struggle with most actively. [Boy, that's an awfully polite way to say that we fight!]

Interdependence is *not* the opposite of independence. It's not an either/or kind of thing. This paradox confuses many people. ✦ When you're in a committed relationship, it's not a choice between commitment and freedom. You don't give up your freedom when you become a couple. If you do, you're either in an immature relationship or a controlling one. Mature relationships are a dynamic interaction of interdependence and independence. True commitment is a voluntary, freely chosen thing. You must be independent in order to make that choice. If you're coerced/intimidated/seduced into making that choice, you don't have true commitment, and you're doomed to failure.

You *must* have the freedom to say "yes" or "no" to your relationship. If you *don't* have this freedom, you have an *arrangement*, or a *contract*, or an *indentured servitude*—but you don't really have a *relationship*. ✦ The decision to say "yes" or "no" is made and re-made every day. You *always* make a choice, regardless of whether it's made consciously or unconsciously. If you let the decision be unconscious or automatic, you're giving-up some of your power, and you're robbing yourself of the joy of re-commitment. Saying "yes" with feeling is an empowering act. One that builds intimacy. ✦ Yes, this freedom is a scary thing, because it gives your partner the power to say "no"! But think about it: He or she always had that power *anyway*! We just rarely *use* that power.

"Marriage is a relationship. When you make the sacrifice in marriage, you're sacrificing not to each other but to unity in a relationship. The Chinese image of the Tao, with the dark and light interacting—that's the relationship of yang and yin, male and female, which is what a marriage is. And that's what you have become when y have married. You're no longer this one alone; your identity is in a relationship. Marriage is not a simple love affair, it's an ordeal, and the ordeal is the sacrificeof ego to a relationship in which two have become one." ✦ Thoughts from Joseph Campbell, in his deeply insightful book *The Power of Myth*.

FYI: Interdependence Defined

* ✳ "Caring without clinging." {Jerry E., Atlanta}
* ✳ "One soul living in two bodies." {Eric L., Chicago}
* ✳ "The dynamics of *relationship ecology*." {Archie C., Syracuse}
* ✳ "Giving *of* yourself without giving *up* yourself." {Marisa M., DuBois}

What are you committed to? Are you committed to your wedding vows—or the terms of your prenuptial agreement? ✦ Are you committed to *forever*—or to *convenience*? ✦ Are you committed to excellence—or to mediocrity? ✦ Are you committed to remaining independent—are you stuck being dependent—or are you committed to the more difficult (but more rewarding) path of *interdependence*?

A key word in any discussion on interdependence is *dynamic*. At its best, a relationship is a dynamic, ever-changing process whereby two people share everything from their joys to their sorrows. In a healthy relationship, that process involves playing different roles for each other at different times. I'm strong while you're weak; you're confident when I'm insecure. In a healthy relationship there's a dynamic shifting of roles that takes place continuously and largely unconsciously. Healthy couples flow into and out of and around each other. ✦ *Un*healthy couples become stuck in their respective roles—often out of comfort, sometimes out of fear. Their inability to be flexible makes the relationship brittle. It can't handle too much stress, or the unexpected, or intense emotions—either positive or negative emotions. Unhealthy relationships that have lost their dynamic qualities no longer support each individual. Change or movement *of any kind* can be of great help to these relationships.

FYI: Pros & Cons

Many Romance Class participants open up and share some pretty intense, intimate feelings with us. We always learn a lot. I hope that these anonymous but truly heartfelt observations strike some familiar chords in you, too.

✓ "I'm afraid that interdependence may lead to *dependence*."
✓ "I fear that my partner won't be there when I need her."
✓ "I'm afraid that I'll lose myself in him."
✓ "I've spent such a long time being single, I'm not sure I *can* learn how to be truly interdependent."
✓ "I value my independence. I'm concerned that I'll lose it in a relationship."

✗ "I find great comfort in the interdependence my husband and I share."
✗ "Discovering that I didn't have to be strong all the time was a tremendous relief for me. —Don't tell the guys I said that, okay?"
✗ "I think that interdependence is one of the benefits of marriage over *any* single relationship, no matter how long-term or committed."
✗ "I was *happy* being independent—but it wasn't very challenging. I'm happy in my marriage, too—but it's complications and situations are *wonderfully* challenging. They spur me on to change and grow."

The dependent youngster yearns to be independent.
The independent adolescent feels all grown-up.
But only the interdependent adult
knows true maturity.

Resources

☆ *Do I Have To Give Up Me To Be Loved By You?* by Jordan & Margaret Paul
☆ *Personhood*, by Leo Buscaglia
☆ *I and Thou*, by Martin Buber
☆ *The Fragile Bond*, by Augustus Y. Napier
☆ *Intimate Partners: Patterns in Love and Marriage*, by Maggie Scarf

---

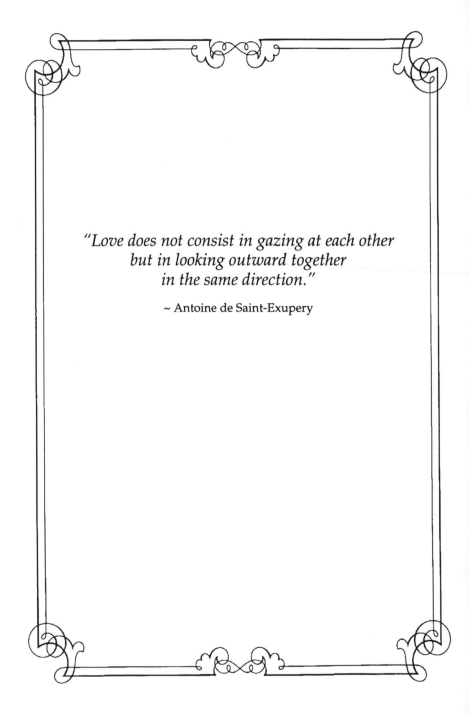

*"Love does not consist in gazing at each other
but in looking outward together
in the same direction."*

~ Antoine de Saint-Exupery

Intimacy

Many of us have an intense love-hate relationship with intimacy. [I know *I* do.] We want it; we need it; we chase it; we lament it's loss. And yet we fear it; we run away from it; we protect ourselves from it. ✦ Why? Well, the price of intimacy is high. And the risk is great. The price is *yourself*. And the risk is abandonment, loss or humiliation. These are major, and understandable, barriers. ✦ What about the reward, the promise of intimacy? People who experience intimacy with their partners are *known*. They've got a safe harbor, and this helps them deal with the world much more effectively. They have more inner peace than most people. They have an inner resource takes them beyond the limits of what one person alone can achieve.

Intimacy must be created and re-created. It's not an accomplishment that sits like a trophy on your mantle. It's a feeling, an experience, that is only alive in the moment, in the *Now*. ✦ This is why long-term intimacy is possible only in committed relationships. It takes most of us a long, long time to master the art of staying in the Now. We keep slipping into the past or the future. We get nostalgic for the intimacy we experienced in the past; we dream of intimacy to come in the future. We need a committed partner who will stay with us while we practice living in the Now.

> *"People need to act toward each other*
> *as though they are making up after a fight—*
> *without having the fight first."*
>
> ~ Jay Uhler

For most people, *creating* intimacy is much easier than *sustaining* intimacy. Why? Because *creating* intimacy only requires an immediate need and short-term desire—whereas *sustaining* intimacy requires commitment, skills, and very often, unlearning early conditioning and a lifetime of bad habits.

There is only one place where intimacy can be found: It's in the *Now*. You can find hints, advice and great quotes in the Past. But intimacy isn't simply an *idea*—it's an *experience*. And experiences happen *now*. Intimacy must be re-created, re-experienced and re-understood all the time.

Exercise: Pillowtalk

○ Light one candle.
○ Get settled into bed together. (Make it early enough so that neither of you will doze off suddenly.)
○ Talk about your relationship. Specifically, about what's working and what's not working. Keep your focus on the recent past—within the past week. This will keep you centered in the present.
○ The purpose here is to connect emotionally with your partner—it's not to hash out problems, deal with heavy issues, or be sexual.

One sign of intimacy is calling each other "pet names." For me, that was one of the subtle signs in my early relationship with Tracey: We *spontaneously* called each other by private, silly names. ✦ *However—* I recently learned a little lesson from Tracey. It seems that over the past four years I've fallen so far into the habit of calling her by one of the twenty-some names I have for her, that I rarely call her *Tracey* any more! I'm now making an effort to balance things. ✦ Beware! Over time, the heartfelt "Honey" can become generic and empty!

Romance is the process—Love is the goal.

Yes, sex can express intimacy in a way that words cannot. But don't lose sight of the fact that words are critically important before and after lovemaking. We need to guide and teach one another; we need to encourage and support one another.

Intimacy can be expressed through a simple gesture; a kind word; a gentle touch; a wink of an eye; a simple gift. The expressions are myriad, the meaning is one: "I love you."

You can't learn intimacy from a book! Not *this* one, not *any* one! Intimacy must be experienced, experimented-with, lived-with. The best we authors and lecturers and experts [*experts*?!—more like fellow travelers] can do is point the way. ✦ [Actually, that's not true. The best we can do is to practice what we preach . . . To live lives that reflect our beliefs. I guess that's the true test of integrity, which applies equally to politicians or televangelists or writers of relationship books.] ✦ Please, *please* remember that *you're* in charge. Take every suggestion and bit of advice with a grain of salt and a dose of skepticism. What's important is how *you* feel and how *you* react and how all of this stuff can be integrated into the unique individual that *you* are.

Studies show that most couples spend less than 30 minutes a week sharing intimate feelings. [I hope *you* weren't among those surveyed.]

Resources

☆ *Challenge of the Heart: Love, Sex and Intimacy in Changing Times*, by John Welwood

☆ *Being Intimate; A Guide To Successful Relationships*, by John Amodeo & Kris Wentworth

☆ *The Transformation of Intimacy: Sexuality, Love, and Eroticism in Modern Societies*, by Anthony Gibbins

---

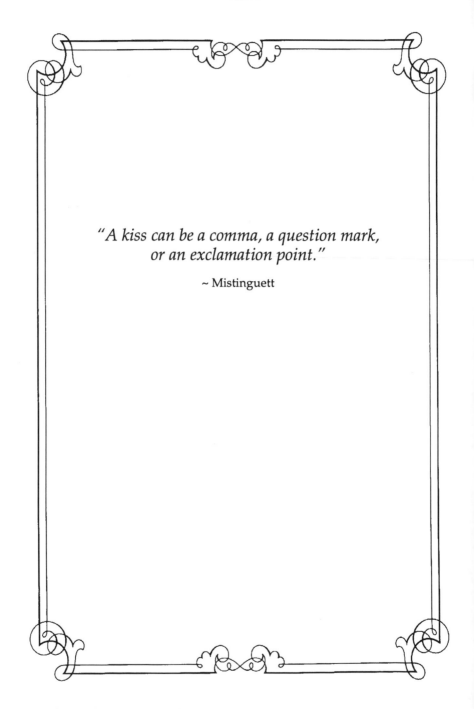

"A kiss can be a comma, a question mark, or an exclamation point."

~ Mistinguett

Kissing

Speaking our feelings is necessary.
But when you reach the point of needing to convey
"I love you more than I can say"
—that's when a kiss says it all.

Do you remember your first kiss? . . . I mean your first *real* kiss! What was his/her name? How old were you? Where were you? Who initiated the kiss? Wasn't it just about the best thing that had ever happened in your life?! ✦ What happened to the anticipation and excitement that used to accompany the act of kissing? Is it possible to regain that electric feeling? Those who have ernestly tried, report back a resounding *yes*! As in many things, it requires a change in mindset, a little willingness from both partners, and a little practice. ✦ Are you ready? [Let me tell you, if you don't have fun in *this* chapter, I suggest that you give up, move to a mountaintop, and devote yourself to a life of contemplation and chastity. The rest of us have signed up for a lesson in *Aerobic Kissing*!]

Homework: Warm-Up Exercises

- ❤ Remember that kissing is an *activity unto itself.*
- ❤ Kissing is not merely the first stop on the road to sex!
- ❤ Remember, there's a lot of kissing to be discovered in the area between a quick peck and passionate French Kiss!
- ❤ When you kiss, stay focused, stay in the moment.
- ❤ Timing is just as important as technique.

Words express passion. Kissing confirms it.

Kissing is a special kind of touching. And all touching conveys messages. What do *your* kisses convey? Caring and love? Passion and excitement? Or merely lust and impatience?

Do you grok kissing? [For an explanation of *grokking* you'll have to read one of the best science fiction books of all time, *Stranger In A Strange Land*, by Robert A. Heinlein.] As I keep saying, if you have the right mindset you can find romance *anywhere*—in the *Wall Street Journal* and in science fiction. The following is an excerpt from *Stranger In A Strange Land* in which Anne is talking with a man about the main character, Michael, a human who was raised by Martians, and thus has some extraordinary abilities... ✦ "'Anne? What's so special about the way that lad kisses?' Anne looked dreamy, then dimpled ... 'Mike gives a kiss his whole attention.' 'Oh, rats! I do myself. Or did.' Anne shook her head. 'No. I've been kissed by men who did a very good job. But they don't give kissing their whole attention. They *can't*. No matter how hard they try parts of their minds are on something else. Missing the last bus—or their chances for making the gal—or their own techniques in kissing—or maybe worry about jobs, or money, or will husband or papa or the neighbors catch on. Mike doesn't have technique ... but when Mike kisses you he isn't doing *anything* else. You're his whole universe ... and the moment is eternal because he doesn't have any plans and isn't going anywhere. Just kissing you.' She shivered. 'It's overwhelming.'" ✦ You may not be able to speak Martian—and therefore will never be able to master grokking fully—but you *can* learn to focus your attention better, and give your partner your undivided attention while you're kissing!

"Miss me. Kiss me. Bliss me."

~ T.E.G.

If your lover is dissatisfied with your kissing, you can be certain that she'll be disappointed with whatever follows after the kiss.

Questions: When, Where & How?
❖ When are you shy—and when are you bold?
❖ When are you the kisser—and when are you the kissee?
❖ When are your kisses planned—and when are they surprises?
❖ When do you kiss tenderly—and when do you kiss with force?
❖ Have you kissed every square inch of your lover's body?

FYI: Kissing Lessons

At last count there were 1001 ways to kiss. Some, but not all, of them have been named. Have you tried all of these? Do you have any others to add to the list?

* *Lip-Only Kiss*: When the only part of your bodies that touch are your lips.
* French Kiss: Lips touching, mouths open, explore each other with your tongues.
* *Nip Kiss*: When you add gentle, little nibbles of your lover's lower lip.
* *Cradling Kiss*: When you hold your lover's face in both hands while kissing.
* *Switch Kiss*: When you kiss your partner's upper lip while she kisses your lower lip.
* *Zorro Kiss*: Also known playfully as the "Dueling Tongues" kiss.
* *Sleep Kiss*: Kissing your partner *gently* while he sleeps.
* *Awakening Kiss*: Kissing your partner's lips gently at first, and then increasing the pressure until she awakens.
* *Butterfly Kiss*: When you lightly brush your eyelashes against your partner's cheek, or other body part.
* *Vacuum Kiss*: Sucking the air out of each other's mouths, and then separating with a *Pop!*
* *Cordial Kiss*: Take a sip of your favorite cordial or liqueur, keep it in your mouth, then kiss your partner and share the liquid.
* *Humming Kiss*: Humming her favorite love song while kissing.

Warning! Oral sex—even between married or consenting adults—is illegal in 23 states!—Alabama, Arizona, Arkansas, Florida, Georgia, Idaho, Kansas, Louisiana, Maryland, Massachusetts, Minnesota, Mississippi, Missouri, Montana, Nevada, North Carolina, Oklahoma, Rhode Island, South Carolina, Tennessee, Texas, Utah, Virginia—and Washington, D.C., and in all branches of the U.S. military!

Resources

☆ *The Clitoral Kiss*, by Kenneth Ray Stubbs
☆ *The Kama Sutra of Vatsyayana*, ed. by W. G. Archer
☆ *The Sensuous Mouth*, by Paul Ableman
☆ *The Best Places to Kiss in New York City: A Romantic Travel Guide*, by Paula Begoun. (Also *Los Angeles* and *San Francisco* and *Southern California* and the *Northwest* and the *Northeast!*)

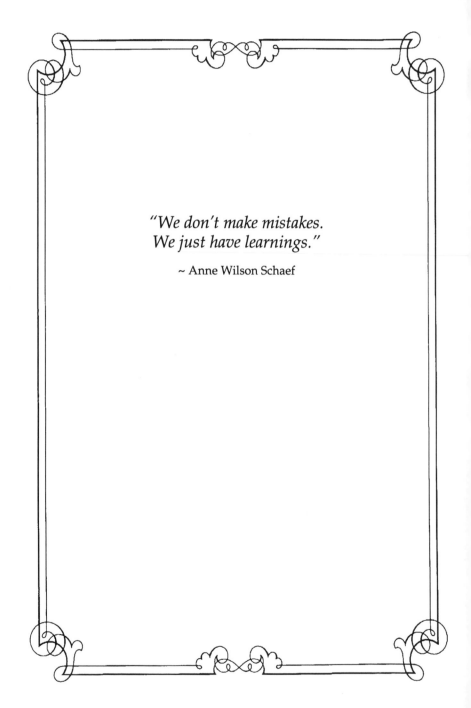

*"We don't make mistakes.
We just have learnings."*

~ Anne Wilson Schaef

Learning

There is *joy* in learning. A joy that most of us had up through kindergarten, when our educational system turned learning into a *job*.—A boring, repetitious, pointless job—and one that didn't pay well, either! We've had the joy of learning squeezed out of us, and many of us choose mindless entertainment over any kind of learning (television vs. books or classes). ✦ If we are to create intimate relationships, we need to re-capture the spirit of joy that was once a part of learning. For learning is an integral part of growth and change.

The first step in learning is . . . *unlearning*. (Young children have the benefit of having little prior experience and no bad habits to overcome, so they can go straight to learning. While we adults have to go through a difficult—and sometime torturous—process of unlearning years of habits, beliefs and patterns.)

FYI: Unlearning
The proper state of mind precedes all unlearning. It helps if you're . . .

- Openminded
- Flexible
- Playful
- Dissatisfied with what you already "know"
- Willing to "let go"
- Non-judgmental

FYI: Learning
Now, what do you need in order to learn? These things enhance learning . . .

- Listening skills
- Focusing skills
- A supportive environment
- Good role models
- Patience
- Good teachers
- Healthy self-esteem

‌

‌

Homework: Unlearning & Learning

What do you need to unlearn? What do you need to learn?

* ✤ Jot down at least four things you need to unlearn. (Behaviors, beliefs, habits, attitudes.)
* ✤ Jot down four things you feel your *partner* needs to unlearn.
* ✤ For each item on your lists, answer these questions:
  * ↔ "How would I benefit from making these changes?"
  * ↔ "How would my partner benefit if I made these changes?"
* ✤ How do your lists compare with your partner's?

An intriguing Truth that I learned several years ago is "In life, you teach what you need to learn." I've always liked this, and I've believed it on a gut level. However, I could never figure out how this applied to my teaching the Romance Class. You see, I'm *already* pretty romantic—so where's the lesson in this for *me*? ✦ Well, I *finally* figured it out. [But I'm not sure I can express it to you adequately without the help of my tone of voice, facial expressions and wild gesturing of my hands.] ✦ It has to do with *subtlety.* I've come to appreciate a more subtle level of the expression of love in my relationship with Tracey. It's an expression that goes "beyond" the roses and bubblebaths. It's more subtle than any gift— any *thing*. It's *quieter* than words. It's *softer* than a whisper. It's like . . . It's like . . . It's more a "look" than anything else. —It has to do with the *eyes.* Or rather, it's a quality/feeling/mindset/attitude that somehow gets communicated through your eyes. You know how it's said that your eyes are the window to your soul? —It's related to *that.* ✦ I think this has to do with the place where love and romance come together. ✦ For example . . . Tracey and I will be in the midst of a heated argument [. . . Yes, of *course* we fight, too!] and a certain *look* will flash between us—and we'll start *laughing.* Or . . . We'll be out somewhere, and Tracey will turn to me and whisper a lyric from our favorite Carly Simon song (*"I'm so in love with you—What else can I do?"*)—and we'll both well up with tears. In *public*! ✦ What in *your* life are you teaching . . . that you need to learn?

‌

John and Trudy W. honored me last year by celebrating their 50th wedding anniversary in my Romance Class. Here's what Trudy had to say: "We've come to share our knowledge and our insights. Here's the most important thing we've learned in our 50 years together: *We're mere beginners!* And the more we act like *students* of our relationship—instead of like its *masters*—the happier we are." And John added: "We've found that when it comes to most so-called experts, well, *the emperor has no clothes!*" ✦ I *wish* you could have been in that class with me!

One of the quickest ways to learn anything is to "model" those who are already successful at the skill you wish to master. Anthony Robbins is a champion of this effective concept. If you want to be a great skier, study and emulate the Olympic champions. If you want to be successful in business, model yourself after any number of successful millionaires. And if you want to have a great relationship, model yourself after the great couples. ✦ This sounds easy—*until* you start looking for some people who *are* great couples. *You can't find any!* [That's slightly overstated, but only *slightly*.] Believe me, I've looked. And I can't find *anyone* in our popular culture who I'd recommend to you. I searched the history books, too. Lots of intrigue and passion, but no one you'd want to model yourself after! Does this mean we're chasing a fairy tale? ✦ No, not at all. It simply means that great couples tend to keep to themselves, and that there are relatively few of them. Don't let this discourage you. First of all, you just might find a great role model living next door to you. And second, there's nothing wrong with aspiring to something that is rare and hard to achieve!

Resources

☆ *Learning to Love*, by H.F. Harlow
☆ *Getting the Love You Want: A Guide for Couples*, by Harville Hendrix
☆ *Mindfulness*, by Ellen J. Langer
☆ *The Potent Self*, by Moshe Feldenkrais

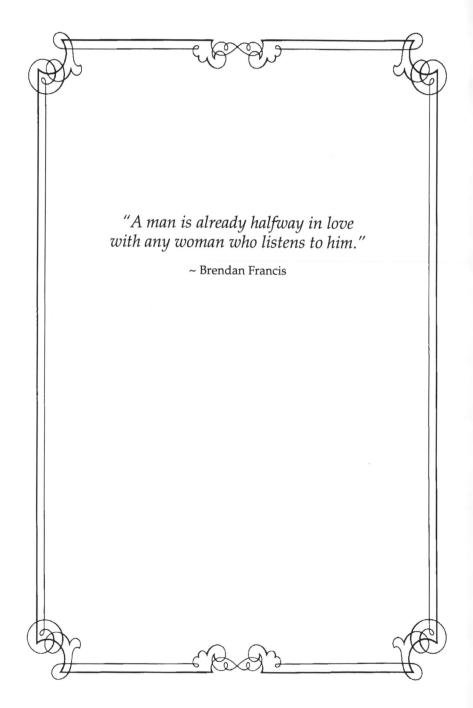

*"A man is already halfway in love
with any woman who listens to him."*

~ Brendan Francis

Listening

The first, and often most *difficult* listening skill is learning to listen to *ourselves*. Few of us take time on a regular basis to quiet our minds and simply *listen*. I'm not talking necessarily about meditating (although it couldn't hurt!), but about simply *listening* to ourselves. To our desires, feelings, intuitions, urges. There is wisdom and direction inside of us that we rarely tap into. ✦ The "real you" is somewhere in there, too.

Homework: Listening to Yourself

* Set aside 20 minutes of uninterrupted time.
* Sit comfortably.
* Close your eyes. Take several deep breaths.
* Let your mind wander.
* Make no effort to direct your thoughts or think about anything in particular.
* Just go with the flow.
* If you find yourself consciously "solving problems" or being upset about certain thoughts:
  * Open your eyes, jot the disturbing thoughts down on a pad, then close your eyes again and continue listening to yourself.
  * You can deal with those issues *later*.
  * Or just wait . . . Insights often pop into your head unexpectedly within a few days if you keep listening.
* Practice this exercise once-a-day for at least a month.
* You'll know yourself better at the end of the month. Guaranteed.

Now let's try listening to our *partners*. ✦ Are you a *passive* listener or an *active* listener? To the outside observer, there's no difference. The passive listener usually gives all the right feedback: Nods of the head and sympathetic responses. But there's a *world* of difference between what goes on *inside the heads* of passive and active listeners. The passive listener is focused on *himself* ("How does what she's saying affect *me*?"). The active listener is focused on his *partner* ("What is she feeling? Do I really understand what she's saying?"). ✦ Active listeners listen with *empathy*. And empathy is the pathway to intimacy.

Homework: Listening with Empathy

☞ Select a time when you have one hour of uninterrupted time, and the energy to deal with a problem.
☞ Sit facing one another, close enough to touch.
☞ Your partner states an issue or problem.
☞ You *listen*.
  ✳ No interrupting, judging or correcting allowed!
  ✳ As much as possible, "put yourself in your partner's shoes."
☞ Now, you repeat back to your partner the essence of what you heard him say. Use your *own* words, *not* his. This will ensure that you really understand what he's saying.
☞ Your partner acknowledges that he was heard correctly, or clarifies as necessary, then continues.
☞ Neither of you attempts to problem-solve during this session. The purpose is simply to be heard and understood.
☞ Being heard and understood is the essence of empathy. And empathy leads to intimacy.

One of the easiest ways to become a better listener is simply to *remove sources of interference*. Interference causes garbled communication, misunderstandings and lapses in receiving information. ✦ The first source of interference is . . . *you* yourself! What's your mindset? Are you really *here* with your partner, or are you somewhere else in your mind? Another way we create our own interference is by doing two or more things at the same time. "Multi-tasking" is a great way to get things accomplished, but it's a poor way to relate to your lover. ✦ The second major source of interference is the outside environment. Are the two of you alone? Are you likely to be interrputed? Is it noisy? Is there a phone anywhere within earshot?

FYI: Some Listening Skills

➤ Give your lover your *undivided attention*. (This is a deceptively simple statement of something that is extremely hard to do!)
➤ Eliminate the phrase "Yes, but . . ." from your vocabulary.
➤ Don't interrupt your partner.
➤ Practice empathy. Put yourself in your partner's place.
➤ Suspend your judgment.
➤ Try to listen with "new ears"—as if you've never heard this before.
➤ Listen with patience.
➤ Listen with your heart, not your head.

Homework: Reducing Fear By *Listening* to Your Lover

One of the most difficult tasks you'll ever undertake is to listen to your partner express negative emotions: Feelings of anger, dissatisfaction or fear. The challenge here is to refrain from becoming defensive, judgmental or threatened while listening. [Easier said than done, I know.] ✦ Here's an exercise in "Open-Minded Listening":

✳ Set aside a specific amount of time, about an hour, when you won't be interrupted. No kids, no phones, no interruptions.

✳ Sit in a comfortable room, in chairs facing one another.

✳ One person at a time "has the floor," and does so until he or she feels ready to trade roles.

✳ The talker expresses his or her feelings uninterrupted by the listener.

✳ The listener is restricted to asking questions only for clarification.

✳ The listener is not allowed to argue—or agree!—rebut, tell his side of the story, snort, sigh or roll his eyes!

✳ The goal of the listener is to be as non-judgmental and accepting as humanly possible.

✳ When the talker decides he is through, switch roles.

✳ You'll find that this exercise dissipates fear, anger and guilt.

One night in the Romance Class . . . A quiet guy in his mid-40s says: "Here's the biggest insight I've had in my 22-year marriage: My wife is an *expert* on me!" ✦ Is this really so surprising? You love someone. You live with him. You pay attention to him. You observe and study him. You learn how to interpret his moods, his tone of voice, his patterns. Of *course* you're going to become an expert on him! ✦ "At first it felt *great*—I felt very special. Then I felt guilty because, to be honest, I was *not* an expert on her. But I started listening more closely to her . . . and let me tell you—it's improved our marriage one hundred percent!" ✦ Doesn't it make you feel *special* to have someone's attention focused on you? As long as it's *loving* attention, and not *critical* attention, you'll benefit from your partner's insights, observations and consideration of you.

Resources

☆ *Born For Love*, by Leo Buscaglia
☆ *I'm OK, You're OK*, by Thomas Harris
☆ *Making Peace With Yourself*, by Harold H. Bloomfield
☆ *You Just Don't Understand*, by Deborah Tannen

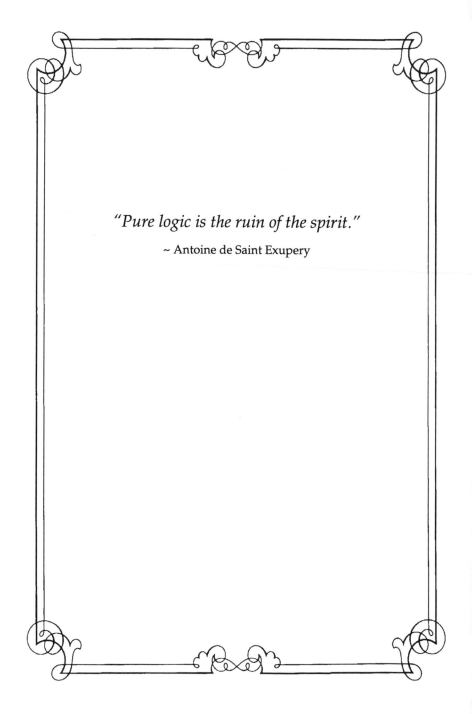

"Pure logic is the ruin of the spirit."

~ Antoine de Saint Exupery

Logic

"I hate to say it, but I fit the stereotype of an engineer. I'm logical, analytical, and somewhat out-of-touch with my emotions. I love my wife a great deal, and I'm not *stupid*—but when she used to tell me that she wished I were more romantic, I didn't really understand what that *meant*. The concept of romance didn't connect with my day-to-day life. I didn't have a vocabulary of romance. It was a great insight to me that romance is *truly* about the little, thoughtful, everyday gestures. *Thanks!*" {Dan B., talking from San Francisco, about his wife Kathy McB.}

Suggestion: A Logical Plan

Let's apply a little logic to love, shall we? Some of us don't believe in Fate, and we're unwilling to wait for luck!

➤ Step 1: *Set your goal.* Define the desired outcome.
➤ Step 2: *Take action.* You gotta do something or nothing will happen!
➤ Step 3: *Observe & analyze.* What reaction do you get? What happens?
➤ Step 4: *Adjust your actions.* Are you flexible enough to change?
➤ Step 5: *Repeat.* Repeat steps 2 through 4 ten times.
➤ Step 6: *Re-evaluate.* Review your original goal. Adjust it if you desire.
➤ Step 7: *Repeat.*

Success in love is *not* an accident. The difference between the Huxtables and the Bundys (between successful, happy couples and miserable, dysfunctional couples) is *not* a matter of Fate. ✦ There are consistent, logical patterns of action that lead to success. There are beliefs and attitudes that create intimacy. There are choices that build trust. There are strategies that lead to long-term happiness. ✦ Just because love is a mysterious, emotional thing doesn't mean you have to approach it like a moonstruck teenager, innocent child or melodramatic movie star. We all have the potential to create incredible loving relationships. It's simple—but it's not *easy*. ✦ The rules and guidelines are few, but their consistent application is difficult and complex. The concepts are simple: Affection, Commitment, Communication, Creativity, Forgiveness, Interdependence, Intimacy, Passion, Playing, Romance, Self-esteem, Time, Togetherness and Trust. We all know this stuff. But the pieces of this wonderful jig-saw puzzle can be put together a million different ways!

I believe that we're witnessing the dawn of a new era. A time in which the tyranny of *logic* is overthrown, and *emotion* is given equal time and more respect. Here at the close of the 20th Century we stand at the pinnacle of technological achievement—*and* at the edge of environmental disaster, and on the brink of moral bankruptcy. I believe that all of this is traceable to the radical separation of emotion from logic. ✦ I'm *not* advocating a rejection of science and logic and progress, or a return to blind mysticism and superstition. But I *do* believe we need to radically change our way of thinking about the place of emotion in our lives. We also need to change some of the paradigms we hold about the nature of humanity, the nature of relationships, and the nature of our minds. For example, a widely-used metaphor of the brain is that it functions like a computer. —We *interface* with the world, we receive *inputs*, we *process* information. This view is okay in a *limited* context. The brain is vastly more complex, mysterious and wonderful than *any* computer. ✦ The danger lies in believing that the brain is *actually*—instead of *metaphorically*—a computer. This leads to the dismissal of emotion—because it can't be understood as programming, and it defies logic. This kind of thinking dehumanizes people, it hurts society, and it really screws-up intimate relationships. ✦ A truly wonderful book deals with the primacy of emotion in our lives from a very unusual perspective—that of *synesthesia,* a rare condition in which people hear colors and smell sounds. In *The Man Who Tasted Shapes*, neurologist Richard E. Cytowic argues convincingly that humans are *irrational* by design: Our emotion, not our logic, is really in charge. I believe that his book forms the foundation of a new era.

> *Some say that emotion defies logic*
> *Well, I say that logic defies emotion!*

Questions: Logic In Your Life

✔ Which one of you is more logical? Which one is more emotional?
  → Do you each respect the other's style?
✔ Do you balance logic and intuition in your life?
✔ Many romantics are quite logical. What logical skills enhance your relationship?
✔ If overdone, logic can stifle a loving relationship. How does your logic sometimes interfere with your expression of love to your partner?

Exercise: Logical Love

Let's apply a little *logic* to our relationship, shall we? Let's see if we can quantify this thing called love . . .

☐ This is *not* a couple's exercise. Wait until he's away, or lock yourself in a closet. You are not going to show this list to your partner. So burn it or eat it when you're done with it! [I don't want any of you calling me, complaining that your (former) lover found your list and got mad!]

☐ Grab a pad and pen.

☐ Make two columns on a sheet of paper. Label one (+) and the other (-).

☐ In the (+) column, list all of the things you like about your partner.

☐ In the (-) column, list all of the things you dislike about your partner.

☐ Rate each item from 1 to 10, with the items that are very important to you receiving high numbers, and those that are minor receiving low numbers.

☐ Tally your columns.

☐ If your (+) column receives the higher score, congratulations! You've got a good base on which to build a relationship. Stay focused on the positive, and keep things in perspective.

☐ If your (-) column receives the higher score, you've got some serious thinking to do.

⤏ First, consider your mindset when you did the exercise: Were you upset or depressed? If so, do the exercise again later.

⤏ Second, think about whether your partner has always had these characteristics, or whether he has changed over time.

⤏ If you're single, think seriously about why you're staying in this relationship. Talk with a good friend or a counselor.

⤏ If you are married, review your commitment to the relationship, and do everything within reason to work things out.

⤏ Be realistic, and don't expect to change things overnight.

⤏ Does your partner share your dissatisfaction? How well do you communicate with one another?

⤏ Try some of the communication and forgiveness exercises elsewhere in this book.

⤏ Consider getting outside help, from a counselor or therapist.

⤏ Don't settle for less than a loving relationship. We all deserve to be loved and appreciated in the context of a safe and supportive relationship. Good luck!

Resources

☆ *Crazy Wisdom*, by Wes "Scoop" Nisker
☆ *The Little Prince*, by Antoine de Saint-Exupery

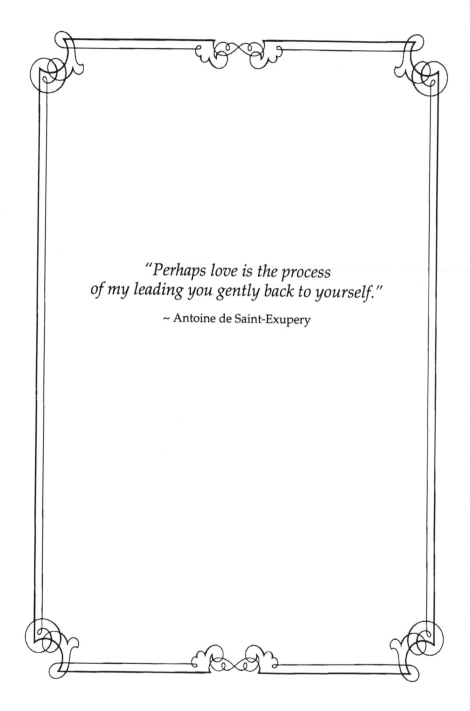

*"Perhaps love is the process
of my leading you gently back to yourself."*

~ Antoine de Saint-Exupery

Love

Alien: So, this thing you call "love" . . . did you learn it in college?
Human: Of *course* not! We all learn about love from our *parents*.
Alien: Ah, so all parents are highly-trained experts in the art of loving their children? What are the qualifications for becoming a parent?
Human: Uh, well, no. *Anybody* can become a parent. There are no qualifications. [*Embarrassed silence.*] But wait! We *also* learn about love from our culture as a whole. Yeah, culture fills-in the missing pieces.
Alien: Culture? You mean like television? Please explain how your most popular shows set a good example. For instance, *The Simpsons* or *Roseanne* or *Married With Children*.
Human: Never mind . . . Wait!—Books! Yeah! We learn about love from *books*. I mean like great literature 'n stuff. Like Shakespeare.
Alien: I'm accessing *Romeo and Juliet* on my computer. [*A three-second pause while he reads the entire play* . . .] So love is about being infatuated with someone you've met only once . . . murdering some of your future in-laws . . . and committing suicide over some miscommunication.
Human: Aaaaaauuuugh!

Aaaaaauuuugh indeed. **Love**. It makes the world go round. Money can't buy it. But it's all you need. Even though it's blind. It will find a way. It will keep us together. It's a many splendored thing. ✦ Love. The most important concept in our lives, in our religions, in our art and literature, in our relationships—and we all get haphazard training, conflicting messages, and dysfunctional role models to guide us on our way. What's a person to do?! ✦ I think the thing to do is to finally get it through our thick skulls that love—like life—is a journey of self-discovery. And even though maps and guides can help you through the journey, the key thing here is that you have to make your own journey. You have to live it. You have to take your own risks. You have to find your own way.

Is there a difference between *loving* someone and being *in love*? Is love a promise? Is love a feeling? Is love a commitment?

———

Creating a loving, intimate relationship is the most difficult, time-consuming and complicated challenge you will face in your entire life. Everything else is easy compared with love. ✦ You can learn the inner working of the atom in a few classes. You can learn to speak five languages if you're determined enough. You can learn how to send a man to the moon. But there's no instruction book [not even this one] or class or guru who can teach you a sure-fire, guaranteed method for achieving lasting love in your life. [Anyone who makes this promise is deluding himself and/or you.] ✦ Why do you think most of our great literature, poetry, theatre and films are devoted to the exploration of love? Because we're endlessly fascinated with the mystery that is love. ✦ Why do humans have such difficulty with the basic concept of sex (while animals take to it so easily)? Because we've entangled sex with love. ✦ Why is world peace so hard to accomplish? Because it, too, is wrapped-up in love. [War is not about territory or resources or power. It's about *fear*. And fear is the lack of love.] ✦ Why am I going on like this? To convince you of the enormity of the task you have undertaken: The task of creating and maintaining a loving relationship. My purpose is not to discourage you, but rather to show you that *no one has all the answers*. In thousands of years of working at it, we have a few guidelines (which no one pays much attention to anyway) and even fewer role models. ✦ The quietly brave, the creatively intimate, the gently strong—they are the lovers, the peacemakers and the saviors of the world.

———

Homework: Defining "Love"

☆ Fill-in the blank: "Love is _____." (More than one answer *is* allowed.)
☆ List 5 characteristics of love.
☆ Fill-in the blank: "Love is *not* _____."
☆ How is love defined by your parents, family and friends? How is love defined in our culture? What definitions do you agree and disagree with?

———

What is love? I don't mean that *philosophically*. I mean it *practically*. What is love to *you*? What *behaviors* make you feel cared-for and loved? What gives you pleasure? What could your partner do—*specifically*—to make you feel more loved? ✦ Love isn't *love* until it's acted-upon.

———

You hear a lot about suppressed anger, suppressed guilt and suppressed desires. But you never hear about "suppressed love," do you? I think suppressed love may be the Great Missing Piece to the relationship puzzle that everyone is struggling with so mightily. ✦ The phrase "suppressed love" conjures up a wonderful, hopeful image, doesn't it? Picture a huge, underground reservoir of love, temporarily covered-over by anger, guilt, misunderstandings and boredom. It seems to me that this reservoir is infinite, as our love for one special person is connected to the universal concept of Love. There is great, great power in this image. Try it on for size and see if it doesn't improve your outlook on life.

Exercises: Overcoming Resistance

☞ What do each of these phrases bring to mind?
  ❖ Unconditional love
  ❖ Physical love
  ❖ Spiritual love
☞ How have you been blocking or resisting love in your life?
  ❖ Write a list of at least five ways. (Are you blaming someone else? Do you close-down your feelings? Do you keep yourself too busy to feel?)
  ❖ Keep this list handy, and add to it over the next week.

I'm very frustrated with the abuse heaped on the word "love." It's manipulated by the media and used sloppily by nearly everyone else. As a colleague of Cupid, it's my duty to set the record straight. ✦ Love *does* not—*cannot*—hurt. It's the *absence* of love that hurts. ✦ Love cannot be used to manipulate. If one person is manipulating another, there is a lack of love. ✦ People do *not* stay in abusive relationships because of love! They stay because they're scared, they believe they don't have options, or they have low self-esteem. ✦ The power of love is always a giving, expansive, joyful, creative thing. It is *impossible* to twist love into a negative purpose. Don't blame love for your problems. Our root of our problems—all of our problems—is a lack of love. It's that simple. And that hard.

Resources

☆ *Rediscovering Love*, by Willard Gaylin
☆ *The Power of Unconditional Love*, by Ken Keyes, Jr.
☆ *This Is My Beloved*, by Walter Benton

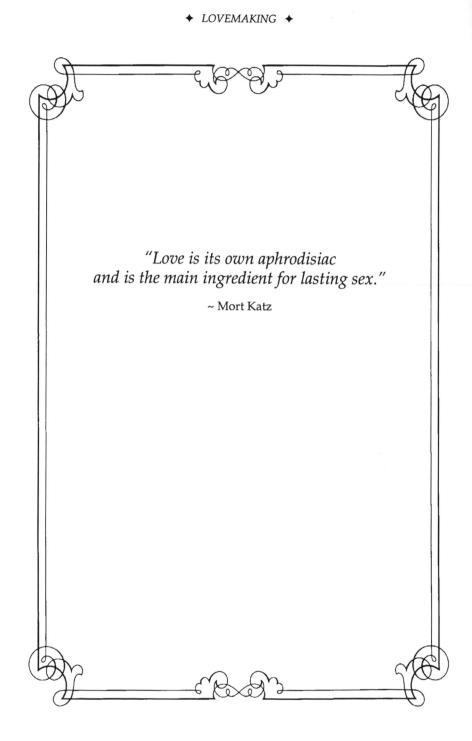

*"Love is its own aphrodisiac
and is the main ingredient for lasting sex."*

~ Mort Katz

Lovemaking

Take a little sex, stir-in a generous portion of love, and you get— *lovemaking.*   ✦   Let's take a moment to appreciate this unique and wonderfully human creation. It's an incredible melding of our animal nature and our spiritual nature. Ain't it *grand*?

Questions: Where & When?

Sometimes we get kinda personal in the Romance Class. "Where would you like to make love that you've never done it before?" I ask every class. You should *see* some of the looks on some people's faces when their partner gives answers like those here!

* In a limousine
* On horseback
* In a Victoria's Secret dressing room
* In the back seat of the car
* In the *front* seat of the car—*while he's driving!*
* On a plane in our seats under a blanket
* In an elevator
* In her office on her desk
* At the top of a ferris wheel
* In a hammock
* In a church
* On the steps of the Lincoln Memorial in Washington, D.C.
* In a movie theatre—during the movie
* In France—anywhere, just so it's in France
* In front of the window of a hotel room in Manhattan—where office workers could potentially see us!

Some people just *think* too much! They've read too many self-help books and sex manuals. Try *letting go*! Trust your instincts! Don't forget that you have an animal nature inside of you, along side your human nature.

"What's wrong with a little quickie now and then?"
Nothing. Absolutely nothing.

Homework: Variations on a Theme

❤ Make love without using your hands.
❤ Make love without touching your partner's genitals.
❤ Make love with your eyes closed. (Blindfold each other!)
❤ Make love without uttering a word.
❤ Make love, talking softly throughout.

Exercises: Looking for Clues

● Pay close attention to your lover's breathing patterns during lovemaking.
● Listen to the noises she makes as she's aroused.
● Notice the muscle tone of your lover's body during different phases of your lovemaking.
● Are you comfortable enough with each other to masturbate in the other's presence? You could learn a *lot* about how to please your partner.

Ideas: Props

How could you use these items as part of your lovemaking?

■ Three pillows
■ Baileys Irish Creme
■ A silk tie or scarf
■ Chocolate pudding
■ Silk stockings (black) (seamed)
■ A blindfold

■ A video camera
■ Two ice cubes
■ A feather
■ Rose petals
■ 100 candles
■ A mirror

Suggestions: Use Your Imagination

How many different kinds of lovemaking can you think of?

▲ Planned or spontaneous
▲ Indoors or outdoors
▲ Slow or fast

▲ Loud or quiet
▲ Clothed or naked or "dressed-up"
▲ Fantasy or kinky

Homework: The Subtleties of Arousal

I'll leave the mechanics and basics to Dr. Ruth, who's covered them quite thoroughly and entertainingly. Let's talk about the subtleties of *arousal*—those very personal feelings, passions, desires and fantasies that we rarely talk about, even with our intimate partner. We're not talking about sexual stimulation, as in direct genital contact. We're talking about *erotic arousal*, which involves more of your senses, more of your body, and more of your time. The payoff is more satisfaction and deeper sexual intimacy. ✦ Let's explore what arouses you:

- ✤ Get that pad and pen ready . . .
- ✤ List five things that turn you on.
- ✤ List five *more*.
- ✤ What's your favorite erotic fantasy?
    - ✳ Have you shared it with your lover?
    - ✳ Have you acted it out?
- ✤ What was the most erotic experience you've ever had?
- ✤ What's your favorite erotic movie, or movie scene?
- ✤ What is the most sexually attractive thing about your lover?
- ✤ Describe the kind of fondling you enjoy most.
- ✤ What sexual activity do you enjoy, but are reluctant to ask for?
    - ✳ What would you be willing to do for your lover in exchange for this special sexual request?
- ✤ What one thing about your partner's lovemaking technique would you like to change?
- ✤ Do you include all five senses in your lovemaking?

Do *not* trade lists with your partner. Discuss these points, but don't rush it! This is sensitive, difficult stuff. Respect each other's shyness, but don't simply skip over uncomfortable topics. You've got the rest of your lives to sort out your sexuality.

Resources

- ☆ *Super Marital Sex: Loving for Life*, by P. Pearsall
- ☆ *The Metaphysics of Sex*, by J. Evola
- ☆ *Masters and Johnson on Sex and Human Living*, by William Masters, Virginia Johnson, and Robert Kolody

---

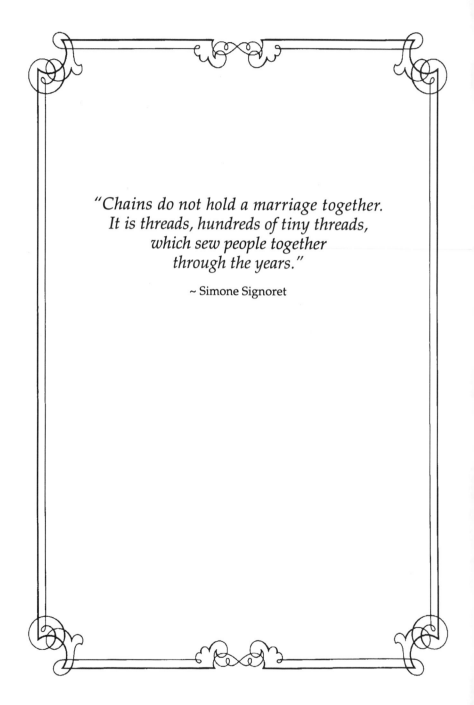

*"Chains do not hold a marriage together.
It is threads, hundreds of tiny threads,
which sew people together
through the years."*

~ Simone Signoret

Marriage

A marriage is a creation of two individuals who turn a *relationship* into a long-term *commitment*. (The wedding merely affirms the marriage.)

FYI: Characteristics of Successful Marriages

"What do you need in order to make a marriage work?" I ask this question in every Romance Class. It's *not* a rhetorical question, and it's not a set-up, because I don't have all the answers. ✦ Here's the best of all the lists we've compiled over 12 years. It's not the Ultimate List, but it's a start!

- ❏ **Love**. It's not *all* you need, but you need it. Otherwise, what's the point?
- ❏ **Self-knowledge**. "Know thyself." Thy feelings, wants, needs and desires. Thy strengths and weaknesses. Thy personality and motivations.
- ❏ **The right partner**. This could actually be the single most important factor in making a long-term relationship work: Choosing well!
- ❏ **Friendship**. Do you *like* each other?! Friendship is often the bond that holds us together when the love falters.
- ❏ **Communication**. Two-way. Continuous. Intimate. Honest. Informative.
- ❏ **Self-esteem**. Inner strength. Self-confidence.
- ❏ **Maturity**. Only the mature have a shot at making it long-term.
- ❏ **Commitment**. A strong commitment can keep you together when everything else fails.
- ❏ **Trust**. If you don't have trust, you have little else.
- ❏ **Respect**. Respect reflects equality. Respect for your differences.
- ❏ **Honesty**. The key building block of intimate communication.
- ❏ **Shared values**. A common core of shared beliefs.
- ❏ **Flexibility**. A little compromise, a little give-and-take.
- ❏ **Patience**. Appreciating her differences; his quirks; her faults; his fears.
- ❏ **Humor**. Taking it lightly! Breaking the tension. Sharing private jokes.
- ❏ **Sex**. Sexual compatibility deepens, strengthens and *energizes*!
- ❏ **Money**. Not necessarily a lot—but "enough." Money reflects security.
- ❏ **Time**. You can have everything else in abundance, but if you don't spend much *time* together, you don't have much of a marriage.
- ❏ **Spirituality**. Recognizing your Oneness. Finding your Way together.
- ❏ **Romance**. Bringing love alive. Expressing feelings.

FYI: "The 7 Marriages of Your Marriage"

A marriage is not a monolithic thing. It changes and grows. Every marriage has many subtle dynamics and patterns over time. ✦ Marriage experts Mel and Patricia Krantzler provide a bookful of unique insights in *The 7 Marriages of Your Marriage*. In a nutshell, here are the "mini-marriages" that comprise our marriages over time:

1. The *Movie-Marriage-In-Your-Mind* Marriage—The first few years of marriage when reality clashes with expectations.
2. The *Our-Careers-Are Everything* Marriage—Job stability, career-building, and adjusting to the demands of the two-career marriage.
3. The *Good-Enough-Parent* Marriage—The result of the tendency to postpone parenthood until after a career is established.
4. The *Time-Is-Running-Out* Marriage—When the realization hits that life is short, and triggers a "mid-life crisis" for one or both partners.
5. The *Is-This-All-There-Is?* Marriage—A time of reflection: When society stereotypes us as too old to try anything new, but too young to give up.
6. *The End-Is-The-Beginning* Marriage—Life after 65: Adjusting to retirement and contending with age.
7. The *After-Death* Marriage—Experiencing grief, despair, and isolation as a widow or widower—and feeling guilty for desiring sex or remarriage.

FYI: 7 Types of Marriages

Seven types of marriages were identified by a University of Minnesota study of 15,000 couples. Where do *you* fit in?

1. Devitalized (40% of couples): Great unhappiness with all aspects of the relationship. High likelihood of divorce.
2. Financially-Focused (14% of couples): Careers come before the relationship. Money holds the marriage together.
3. Conflicted (14%): Dissatisfied in many facets of the relationship. Couples fail to resolve issues. Pleasure is derived from outside the relationship.
4. Traditional (10%): Moderately satisfied with many aspects, but sex and communication are troubled.
5. Balanced (8%): Moderately satisfied. Strong in problem-solving and communication. Money tends to be a problem.
6. Harmonious (8%): Highly satisfied with each other, but view children as a burden. Family problems focused on the kids.
7. Vitalized (9%) Highly satisfied with most aspects of the relationship. They resolve conflicts well, and each has strong internal resources.

{From *Spectrum News Magazine*, March/April, 1993.}

Homework: "Name" Your Marriage

In every Romance Class, I ask the married folks to give their marriage a name, or "title." Here are the most frequent and interesting answers:

- ❏ The "Soulmate" Marriage
- ❏ The "Opposites Attract" Marriage
- ❏ The "Settling For Less" Marriage
- ❏ The "Best Friends" Marriage
- ❏ The "Business Arrangement" Marriage
- ❏ The "We're Here For The Kids" Marriage
- ❏ The "Platonic" Marriage
- ❏ The "Passionate" Marriage
- ❏ What about *your* marriage? _____
- ❏ The "Last Chance" Marriage
- ❏ The "Two Peas In A Pod" Marriage
- ❏ The "Automatic Pilot" Marriage
- ❏ The "Fairy Tale" Marriage
- ❏ The "Just Like My Parents' Marriage" Marriage

Passion is a fire. In young lovers it rages out of control, like a forest fire. In mature lovers, it burns quietly—yet still brightly. Marriage is a fireplace.

Questions

▲ How would you "title" your marriage? (Does it have *more* than one title?)
- ♥ Do you and your partner agree?
- ♥ How does your title help explain the state of your relationship?
- ♥ Would you like to re-title your marriage? What changes would need to be made?

▲ Discuss the major characteristics of your marriage. (You may want to refer to the list at the beginning of this chapter.)
- ♥ Which characteristics are you good at?
- ♥ How can we celebrate—and support—our strong points?
- ♥ Where do you fall short? What would you like to change?

Resources

☆ *Marriage and Personal Development*, by Rubin & Gertrude Blanck
☆ *Married People*, by Francine Klagsbrun
☆ *The Book of Marriage*, by Hermann Von Keyserling
☆ *The Mirages of Marriage*, by William J. Lederer & Don D. Jackson

---

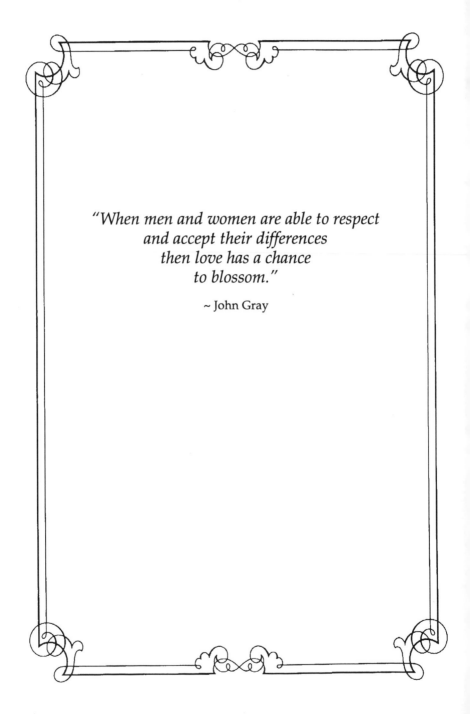

*"When men and women are able to respect
and accept their differences
then love has a chance
to blossom."*

~ John Gray

Masculinity/Femininity

Except for the obvious physical and sexual differences between men and women, there is no firm ground from which to declare with certainty and clarity the differences between masculinity and femininity. It's mostly a matter of opinion, cultural tradition, beliefs, trends, preferences and habit. Having said that, I, too, shall leap into the fray!

FYI: Some Differences

The following are generalizations, trends and observations. They are *not* Truths or prescriptions or my beliefs [well, *maybe* some of them]. Which statements do you agree/disagree with? Discuss your views with your partner.

XX Women hear "love" when you say "romance."
XY Men hear "sex" when you say "romance."

XX Women connect many emotional issues with their sexuality.
XY Men can easily separate their sexuality from their feelings.

XX Women communicate to create relationships.
XY Men communicate to gather information.

XX Women cooperate.
XY Men compete.

XX Women view relationships as a vast interlocking network.
XY Men view relationships in a hierarchical manner.

XX Women tend to be "right-brained"/emotional, holistic, creative thinkers.
XY Men tend to be "left-brained"/logical, linear, compartmentalized thinkers.

XX Women often treat men as emotional children.
XY Men often treat women as incompetents in the real world.

XX Women put men in shining armor on a white horse.
XY Men put women on a pedestal.

XX Women are aroused through sensation—and slowly.
XY Men are aroused visually—and quickly.

XX Women have been taught to hide their angry feelings.
XY Men have been taught to hide their tender feelings.

XX Women have been taught to suppress their aggressive side.
XY Men have been taught to suppress their gentle side.

If you ever want to send a little boy into orbit, just call him weak, a sissy, or worst of all, "a girl". This insecurity persists into adulthood for many men. We fear that if we're too sensitive, vulnerable—*feminine*—that we'll be perceived as weak-willed wimps. ✦ While it's true that no one respects a weak-willed wimp, it is *not* true that being sensitive and vulnerable makes you a wimp. Sensitivity and vulnerability are *human* traits, not feminine traits. If you weren't sensitive you wouldn't make a very good father, would you? And if you weren't vulnerable you'd never be able to experience love at all! ✦ [What *does* make you a wimp? Not sticking to your principles. Reneging on your promises. Lying. Cheating. Refusing to accept responsibility for yourself and your actions.]

My conclusion, after talking with thousands of people in the Romance Class over more than a decade, is that the most important differences between us are *not* those that are gender-based, but those that arise from the fact that we are distinct, unique individuals.

Question: What *Is* a "Real Man"?

Here's an assignment for *both* of you:

➤ Grab a pad and pen.
➤ Answer this question: "What is a *real man*?"
   ❖ An essay isn't necessary—a list of adjectives will be fine.
➤ Compare lists.
➤ Discuss!

If this exercise doesn't generate some eye-opening, insightful conversation, I'll eat my hat!

FYI: Masculine Traits to Beware Of

☞ Withdrawing from conversations that involve feelings.

☞ Independence. Too much of a good thing is *bad*! If you're *too* independent—with an attitude of "I am a rock/I am an island"— you'll isolate yourself. [In fact, one woman in the Romance Class described her husband as "sentencing himself to *solitary confinement*" when he withdraws into an overly-independent mode."]

☞ Over-confidence. We think we can do *anything* . Yeah, right!

☞ Large—yet fragile—egos. What a dumb combination!

Common problems when some men deal with confident women: They regard her assertiveness as anger; her strength as competitiveness; her independence as indifference. ✦ Common problems when some women deal with honest men: They regard his feelings as wimpiness; his confusion as evasiveness; his assertiveness as aggressiveness.

Let's think about the differences between the sexes for a moment, shall we? ✦ It seems to me that there are three basic positions you can hold regarding our differences: 1) You can believe we have "irreconcilable differences," and be resentful about them, 2) You can deny our differences, striving for total equality [androgyny?], 3) You can *celebrate* our differences. ✦ Guess which position is shared by every romantic who ever lived?

Resources

☆ *Brain Sex: The Real Difference Between Men and Women*, by A. Moir & D. Jessel

☆ *The Cinderella Complex*, by Colette Dowling

☆ *Unfinished Business: Pressure Points in the Lives of Women*, by Maggie Scarf

☆ *A Modern Man's Guide to Modern Women*, by Dennis Boyles

☆ *The Feminine Mystique*, by Betty Friedan

☆ *Iron John*, by Robert Bly

☆ *Secrets Men Keep*, by Ken Druck

☆ *What Every Woman Should Know About Men*, by Dr. Joyce Brothers

☆ *Fire In The Belly*, by Sam Keen

☆ *In The Company of Men: Freeing the Masculine Heart*, by Marvin Allen & Jo Robinson

"One is the loneliest number."

~ Three Dog Night

Math

How happy are you? This is *not* a rhetorical question. *How happy are you?*
. . . No, no—we want more than vague descriptions like *"fairly* happy"
or *"very* happy" or "Huh??" ✦ This is the *Math Chapter*, for crying
out loud!—We want *concrete, quantifiable* answers here! No right-brain
fuzziness allowed! We want the logical and measurable! ✦ On a scale
of one to ten, how happy are you? *How* in love are you? Rate your
relationship. Chart your feelings. ✦ {"Yeah, *right."*} Okay, so math and
love don't usually show up on the same page together, much less in the
same *book*. That's exactly why we might be able to create some unexpected
insights if we try.

Idea: The "Relationship Report Card"

Well, if we're going to be mathematically-minded, it makes sense to start by
getting an objective evaluation of where our relationship stands, right?! If you
were going to get a report card on your relationship, what would your grades
be? Grab a pad and pen and . . .

➤ Grade yourself. Grade your partner. Grade the relationship.
➤ Here are some categories for your report card. (What *other* categories
are appropriate for your relationship?)

❑ Listening skills	❑ Self-esteem
❑ Communicating skills	❑ Lovemaking skills
❑ Spontaneity	❑ Sex appeal
❑ Playfulness	❑ Commitment
❑ Loyalty	❑ Responsibility
❑ Self-knowledge	❑ Trust
❑ Friendship	❑ Respect
❑ Maturity	❑ Attendance
❑ Creativity	❑ Values
❑ Handwriting	❑ Flexibility
❑ Humor	❑ Gym
❑ Romance	❑ Patience

➤ Trade and compare. Discuss.
➤ How could you improve your grades? Do you need some remedial
classes?!

FYI: The Bell Curve

Do you remember the Bell Curve from statistics class?—Or from any class in school that graded on a "curve"? Remember that bell-shaped curve that illustrates how 16% falls in the low end, 16% falls in the high end, and 68% is spread-out along the middle? ✦ Our emotional lives, too, follow a Bell Curve. A relatively small portion of our lives are *peak* experiences (weddings, births, incredible sex, job promotions); but, thankfully, a small portion are *awful* experiences (accidents, deaths, bankruptcy, disasters). For the most part, you can't control the two extremes. But most of our lives are spent in the *middle*—where there's a mix of good and bad, where we have much more control.

✳ How could you take more control of your life?
✳ Pick one area—just *one*—that you'd like to change or improve.
✳ Start small. Keep your goal realistic.

"Sex is 90% of a bad relationship, and 10% of a good relationship."

~ Anonymous

FYI: 80/20

The "80/20 Rule" applies to relationships and romance just as it does to business and life in general. All salespeople know that "80% of your business comes from 20% of your customers." Stated more generally: "Eighty percent of your results will come from 20 percent of your effort."

■ Obviously, the smart person focuses his or her time, energy and resources on the 20% that will provide the most benefit, or is most sure of producing the desired effect.
■ If you know your partner is a movie buff . . .
  ❏ It makes sense to make a lot of movie dates, right?!
  ❏ Turn your living room into a "Theatre for Two"—Get a high quality video disc projection system!
  ❏ Plan a vacation to an international film festival!
  ❏ Get tickets to attend the Academy Awards!
  ❏ Get movie posters.
  ❏ Find books on favorite films.
■ Don't waste your time (or money!) on presents, gifts and gestures that may not please your partner!

What *is it* about the number "7" that is so intriguing? There are four excellent books on the market with 7 in their titles. Two are relationship books, and two are more psychological—but they *all* are helpful resources to romantics. ✦ You'll find descriptions of each book in a different chapter: 1) *The 7 Habits of Highly Effective People*—Habits chapter, 2) *The 7 Marriages of Your Marriage*—Marriage chapter, 3) *7 Kinds of Smart*—Uniqueness chapter, and 4) *The Seven Basic Quarrels of Marriage*—Arguing chapter. [I was tempted to title this book *The 7 Basic Lessons of Love*—but I just couldn't limit myself to seven lessons!]

---

*Communicating in an intimate relationship is 10% about relating **facts** and 90% about relating **feelings**.*

How do you rate your relationship? —Relative to your imaginary ideal? —Relative to the people you know? —Compared to *all* relationships?

A relationship made in Heaven
Fantastic
Great
Good
Fair
Poor
Terrible
The relationship from Hell

What level do you reasonably feel you can attain? Is your evaluation the same as your partner's? What's your guess as to how many couples fall into each category? Nobody knows for sure, but it makes for some insightful—and sometimes *passionate*—discussions!

Resources

☆ *The 7 Habits of Highly Effective People: Powerful Lessons in Personal Change*, by Stephen Covey
☆ *7 Kinds of Smart*, by Thomas Armstrong
☆ *The Seven Basic Quarrels of Marriage: Recognize, Defuse, Negotiate, and Resolve Your Conflicts*, by William Betcher & Robie Macauley
☆ *1001 Ways To Be Romantic*, by some guy named Godek
☆ *1001 **More** Ways To Be Romantic*, ditto
☆ *The 7 Marriages of Your Marriage*, by Mel & Patricia Krantzler

---

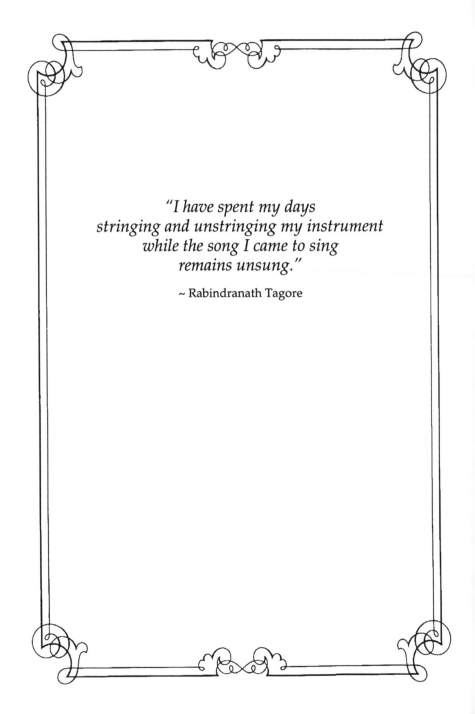

*"I have spent my days
stringing and unstringing my instrument
while the song I came to sing
remains unsung."*

~ Rabindranath Tagore

Mistakes

The Number One mistake I see people making in the Romance Class is having the attitude that "I shouldn't have to *ask* my partner to express his/ her love." They believe that "If the gesture or gift is given only in response to my request, then it doesn't count." ✦ Some of you are not going to want to hear this, but *If your partner is taking you for granted, it is* **your** *responsibility to initiate the change in his or her behavior!* You see, your partner is *happy* with the status quo!—So why should *he* change?! The partner who is unhappy with *any* relationship situation has the responsibility for initiating the conversation that will bring about change. You have the *right* to be appreciated. You also have the *responsibility* for looking out for your own best interests. If you don't take some action, you're playing the martyr. ✦ Here's why most people in this situation hold back: "I'm afraid she just won't respond. And I don't really have much hope she'll change. If I push the issue, then we'd be face-to-face with a *real* problem. So I guess it's better to not rock the boat." This approach will keep the peace for a while, but the price will be high: The passion will drain from your relationship, to be replaced with building resentment. I understand that the fear of rejection is strong, but believe me, it's better to face the Truth about your relationship than to continue living in a fantasy. ✦ It may help to remember this: Once you've fulfilled *your* responsibility by raising the issue, your *partner* has the responsibility for responding. And how she responds will tell you a great deal about the state of your relationship. Good luck!

Do you believe everything you read? [What are ya, stupid or what?!?] Of course not! There are a lot of us so-called "experts" in the world offering advice, hawking books and tapes and workshops and all kinds of stuff. How do you know who to believe? ✦ Some wise words from Sam—a sage counselor-friend of mine—have guided me in questions like this. He said, in his enigmatic way: "Only *half* of what I say is true. The problem is, *I* happen to believe that *all* of it is true. *Your* challenge is to figure-out which half is true for you!"

One of the biggest mistakes couples make is to believe that you and your partner are supposed to make each other happy. To believe this is to put both of you in an impossible, no-win situation. *You are responsible for creating your own happiness.*

Note: 1001 Ways to Communicate Poorly

Here are some common mistakes we all make when dealing with our partners. How many do you recognize in yourself? Does your partner experience some of these from you that you're unaware of? (The purpose here is not to place blame. It's to raise your awareness. Awareness must be achieved before change can be made.) ✦ Here are some dysfunctional, non-productive and downright nasty communication techniques:

+ Pretending to be above it all
+ Playing the victim
+ Changing the topic
+ Playing innocent
+ Making counter-accusations
+ Pretending you don't understand
+ Making excuses
+ Exaggerating
+ Mimicking your partner
+ Withholding
+ Denying your feelings
+ Denying your partner's feelings
+ Threatening your partner
+ Escalating the conflict
+ Analyzing your partner's motives
+ Being sullen
+ Being dogmatic
+ Name-calling
+ Evading the issue
+ Piling-on too many issues
+ Refusing to take any responsibility
+ Bullying your partner
+ Being contemptuous
+ Being sarcastic
+ Being totally logical
+ Being totally emotional
+ Being parental
+ Stonewalling your partner
+ Stonewalling information
+ Blackmailing your partner
+ Demeaning your partner
+ Ridiculing your partner
+ Being rigid and inflexible
+ Being philosophical

Mistakes—don't be afraid to make them! The goal is *not* to be perfect. And you do *not* need to be perfect in order for someone to love you! ✦ If you're afraid to make mistakes, you'll never take any risks. And if you never take any risks, you'll never grow. And if you never grow, you'll never fulfill your dreams or achieve much happiness. ✦ This may sound odd, but if you never make mistakes in your relationship, you'll never give your partner the opportunity to practice forgiveness. You see, you're actually doing her a *favor* by making mistakes!

[An excerpt from an article on the Dallas Cowboys' head coach Jimmy Johnson. From *USA Weekend Magazine*, presented without editorial comment.] ✦ "There are some key ingredients for NFL head coaches. No. 1: Jettison all influences and experiences that don't have to do with winning. Johnson divorced his wife, Linda Kay, after taking the Cowboys job because they'd grown apart and because he didn't want family stuff getting in the way of the biggest job of his life . . . He doesn't remember birthdays, not even his two sons', and doesn't do Christmas . . . 'I've prepared my entire life—48 years, 24 hours a day, 365 days a year—for 16 Sundays. Everybody out there in the world judges whether I'm a successful human being based on how I do on those Sundays. If we lose, I'm a complete bum, a worthless human being. If we win, I'm a success. That's the way this business is. I will not be a loser.'"

Beware of "The 10 *Secrets* of Marital Happiness"; "The Dozen *Rules* of Successful Relationships"; "How To Stay In Love *Forever*"; "The *Only* Relationship Workbook You'll Ever Need." ✦ I've learned that books and advice can be like junk mail promises: *If it sounds too good to be true, it probably is.*

Questions: Your Mistakes

Ask your partner these questions. Then answer them for yourself.

* What's the biggest mistake you've ever made in your life?
* What's the biggest *relationship* mistake you've ever made? How did you fix it or resolve it?
* What's your typical reaction to making a mistake?
* Do you *learn* from your mistakes?

Resources

☆ *Love Knots: A Laundry List of Marital Mishaps, Marital Knots, Etc.*, by Lori H. Gordon
☆ *The Seven Basic Quarrels of Marriage*, by William Betcher & Robie Macauley
☆ *Unlimited Power*, by Anthony Robbins

---

*"What a piece of work is a man,
How infinte in faculty.
In form and moving how express and admirable.
In action how like an angel."*

~ William Shakespeare

Movement

This is like the "Gym Class" portion of the Romance Class. We're going to stretch our minds, move our bodies, and exercise our emotions.

What do you think of when you hear the word *movement*? Do you think of moving your body physically? Do you think of moving through your life? Do you think of psychological change as movement? Do you think of intellectual and emotional growth as movement? ✦ Movement is *all* of these things. *Movement is the essence of Life.* Movement is also an integral part of Love, as Love is always growing, moving, expanding. Love, like Life, is a creative force. In fact, many people believe that Life and Love are inextricably bound. ✦ Movement is a key concept for romantics. If you're not moving, you're not loving. So let's move on and explore this concept a bit.

Is your relationship coasting? If so, you're either going downhill fast, or you're slowing down. Neither choice is very appealing, is it? You can't grow if you're coasting. You can't "take it easy" and expect your relationship to flourish. ✦ If you're not *actively* participating in your relationship, not only have you surrendered its full potential, but the part that you have left is deteriorating. There is no such thing as standing still!

Homework: Your "Movement Characteristics"

It's list time again . . .

→→ Where and how do you move well? Where and how are you stuck?
- → Do you move through your work smoothly, and have trouble at home?
- → Do you move well on the dance floor, but not on the tennis court?
- → Can you touch your toes, but not your deeper emotions?

→→ Are you a flexible or a rigid person? (Physically, emotionally, psychologically, intellectually)

→→ How do your "movement characteristics" compare with your partner's? What could you learn from one another's style?

Your body responds directly to your thoughts, moods and emotions. This is largely an unconscious process. An incredible amount of information is communicated via body language. If you tune-in to your *own* body, it will help you stay in touch with your feelings. If you tune-in to your *partner's* body , you will discover another avenue for understanding andempathizing with him or her.

Exercise: Expressing Emotion Through Movement

In order to be able to recognize an emotional state in another person, you first have to experience it within yourself. This exercise will help you express emotions and also identify them in your partner.

❖ This is a couple's exercise.

❖ Choose one emotion from the following list.

❖ You're going to act out this emotion using body language *only*, in the following scenario: *The simple act of putting on your coat and walking out the door.*

❖ Your partner's task is to guess which emtion you are expressing.

❖ Trade roles and play three rounds.

❖ Then discuss your observations and insights.

❖ Here are a few emotions to choose among:

✛ Overjoyed	✛ Exhausted	✛ Confident
✛ Stressed	✛ Powerful	✛ Carefree
✛ Depressed	✛ Scared	✛ Anxious
✛ Expectant	✛ Calm	✛ Sexy
✛ Curious	✛ Angry	✛ Lazy
✛ Playful	✛ Happy	✛ Bored

❖ You may want to expand this list and do this exercise again later.

As we move through our lives, we tend to move less and less. As we "grow up" we seek to leave behind the things of childhood. What we've forgotten is that the playfulness of childhood is life-affirming, and the attitudes of adulthood are deadening. ✦ "Kids run, but we adults walk. Kids climb, but we take the elevator . . . Kids stand on their heads, but we sit on our bottoms . . . Kids laugh with joy, but we smile with restraint. Kids are exuberant, but we are careful. Kids want to have fun, but we wnat to have security," says Thomas Hanna in *Somatics: Reawakening the Mind's Control of Movement, Flexibility and Health.*

Another type of "movement" is the "Get-off-your-butt-and-get-something-done!" movement. So, for all of you procrastinators out there, I've discovered DO IT! DAY. Yes, September 8th is DO IT! DAY. Mark it on your calendars! ✦ Ethel Cook, founder of DO IT! DAY, explains that "The objective is to complete one specific task that may have languished too long on the back burner—perhaps for so long that it has developed a personality all its own!" Ethel is a lecturer and office organizational expert who helps people increase their efficiency. ✦ "There is definitely a link between your efficiency at work and your happiness at home," Ethel says. "A great way to expand the concept of DO IT! DAY into your life on an ongoing basis is to assign one day each month as your own personal DO IT! DAY." Sounds good to me!

"To be alive is to be moving.
Inhibit the movement and you create illness . . .
To block movement is to block change . . .
The moving body freely channels the energy of life."

~ John Travis & Regina Sara Ryan

A marvelous method of helping people move more freely—both physically and psychologically—is Awareness Through Movement, also referred to as *Feldenkrais*, after its creator, Dr. Moshe Feldendrais. The method employs gentle, directed body movements as a way to help people get in touch with their organic wisdom, their deeper feelings and motivations, and their unique way of organizing their body for movement. ✦ For more information, or to find a Feldenkrais practitioner in your area, contact The Feldenkrais Guild at 524 Ellsworth Street, P.O. Box 489, Albany, Oregon 97321; 503-926-0981.

Resources

☆ *Be Alive as Long as You Live*, by L.J. Frankel & B.B. Richard
☆ *Mindful Spontaneity*, by Ruthy Alon
☆ *Minding the Body, Mending the Mind*, by J. Borysenko
☆ *Relaxercise*, by David and Kaethe Zemach-Bersin & Mark Reese
☆ *The Ultimate Athlete*, by G. Leonard
☆ *The Wellness Workbook*, by John W. Travis & Regina Sara Ryan

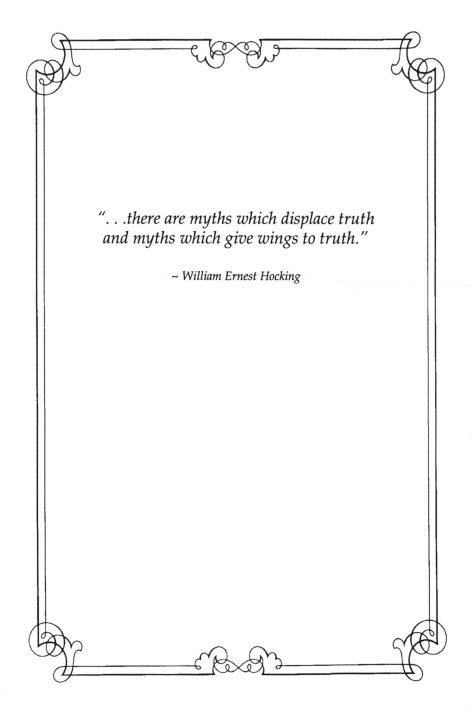

*". . .there are myths which displace truth
and myths which give wings to truth."*

~ William Ernest Hocking

Mythology

Prince Charming lives! He lives on in our imaginations and in our fairy tales. We can't seem to be able to get rid of him: Education can't eradicate him; sophistication doesn't stop him; and liberation hasn't licked him. So why don't we try to learn what he has to teach us, instead of trying to banish him by decree?   ✦   We all have, consciously or unconsciously, an image of the Perfect Partner, a dream of the Ideal Relationship. Instead of denying our wishes and desires, let's look at them and learn from them.

Exercise: The Perfect Partner

✢ Create two columns on a sheet of paper. Title the columns: "The Perfect Partner" and "The Perfect Relationship."

✢ List *at least* 10 characteristics in each column.

✢ Be *perfectly honest.* Don't edit your answers for fear of displeasing your partner! [I *guarantee* that you'll *both* fall short of Perfect—so you're both in good company!]

✢ Now, tell your partner about those characteristics that he or she *does* fulfill! [If he or she doesn't match *anything* on your list, you need either a new list or a new partner!]

✢ Second, talk about those *other* characteristics.

✢ How realistic are some of those items? How important are they to you?

✢ If you approach this exercise seriously, you'll generate some very insightful conversation with your lover. It could open the door to discussing some issues that you've been reluctant to talk about.

✢ (One creative couple in the Romance Class used the "unfulfilled characteristics" as the basis for some very fun fantasies!)

Let's back up for a moment and clarify what I mean when I talk about *myths* and *mythology.* Myths are *not* fairy tales, and mythology does *not* refer to ancient Roman gods.   ✦   *Myths* are stories that we live by, or pattern our lives after. They are based on archetypal characters and real-life people, combined in our minds in unique ways. *Mythology* refers to a larger pattern/philosophy/vision that encompasses and explains our lives, our experiences and our world.

Throughout history, a culture's mythology was created over long stretches of time, it was communicated by word-of-mouth, and it was reflected in people's everyday experiences. ✦ Our modern culture has radically changed this—and for the worse, I think. Our mythologies are created by TV, advertising and the other mass media—not by people we know or can interact with. Our mythologies are communicated at the speed of light, via cable TV and the airwaves—giving us little time to think, react or synthesize. And, our mythologies are largely removed from our everyday experiences. The media images *tell* us what we think and believe. I'm always struck by those little charts in *USA Today*, giving the results of today's poll. They're always headlined "What We Believe," or "How We Feel About..." I don't know about *you*, but I'd like to know who this "we" is! Those faceless people don't speak for me! The point here is that we are further and further removed from the sources of our own cultural mythologies. ✦ Why is this bad? Because it encourages us to be out-of-touch with our *own* feelings and our *own* experiences. When the latest (unsubstantiated) poll informs us that "Eighty percent of married American men have affairs" it has subtle—but pervasive and powerful—effects on our values, beliefs, and how we view the world. What I object to is opinion masquerading as facts, and gossip presented as news. ✦ I'm discussing this because it has a *profound* effect on our intimate relationships. It is becoming increasingly difficult to hold onto loving values and genuine beliefs amid the media barrage. Because solid, loving relationships generally don't have much news value, we rarely see them communicated. And thus, our culture's shallow values and ever-changing images are shoved down our throats. ✦ Sorry to rant and rave. —You should *hear* me in the *Romance Class*! Anyway, I encourage you to trust in your own experience, hold to values that you feel in your heart, and express your individuality.

Do you realize that you have the power to *define* your life? ✦ "At first, Gerry and I were *lovers*. Then we became a *couple*. Then we became *spouses*. And then we became *parents*. ✦ At each stage we *unconsciously* redefined ourselves. And unfortunately, each stage became less exciting, and more boring. After our third child was born, and our relationship was skidding, we decided to *consciously redefine* ourselves. We became *lovers who happened to have kids*. It made all the difference in the world! It's revitalized our relationship."

Homework: Discovering Your Family's Mythology

It is surprising how little we know about our own families. Most of us don't even know the "stories" of our parents . . .

* Ask your parents to relate the story of their courtship and wedding.
* If you're lucky enough to have living grandparents, ask them about their story.
* Interview various members of your extended family.
  * Write-down the story outlines, the patterns and themes that run through your family.
  * From this, write-out the myths and mythologies of your family.
* How much of this information is new to you?
* How have you been influenced by your family's mythologies?
* Compare your family's mythologies with your partner's.

"What is marriage? The myth tells you what it is. It's the reunion of the separated duad. Originally you were one. You are now two in the world, but the recognition of the spiritual identity is what marriage is. It's different from a love affair. It has nothing to do with that. It's another mythological plane of experience. When people get married because they think it's a long-time love affair, they'll be divorced very soon, because all love affairs end in disappointment. But marriage is recognition of a spiritual identity. If we live a proper life, if our minds are on the right qualities in regarding the person of the opposite sex, we will find our proper male or female counterpart. But if we are distracted by certain sensuous interests, we'll marry the wrong person. By marrying the right person, we reconstruct the image of the incarnate God, and that's what marriage is." ✦ From Joseph Campbell's fantastic book *The Power of Myth*. This book belongs in every romantic's library.

Resources

☆ *The Power of Myth*, by Joseph Campbell & Bill Moyers
☆ *The Hero With A Thousand Faces*, by Joseph Campbell
☆ *The Myth of Masculinity*, by Joseph H. Pleck
☆ *The Myth of the Monstrous Male*, by John Gordon
☆ *The Hero Within*, by Carol S. Pearson

"Love creates an 'us' without destroying a 'me'."

~ Leo Buscaglia

Oneness

The search for wholeness permeates our lives. Whether we're conscious of it or not, our motivations, decisions and actions move us toward the achievement of this ultimate goal. Growth. Fulfillment. Wholeness. Inner Peace. Flow. Centeredness. *Oneness.* ✦ Our love relationships are intimately connected to this goal. Literally and figuratively, physically and spiritually, specifically and symbolically, our love relationships are all about the struggles of oneness vs. separateness. ✦ We seem to be drawn naturally toward things that promote oneness. We desire connection. We are drawn to be in couples. We struggle to communicate. Our desire is strong, but our skills are often weak.

{"This concept of *Oneness* is rather esoteric, don't you think?? I'm just a regular guy who wants to have a good relationship. What's with all this philosophical bull!?"} ✦ This *isn't* philosophical. It's *practical.* But it's not intuitively obvious, so you gotta think it through. *Ready?...* ✦ To begin with, you're two separate, independent individuals. You meet; you're attracted to one another; you create a "bond" between you; this bond becomes a *relationship.* As you become a full-fledged couple, your relationship grows. Now, let's take a look at this *relationship.* What exactly *is* it? You can't touch it, but it certainly has energy, force, direction and influence over you. Thus, it is Real. It exists. It is a "thing"—an "entity," if you will. It exists on the same plane that "consciousness" and "love" exist. They're hard to define, difficult to grasp, but they're definitely there. Got all that? *Onward...* ✦ Here's the practical part. Through this relationship, you and your partner experience the beginnings of Oneness. Think about it. Why is it that *you* are affected when *she* feels sad? Why does *she* feel joy in *your* accomplishments? Because you are connected through your relationship. ✦ Your intimate relationship is a pathway to inner peace. Your partner is an integral part of your self-discovery and personal growth. Some define a *couple* as "Two, in the process of becoming one." ✦ [Does this make sense to you? Does it fascinate anyone else, as it does me? I suspect that there's an entire book waiting to be written on this concept.]

The desire for Oneness should not be confused with the desire to change your partner to make her more like you! The spiritual connection takes place on another level altogether, which leaves your differences in place, yet transcends them.

FYI: Defining Oneness

When do you feel "at one" with your lover? Here are some answers from Romance Class participants through the years:

☐ "When I feel a sense of inner peace."
☐ "After the two of us have shared a hot, luxurious bath."
☐ "In the midst of making love. Especially during orgasm."
☐ "When we're at a party talking with other people, and my wife and I talk as if we were one person: We finish each other's sentences and anticipate what the other is thinking. We call it being *In Sync*"
☐ "When he gazes intensely into my eyes in that way that always makes me well up with tears."

Suggestions: Approaching Oneness

Here are a few suggestions to move you in the right direction:

○ *Slow down!* Most of us are moving so quickly in our lives that we don't stand a chance of experiencing calmness, much less the inner peace and joy that characterize Oneness.
○ *Simplify!* Simplify your life. Most of us do too much. [I know *I* do!] We have too many possessions that don't really satisfy us or bring us the fulfillment we'd hoped they would. We have too much *stuff!*
○ *Experience solitude.* Make time and space for yourself. There's a big difference between being *alone* and being *lonely.*
○ *Focus.* Focus your love and passion *where your heart is.* If you've chosen well, your focus will include your partner.

> *"The ultimate oneness is mutuality, not the erasure of self."*
>
> ~ Emmanuel/Pat Rodegast

During the past few years a number of people have asked me about something I wrote in my first book, and this chapter is the perfect place in which to explain the meaning of the word "Namaste." ✦ The word originates in Asia, and is shared by a number of languages and cultures. I learned it in 1990 while trekking in the Himalaya Mountains of Nepal. "Namaste" literally means "I honor the god within you." It is the most common greeting among the Nepalese, who usually accompany the word with the gesture of putting their palms together in front of their chests. ✦ I asked some Sherpas to explain further, and they said that *Namaste* refers to the Oneness that we all share; the part that connects us to one another and to the entire universe. ✦ Among all the memorabilia and memories I brought back from Nepal, *Namaste* is my most cherished. And I share it with all of you.

Resources

☆ *The Halved Soul: Retelling the Myths of Romantic Love*, by Judith Pintar
☆ *The Search for Oneness*, by Lloyd H. Silverman & Frank M. Lachmann
☆ *Peace, Love & Healing*, by Bernie S. Siegel
☆ *The Road Less Traveled*, by Scott Peck
☆ *A Course In Miracles*, Foundation For Inner Peace
☆ *Emmanuel's Book: A Manual for Living Comfortably in the Cosmos*,
  by Pat Redegast & Judith Stanton
☆ The Quiet Answer, by Hugh Prather
☆ *The Inner Lover: Using Passion as a Way to Self-Empowerment*,
  by Valerie Harms
☆ *365 Tao Daily Meditations*, by Deng Ming-Dao

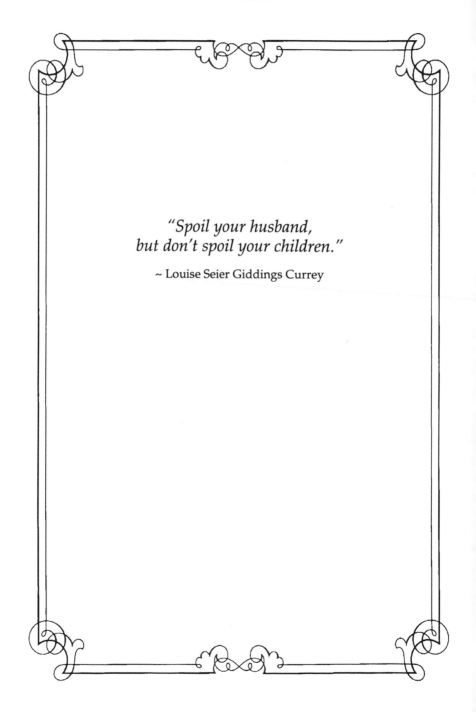

*"Spoil your husband,
but don't spoil your children."*

~ Louise Seier Giddings Currey

Parenting

No, I *don't* have children. [Yet.] So how do I presume to give advice to parents? I *don't*! ✦ I'm merely going to pass along to you some suggestions from parents I've had in the Romance Class, and parents who have written to me. [Well, and maybe one or two of my own opinions—but only one or two.] ✦ Here, in a nutshell, is what I've learned: 1) Children can drain the romance from a relationship *real fast*, 2) But *only* if the parents *allow* it to happen. ✦ Parents tell me all the time that kids are incredibly needy, demanding and time-consuming. But some of them add that parenting shouldn't be used as an *excuse* for ignoring your own needs for intimacy, and your partner's needs for love. Don't forget that you can't *give* what you don't *have*—and if you're not filled with love, warmth and peace (which hopefully you generate with your partner), then you've got little to give to the kids.

Tips: Do's and Don'ts

✳ *Don't* refer to one another as "Mom" and "Dad"—it's cute for awhile, but it soon comes to define you. Referring to your partner in this way makes it difficult to relate to her in a sexual, passionate way.
✳ *Do* make time for each other. Go out on at least two dates every month.
✳ *Don't* smother your kids. They need time away from you just as much as you need time away from them!
✳ *Don't* feel guilty for wanting to escape from your kids occasionally. I'm told it's completely normal.
✳ *Do* learn from your children. *Observe them!* They reflect back to you what you teach them. They pick-up on your wants and needs in amazing ways. They know your personality very, very well.

Those who define themselves primarily as *parents* often find that they have no relevant identity when the kids grow up and move out. Some of them live in the past, in the comfort of nostalgia and their familiar roles as parents. Others shift quickly into grandparenthood. The lucky ones rediscover their partners and resume the love affair that began years ago.

Couples who define themselves first and foremost as *parents* are setting themselves up for a life devoid of romance. Yes, of *course* parenting is important and rewarding and all that good stuff. But the parents who keep their intimate partner as their primary focus seem to derive two benefits: First, they are happier; and second, they are better parents! ✦ Those who define themselves first and foremost as *lovers* retain the intimate connection that supports and nurtures them. Those who do this emphasize that it is an attitude, not a behavior. No one is advocating that you abandon your baby to go on a three-day escape weekend to the Bahamas!

> *"I will **not** allow these tiny human beings*
> *to ruin **my** love affair with **my** husband!"*
>
> ~ Sandy W., mother of three

I always ask Romance Class participants why they're taking the class and what they hope to gain from it. ✦ "Children are a *drain on your energy,* plain and simple. Don't let anyone tell you otherwise. It's exhilarating— but *exhausting* work!" said Martha H., mother of three. "You *must* get out of your parenting role occasionally in order to re-charge your batteries. That's the reason I'm taking this class ... Because romance has always been a source of energy, inspiration and creativity for me. And since the kids arrived, I've *lost* romance as a source of energy. It may not sound *romantic* to you, but that's why I'm here. It's not a matter of *love*—it's a matter of *survival!"*

Homework: Parenting *Yourself*

❖ Sit and watch your kids. Imagine that you, *at their age*, are there with them. Playing. Talking. Would your children like you? What do you remember about yourself at their age?

❖ From an emotional point-of-view, what did you *not* get as a child? Make sure you give it to your children (without overdoing it). How can you give it to yourself right *now*? How might your lover help you?

From Susan A., mother of two: "I grew up reading *Cosmopolitan Magazine*, and I really believed that I could 'Have it all'. I was in for a rude awakening! I had my Harvard MBA, my high-stress, my high-paying career, my devoted-but-workaholic-husband, and my two children. I also had crippling migraines.   ◆   It took me five years of hell and two years of therapy to get my priorities straight. But now my life is in much better balance. My Number 1 Priority is . . . *my job!* Are you surprised? Well good! Because this isn't a fairy tale, it's my *life*. Now, I want you to know that I didn't leave my husband or abandon my children. But I did restructure my time and my commitments radically.   ◆   My conclusion is that you *can* 'Have it all'—as long as you're willing to live with *little bits* of it all."

From Gerrald F., father of four, grandfather to sixteen: "You *can* re-ignite the romance once the kids have grown-up . . . but you *can't* regain the time you lost by over-parenting your children.   ◆   I *love* my kids, but if we had it to do over again, my wife and I agree that we'd change one little thing: We would let the children play outside one half-hour *longer* every day, and use that half-hour to lock ourselves in our bedroom or den, to maintain our intimacy better. We missed this lesson, and I fear it's too late for our children to learn it well enough to practice it. But we're going to make sure our *grandkids* learn it!"

Resources

☆ *The Two-Career Family*, by Lynda Lytle Holmstrom
☆ *Emotional Child Abuse*, by Joel Covitz
☆ *Megaskills*, by Dorothy Rich
☆ *Parent Effectiveness Training*, by Thomas Gordon

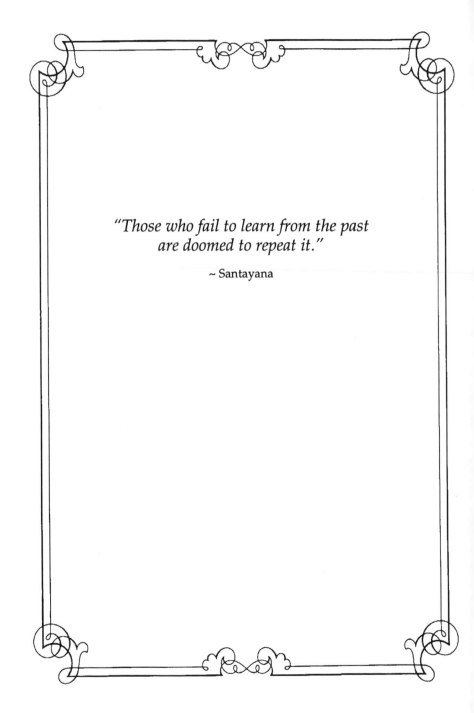

*"Those who fail to learn from the past
are doomed to repeat it."*

~ Santayana

Past

This is where nostalgia lives. The past is home to fond memories. The past is a vast and rich reservoir of experiences and learnings for us to draw from. ✦ Tapping into your past together can be a powerful romantic resource. If you honor your past, you can use it to help you appreciate the present and build a fulfilling future. Your shared experiences and joint memories weave a tapestry that combines your two lives into one.

Do you want a relationship just like your parents'? Studies show that the state of your parents' marriage is one of the most important factors affecting the quality of *your* intimate relationship. We learn our most deeply ingrained values, expectations and lessons from our parents. The healthy ones help us, and the unhealthy ones screw us up. ✦ Unthinking people are carbon copies of their parents—and they're stuck repeating the same mistakes. Immature people rebel—living lives in defiance of their parents—and make mistakes on the *opposite* end of the spectrum. Healthy people keep the *good*, and replace or modify the *bad* that they grew up with.

Suggestion: Recalling the Good Times

Memories of your good times together are a great source of romantic ideas. Tap into them!

❖ Recall with your partner memories that are . . .
  - ➤ Funny
  - ➤ Absolutely *hysterical*
  - ➤ Sexy
  - ➤ Erotic
  - ➤ Tender
  - ➤ Wild & crazy
  - ➤ Loving
  - ➤ Gentle
❖ Brainstorm at least three romantic ideas based on your favorite three memories.

People are always skeptical when I claim that I find romance in the *Wall Street Journal*. Here is an excerpt from an editorial page article I found intriguing. ✦ "Although it was little noticed, last week marked the 81st anniversary of the sinking of the Titanic, and with it the last gasp of Victorian chivalry . . . The erosion of civility in our era is due in part to feminists who saw chivalry as tyranny dressed in kid gloves. But feminists deserve only part of the blame. Since the 1960s, an entire generation has gleefully obliterated all vestiges of Victorian manners . . . In our era we have opted to replace that code [of common courtesy] with cultural anarchy that encourages every individual to maximize self-expression, whatever the cost. Yet I venture that there are many women like me who would welcome a little old-fashioned restraint. . . . We cannot recapture the past any more than we can escape it. Nor should we. But women can demand civility with the same fervor with which we demand our civil rights." {From "Chivalry Went Down With the Titanic," by Linda Lichter, April 21, 1993.}

Homework: The Photo Album Exercise

❖ Collect all the family photo albums and miscellaneous photos you can find—from both of your families.

❖ As you flip through them, and various memories are triggered, relate some stories of your family to your partner.

❖ Keep in mind these questions:

  ♥ From an emotional point-of-view, what was your childhood like?

  ♥ What kind of relationship did you have with your parents at different times in your life? (Don't forget that relationships change over time.)

  ♥ What was your best/worst age? Why?

  ♥ What were your greatest achievements/embarrassments at each age?

  ♥ Who were your favorite relatives? Why?

❖ You've got to *understand* your past before you can *accept* your past. And only *then* you can *learn* from your past.

❖ How do you see your past reflected in your present relationship?

❖ What insights can your partner add? (We sometimes overlook the obvious about ourselves, and we *often* miss the subtleties that a loving observer can see.)

Idea: ✳▲➢•✳✳♠△¬...♥

Speaking of the *past* . . . Have you ever considered using *ancient Egyptian hieroglyphics* to communicate with your lover? You can get personalized jewelry made with your lover's name translated into hieroglyphs. Cool, huh?! You can get pendants, rings, bracelets and earrings—called *cartouches*, meaning an ornamental design that includes a representation of a person's name. Call Discoveries for a free brochure (with a hieroglyphic alphabet): 800-237-3358; or write to 207 Ramsay Alley, Department 101, Alexandria, Virginia 22314.

There is, of course, a *negative* side to the past. We can harbor pain, resentment and anger—all of which come from past occurrences. We can't, of course, *change* the past—but we certainly can change the way we *react* to the past. ✦ The key to letting go of the past is through forgiveness. Check out the Forgiveness chapter.

They say that hindsight is 20/20. ✦ Take a look at your past, your various intimate relationships, your special intimate relationship right now . . . and ask yourself what you've learned; what you'd do differently; what you've done *right*; what your habits and patterns are; what you want to change.

Homework: Another List

❑ What was true yesterday may not be true today. The past can trap us in outdated ways of thinking, and trip us up with false images of our partners.

❑ Write a list of 10 things about yourself that have changed over the past 10 or 20 years: Likes and dislikes; goals and dreams; hobbies and interests; attitudes and feelings.

❑ Are you *happy* with all of these changes? Which do you want to keep? Which do you want to modify? Which do you want to eliminate from your life?

Resources

☆ *Love Through the Ages: Love Stories of All Nations*, by Robert Lynd

☆ *The Natural History of Love*, by M. Hunt

☆ *Your Inner Child of the Past*, by Hugh W. Missildine

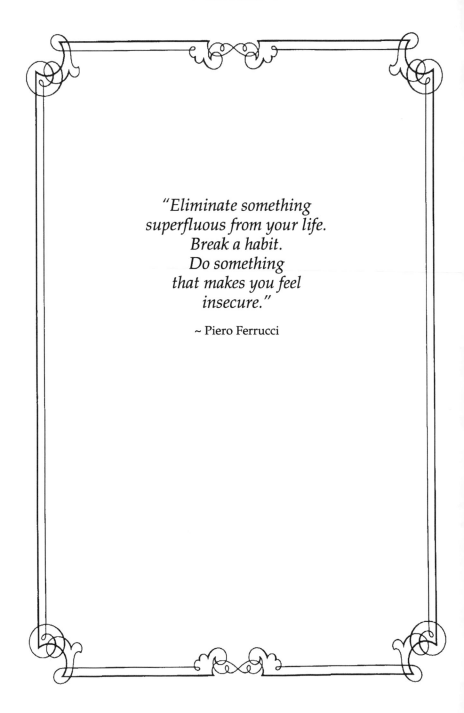

*"Eliminate something
superfluous from your life.
Break a habit.
Do something
that makes you feel
insecure."*

~ Piero Ferrucci

Patterns

There are thought patterns—and patterns of behavior. There are positive patterns—and negative. There are obvious patterns—and subtle, hidden patterns. We have personal, individual patterns—and couple patterns. There are masculine patterns—and feminine. ✦ Our lives are awash in patterns—flowing, blending and overlapping one another. The better we understand them, the more we can appreciate the ones we like, and the more able we'll be to change the ones we don't. ✦ Patterns are created by beliefs, both conscious and unconscious.

Questions: Sources of Patterns

➤ Where do your patterns/tendencies come from? Try looking at . . .
  ✳ Your parents' relationship
  ✳ Your birth order
  ✳ Your relationship with siblings
  ✳ Your relatives/extended family
  ✳ Your ethnic background
  ✳ The rules you grew up with
  ✳ Your schooling/teachers
➤ How do your patterns compare with your partner's?
  ✳ Which patterns coincide? Which ones conflict?
  ✳ Which patterns are major, core patterns? Which are incidental?

Idea: "The Week In Review"

While reading the Sunday newspaper one morning, the headline "The Week In Review" struck me as a good relationship concept.

❖ Review a typical week in your life.
❖ What *relationship patterns* do you see?
  ➤ What issues do you deal with regularly?
  ➤ What kinds of issues do you deal with *well*?
  ➤ Where do you and your lover get *stuck*?
❖ What *time patterns* do you see in your typical week?
  ➤ How do you spend your time?
  ➤ How much time do you spend together? [I mean really *together*.]

We don't live in a vacuum. Our society's many patterns affect us, too. The economy and our choice of lifestyles have a *tremendous* effect on our relationships. Take, for example, the fact that many of us are in two-career couples. This one factor is having far-reaching and negative effects on our relationships. We now have to deal with stresses that previous generations didn't have to contend with. [I am *not* saying romance was *easier* to achieve in the past. I *am* saying that things are significantly *different* now—and we as a society and as individuals haven't yet come to terms with the flood of changes that are washing over us.] ✦ If you're a member of a two-career couple, it's common for you to spend 10 or 12 hours apart from—*and out of communication with*—your partner every day! Have you thought about the long-term effects of this arrangement? Are you doing anything to bridge the gap? How often do you call each other? Do you send notes in the mail? Do you use e-mail? Do you fax? If you don't act to counteract the divisive forces in our society, your relationship will suffer greatly. ✦ The primary forces in our society are pushing us apart, they're not keeping us together. We must work harder, longer, and more creatively than ever before if we are to preserve the values, the lives, and the relationships that we profess to prize so greatly.

FYI: Different Relationship Paradigms

Let's break our habitual patterns of how we view our relationships. Choose two of the following items and describe your relationship as if it were . . .

* ✷ *A business* (Fortune 500 or entrepreneurial? Profitable? Industry? Products?)
* ✷ *A country* (Name? What continent? Terrain? Weather? Politics? What kind of people live there? How do they live?)
* ✷ *A building* (Big or small? Location? Purpose? Height? Material?)
* ✷ *A painting* (What style? Who's the artist? Describe the painting. What kind of frame? Where is it hanging. Value at auction?)
* ✷ *A movie* (Title? Director? Comedy or drama or science fiction or mystery or documentary? Who stars in it? What's it rated?)
* ✷ *A plant* (Describe it. Where does it grow? What kind of seeds does it have? What kind of flowers? Fruit?)

In your interactions with your lover, do you fall into a pattern of cooperation or competition? Those with a competitive mindset create win-lose situations. Those with a cooperative mindset strive for win-win situations.

Homework: Patterns of Success

Where can you identify patterns of success around you?

+ What successful people do you know? What are their patterns?
+ In what areas of your own life have you been most successful? Most comfortable? What patterns can you identify?
+ What patterns of success can you identify from doctors, plumbers, writers, children, factories, dogs, cats and Japan?

Look for "patterns of success" everywhere in your life: In your work, in your garden, in your relationship, in books, in the news, in your parents, in school. Look for patterns, models, strategies that work in one area, and try them out in your relationship. + Look for what makes sense to you, what *feels right* to you. + Jill M. is a successful manager. She decided to apply some of the knowledge from her M.B.A. to her relationship. She realized that there was nothing wrong with applying a little logic and structure to her personal life—which she'd always left to "pure emotion." Here's what she did: She created a "Love Plan" based on a "Business Plan." It included Goals, Strategies, Tactics, Timeframe, Competition, and, of course, a Budget. + Sidney W. is a gardener. He applied patterns of organic growth to his marriage. "I have to admit that I've been using the phrase 'withered on the vine' to describe my marriage for the past 10 years. I know we have strong roots, so I'm not too worried. But I guess we need to weed the garden; share more sunshine; and water one another much more regularly!"

Resources

☆ *Intimate Partners, Patterns in Love and Marriage*, by Maggie Scarf
☆ *The New Peoplemaking*, by Virginia Satir
☆ *American Couples: Money Work Sex*, by Philip Blumstein

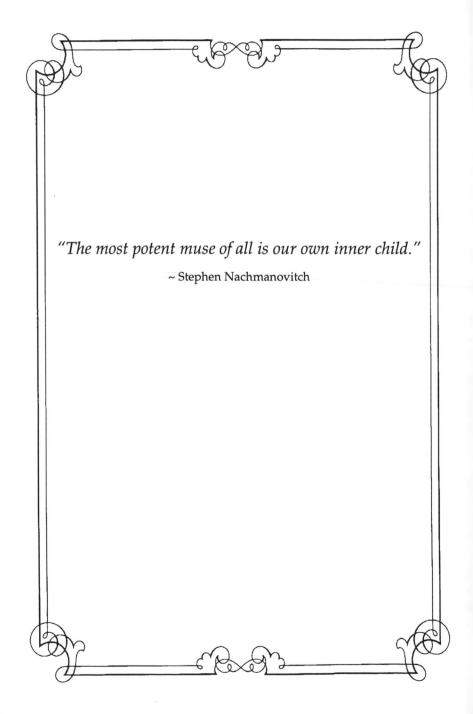

"The most potent muse of all is our own inner child."

~ Stephen Nachmanovitch

Playing

"Couples who *play* together, *stay* together!" said Mrs. Margaret Stanford, a caller on a radio talk show in Chicago recently. And thus this chapter was born. ✦ One of my favorite definitions of romance is that it is "Adult Play." It's doing something very adult (building intimacy) in a very childlike (fun) way.

Homework: An "Inner Child" Exercise

Getting in touch with your "Inner Child" will quickly get you into the proper mindframe for playing. Think of the qualities that characterize children:

* Spontaneous
* Energetic
* Open to new ideas
* Enjoy games for the pure fun of it
* Flexible
* Eager to learn
* Feel their emotions
* Willing to ask for love

* Curious
* Imaginative
* Trusting of others
* Willingness to experiment
* Honest
* Playful
* Express their feelings
* Unafraid to show love

Now, choose any three of these qualities, and use them to brainstorm some ways that you and your lover can bring those qualities into your lives.

If you want to play, it might help to get yourself into an environment that's *conducive* to playing. ✦ Find the nearest playground. {"Okay, now what?"} *Aaaaauuugh! Kids* don't need to be taught how to play, why do *adults*?! Hop on the swings. Take turns pushing each other. Take off your shoes and socks, roll-up your pants, and play in the sandbox. Discuss the balance in your life while riding the teeter-totter. ✦ Find the nearest toy store. Go shopping for the two most special kids in the world: The Child in you, and the Child in your lover. Spend $12 on each of you. If you have difficulty getting yourself into a silly enough frame of mind to do this exercise, you need to *loosen up!*

FYI: Relationship Paradigms

We all have images in our heads that define what a relationship is *supposed* to be like. These paradigms are often based on unhealthy role models we observed as children, or on unrealistic/fantasy images we've absorbed from our culture.

❒ How do you react to the statements below? Discuss them with your partner. On which issues do you agree and disagree?

   ○ Relationships are *hard work.*
   ○ Relationships are *great adventures.*
   ○ I would do *anything* to maintain this relationship.
   ○ People in relationships need private time and their own space.
   ○ In a family, the *kids'* needs come first.

❒ Does your idea of what a relationship is all about include *play?* We all *need* play in our lives. It re-energizes our bodies and puts laughter into our hearts.

❒ In your relationship, which one of you is more playful? Think-up two ways that you can share more playfulness with, or elicit more playfulness from, your partner—*without threatening* him or her. (You need to be *creative*, because you can't *order* someone to play. You can't generate fun by decree!)

Note: Mail-Order Fun

"The biggest difference between adults and children is that adults have the ability to buy their *own* toys!" declared Joseph G., in the Romance Class one day. In honor of Joseph's insight, here are some catalogs that will help bring out the fun, joyous, crazy, frivolous side of your personality:

•• *The Whole Toon Catalog*—The largest selection of animated cartoons on earth! Thousands of video titles—from turn-of-the-century silents to the latest Disney features. (Posters and other stuff, too!) $2.
•• *Cats In The Mail*—For the cat lover in your life. $1.
•• *The Advertising Flag Company*—State flags, sports teams' flags, historical flags, and custom flags! $1.
•• *Badge-A-Minit*—Make your own custom 2-1/4-inch buttons! $1.
•• *Tropical Adventure*—Lingerie & swimwear. An 80-page catalog! $9.
•• *Plane Stuff*—For the aviation buff or balloon enthusiast! $2.

All of these catalogs can be ordered from: Publisher Inquiry Services, 951 Broken Sound Parkway NW, Building 190, P.O. Box 5057, Boca Raton, Florida 33431.

Look at what adults have done with the concept of *playing*. We've structured it, we've removed the spontaneity, we've raised our expectations unreasonably high, we keep score and we've turned it into a businesslike competitive exercise. When's the last time you rolled down a hill or skipped? ✦ Don't wait until *tomorrow*. Play *today*!

*One of the best things about being an adult
is that you can include **sex** as part of your playing!*

FYI: Playing With Language

✻ Favorite license plates recently spotted:
  ✳ IMZ14U
  ✳ SPO-KN4
  ✳ 2DI4
  ✳ UQT-PIE
✻ Type this on your typewriter or computer: Colon, dash, right parenthesis. What does it spell? When you tilt your head sideways . . .
:-)
You get a smiley face. Actually it's an "emoticon"—or *smiley* for short. It's an invention of people who talk to each other on computer networks. Smileys are an agreed-upon shorthand to replace the emotional shadings that are lost in computer conversations. You might be able to incorporate smileys into your next love note. Here are a few more:
:-(:-/   :-o

Resources

☆ *Everything I Ever Needed To Know I Learned In Kindergarten*, by Robert Fulghm
☆ *Homecoming: Reclaiming and Championing Your Inner Child*, by John Bradshaw
☆ *Intimate Play*, by William Betcher
☆ *Wishcraft: How To Get What You Really Want*, by Barbara Sher
☆ *Healing the Child Within*, by Charles Whitfield
☆ *Office Work Can Be Dangerous to Your Health*, by J. Stellman & M. Henifin
☆ *Intimate Play: Playful Secrets for Falling and Staying in Love*, by William Betcher

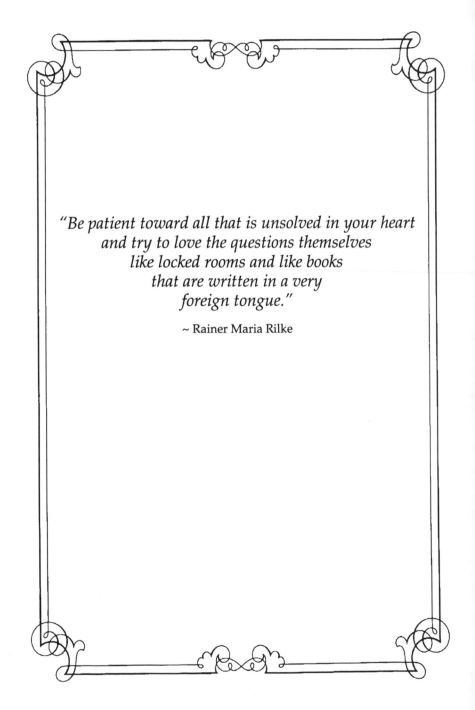

*"Be patient toward all that is unsolved in your heart
and try to love the questions themselves
like locked rooms and like books
that are written in a very
foreign tongue."*

~ Rainer Maria Rilke

Questions

☞ You're going to be on *The Oprah Winfrey Show* . . . What would the title of the show be?

☞ What is your *very best* quality?

☞ How much money would you need to have in the bank before you'd feel financially secure?

☞ If you could save just one object from your burning home, what would it be?

☞ Ideally, how often would you like to have sex?

☞ What movie or TV scene last brought tears to your eyes?

☞ What TV show are you embarrassed to admit that you enjoy?

☞ If you were to change your name, what would you change it to?

☞ What's your favorite number?

☞ If you could be any famous person in history, who would it be?

☞ What is the Greatest Movie of All Time?

☞ If you won $10 million in the lottery today, what's the first thing you'd do tomorrow?

☞ If you could change one thing about your body, what would it be?

☞ If you were a musical instrument, what kind would you be?

☞ What's your favorite erotic fantasy?

☞ If you were going to get a tattoo . . .What would it be? And where on your body would it be?

☞ If you were an animal, what kind would you be?

There's no such thing as a stupid question.

✛ What's your favorite foreplay activity?

✛ Do you know what your partner's favorite foreplay activity is?

✛ Describe an orgasm. (What color is it? Does it tingle, explode, flow? Does it linger? How long? How *else* would you describe it?)

✛ What's the difference between *having sex* and *making love*?

✛ What's your favorite sexual fantasy?

✛ Do you feel comfortable asking your partner for specific kinds of stimulation?

✛ How often would you like to have sex?

✛ What's your favorite erotic movie?

✛ Have you ever had sex outside? In the living room? In the kitchen?

✤ If you were stranded on a desert island . . .
  ✻ What 3 music albums would you like to have?
  ✻ What food would you miss the most?
  ✻ Would you wear clothes?
  ✻ What 3 books would you take along?

✳ Do you believe that you and your partner were *destined* to be together?
✳ Do you believe there's such a thing as *soulmates*?
✳ Do you remember your very first kiss?
✳ Do you believe in heaven? What's it like?
✳ What was your favorite game as a child?
✳ How many years would you like to live?
✳ What would you like your epitaph to read?
✳ Have you ever gone skinny dipping?
✳ Have you ever been infatuated?
✳ Which is more romantic: Sitting face-to-face or side-by-side?
✳ Can a person be *too much* in love?
✳ Can you read your lover's mind?
✳ If you could dress your partner, how would you dress him/her?
✳ What's the most romantic thing you've ever done?
✳ What's the most romantic thing anyone's ever done for you?
✳ Have you ever had a broken heart? How long did it take to heal?
✳ What songs make you think of making love? Do you own them?
✳ Would you like your lover to be more sexually assertive?
✳ If there were 8 days in a week, what would you do with that day?
✳ What's the most erotic movie scene you've ever seen?
✳ Do you talk during lovemaking?
✳ What was your favorite childhood toy?
✳ What was your best subject in Grade School? High School? College?
✳ Do you know what your lover's tears taste like?

"No man really becomes a fool until he stops asking questions."
~ Charles Proteus Steinmitz

❏ What 5 *adjectives* best describe you? Your partner?
❏ What 5 *nouns* best describe you? Your partner?
❏ What 5 *verbs* best describe you? Your partner?

✛ Have you ever told something to a stranger on a plane that you haven't told your partner?
✛ Do you think it's possible for a man and a woman to have a completely platonic relationship?
✛ If you were going to direct "The Best X-Rated Movie of All Time," what would it be like? What would its title be?
✛ If you could give the president of the United States one piece of advice, what would it be?

"Einstein was a man who could ask immensely simple questions."
~ Jacob Bronowski

➤ If you're so smart, how come you're not a millionaire?
➤ How are you *just like* your father? Your mother?
➤ Who's your best friend?
➤ God wants an even dozen instead of only Ten Commandments . . . What are the additional two Commandments?
➤ What's your biggest pet peeve?
➤ If you could commit one crime with the absolute assurance that you would never be caught, what would it be?
➤ What's your favorite joke?
➤ What piece of advice in this book is just plain *wrong?*
➤ What quote in this book should be taped to your refrigerator?
➤ Have you ever faked an orgasm?
➤ Whose ego is more fragile—yours or your partner's?
➤ What book have you been meaning to read?
➤ Where in the world have you always wanted to visit?
➤ If you were a member of the opposite sex, what would your name be?

Resources

☆ *237 Intimate Questions . . . Every Woman Should Ask a Man,* by Laura Corn
☆ *If Love Is the Answer, What Is the Question?* by Uta West
☆ *Is This Where I Was Going?* by Natasha Josefowitz
☆ *Why Did I Marry You Anyway?* by Arlene Modica Matthews
☆ *Is There Sex After Marriage?* by Carol Botwin

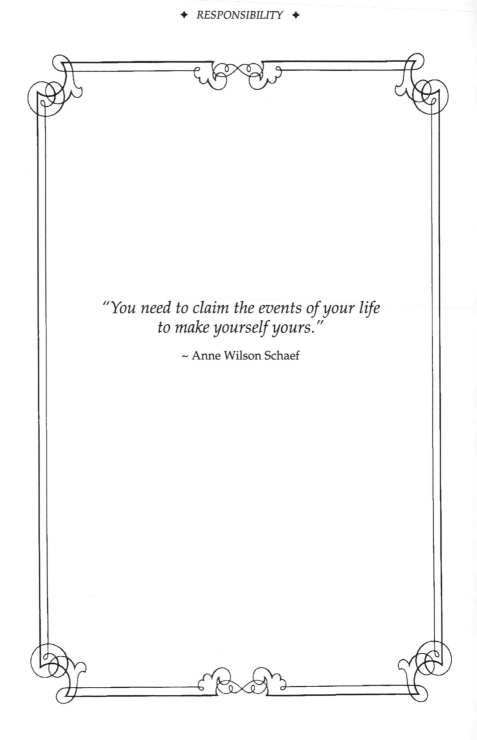

*"You need to claim the events of your life
to make yourself yours."*

~ Anne Wilson Schaef

Responsibility

Which of you is more responsible? ✦ [... *Time to think*...] ✦ That was a trick question, because regardless of which of you is more "responsible"—meaning "conscientious"—you are both *equally* responsible for your relationship. And I don't mean 50/50—a nice, equally-balanced equation; I mean 100/100—you're both 100% responsible for the relationship. ✦ This holds true *regardless* of whether or not you accept this responsibility!

Are you taking full responsibility *for your own happiness* in your relationship, or are you dumping the responsibility on your partner? ✦ It takes *both* of you working hard to create a great relationship. One person working alone can't do it! If you have an unresponsive, uncaring partner, you can only do so much! And while I certainly encourage everyone to work like *hell* to preserve, repair and improve their existing relationship, if your partner isn't participating, there's definitely a point where persistence becomes pointless. One of life's Challenges for some of us is to recognize, accept and act on that reality if it befalls us.

Tips: When Love Is a Heavy Responsibility

When does love become a burden? And what do you do about it?

☞ Love is a burden when it is *clinging*.
  ☛ *What to do*? Work on your independence.
☞ Love is a burden when it is *desperate*.
  ☛ *What to do*? Focus on issues of maturity.
☞ Love is a burden when it is *one-sided*.
  ☛ *What to do*? Talk it through with your partner.
☞ Love is a burden when it is *insecure*.
  ☛ *What to do*? Work on your self-esteem.

"Isn't it interesting that before you can accept responsibility for a relationship, you must accept responsibility for *yourself*?" said Mary in the Romance Class. This is why immature people rarely have long-lasting relationships. This is why those who marry young often struggle so much.

Questions: To Ask Yourself

✹ Are you *cheating* on your partner? No, no—I don't mean being *unfaithful* . . . I mean are you cheating from within; are you not accepting 100% of your responsibility?

✹ Are you being a *martyr*? Martyrs think they're giving 110% . . . That's what gives them the right to suffer and feel superior. The truth is—martyrs are taking *less* than 100% of their own responsibility! What they're trying to do with the martyr act is to pressure the partner into giving more.

✹ Are you playing the "savior"? Are you trying to save your partner from the harshness of the real world? Are you protecting him or her from your true feelings? If so, you're attempting the impossible. You can't take on 200% of the load. You'll fail, you'll resent your partner, and you'll leave him or her feeling powerless and distrusted.

FYI: Scapegoats

Who's to blame for your problems?

↦ Let's stop blaming our parents for our problems, okay?

↦ Your kids aren't the cause of your problems, either.

↦ Your lack of money isn't to blame for your problems.

↦ And let's not blame "society."

↦ Or TV. Or rock n' roll bands with subliminal messages in their songs.

↦ You boss isn't to blame, either.

↦ (You're not gonna try to blame it on *God*, are you? —*Major* cop-out!)

↦ And last but not least—let's stop blaming our *partner* for our problems!

So who's to blame for your problems? There are only two possibilities left: Either *you* or *no one*! Here's my observation about most people:

↦ Our minor problems and screw-ups are clearly our own fault.

↦ Our major problems are . . . *no one's* fault.

Our minor problems are caused by various neuroses, unlearned lessons, stubbornness, and/or just plain foolishness. ✦ Our *major* problems in life are really *just the way things are*. They're "just life!" The attempt to search for someone or something to blame is really a dodge, a delaying tactic that keeps us from moving ahead and getting on with our lives. Our problem is that we insist on calling the situations and challenges of our lives "problems." The problem with "problems" is that they demand *answers*. And you see, life isn't about *finding answers*—it's about *experiencing love*. When you live your life out of love, you automatically act responsibly.

We all have a lot of responsibilities to many people in our lives. We have many conflicting goals, desires, responsibilities, wants and needs. How do you prioritize them? The following is a hierarchy that tends to be shared by the people who seem to be happier in their lives and in their intimate relationships than the average person is:

> *God or your "Higher Purpose"*
> *Yourself*
> *Your intimate partner*
> *Your children*
> *Your parents & siblings*
> *Your very best friends*
> *Your employer*
> *Career colleagues*
> *Other friends*
> *Everybody else*

Many people will quibble with this list a *little*, but I've found that most people agree in theory that this hierarchy promotes loving relationships and balanced lives. The challenge is to live our lives—spend our time—in a manner that parallels this list. [Hey, I never *said* this was going to be *easy!*]

Some people turn "responsibility" into a *somber duty. Yo!—Lighten-up, huh!?* This is a brief reminder that in addition to your serious responsibilities as a spouse/parent/breadwinner, it is also your responsibility to keep your relationship fun, passionate and playful! Your commitment to your partner will never become a heavy burden if you keep in mind your commitment to the Lighter Side of Life, too!

Resources

☆ *Pathfinders: Overcoming the Crises of Adult Life and Finding Your Own Path to Well-Being,* by Gail Sheehy

☆ *Composing A Life,* by Mary Catherine Bateson

☆ *Pulling Your Own Strings,* by Wayne W. Dyer

☆ *Taking Charge Of Our Lives: Living Responsibly in a Troubled World,* ed. by Joan Bodner

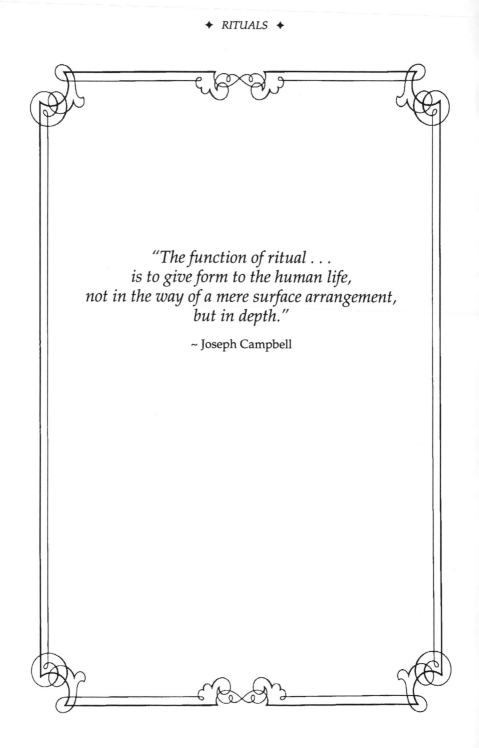

"The function of ritual . . .
is to give form to the human life,
not in the way of a mere surface arrangement,
but in depth."

~ Joseph Campbell

Rituals

Rituals are special ways of celebrating life's significant events. Rituals bring us together and remind us of what's really important in our lives. Modern society is barren of meaningful rituals, with its focus on material gain and relentless change. ✦ Rituals have helped people throughout the ages deal with issues of change. As we move farther and farther away from our rich cultural heritages (from our European, African and Asian ancestors), and into a fragmented pop culture of rapidly changing values, it is more important than ever that we commemorate special times with symbolic events. Many people in the Romance Class have had lots of fun creating and celebrating their own rituals. You have a jump over most people because a romantic mindset is extremely useful in helping you express deep feelings in creative ways.

FYI: Types of Rituals

There are several basic types of rituals:

✤ Beginnings: Celebrating births, new jobs, new homes
✤ Joinings: Celebrating marriages, adoptions, business partnerships
✤ Cycles: Celebrating the seasons, menstrual cycles, yearly events
✤ Endings: Recognizing deaths, losses, the end of relationships
✤ Healings: Dealing with physical and emotional ills

Homework: Create Your Own Ritual

This is a brief outline of a process that should take considerable time and thought. (If you want to delve more deeply into rituals, I strongly recommend *The Art Of Ritual,* by Renee Beck & Sydney Barbara Metrlck.)

❦ Identify your purpose: What are you celebrating? What do you want to accomplish?
❦ Plan your ritual: What symbols will you use? Where will it take place? When will you enact your ritual? Who will participate? What props will you use?
❦ Consider these elements: Color, sounds (silence, music, words, singing), scents, food, drink, body position and movement (standing, sitting, dancing), symbols, readings, vows, interaction between participants, touching, length of ritual, time of day.

FYI: The "Remembrance Ritual"

🐛 *Do you remember what first attracted you to your partner?*

🐛 Sit together for half an hour. No phones. No kids. No interruptions.

🐛 Talk for a few minutes about some of your fondest memories of each other: About your early dates; how you met; how you felt.

🐛 Then close your eyes and let your mind wander for about five minutes.

🐛 Open your eyes. Talk about the qualities that first attracted you to your partner. Talk about the underlying feelings. What qualities or feelings have remained constant over time?

🐛 You'll feel the love, intimacy and passion that are the true foundations of your relationship.

———————

Incense can enhance nearly any ritual. We often neglect our sense of smell, and focus instead on the overpowering senses of sight and sound. Don't forget that your sense of smell taps directly into your memories and emotions—which is perfect for the purpose of creating meaningful rituals. ✦ It's no coincidence that throughout history and across cultures, incense has been used as part of religious traditions, family celebrations and sexual rituals. Choosing incense is best done simply by "following your nose"—literally. It's not an intellectual decision, but an emotional one.

———————

FYI: An Anniversary Ritual

Here's how Tracey and I celebrated our third wedding anniversary:

▲ We gathered these items:
- ■ A copy of our wedding vows
- ■ Our wedding photo album
- ■ A bottle of Korbel Brut champagne
- ■ The CD of Andreas Vollenweider's *Down to the Moon*

▲ We sat in bed and . . .
- ● Paged through the photo album, recalling the events.
- ● Read our vows aloud.
- ● Toasted one another.
- ● And listened to the music.

———————

"Rituals are not the path. They are the reminder that there is a path."

~ Emmanuel/Pat Rodegast

———————

Idea: A Re-Dedication

The most romantic ceremony in most people's lives is their wedding. Why should you settle for just *one*? Creating a second/"re-dedication" wedding ceremony could revive the romance in your relationship in a truly unique way.

➤ You can create the *perfect* wedding—without the glitches that marred your first one.
➤ You can take all the time you like to create it—no pressure!
➤ You can be as creative, unique, eccentric or loving as you like.
➤ You can invite all the people who are special in your life *today*.
➤ You can hold it in a very special place.
➤ You can write your own vows.

Want some help? Get a copy of *I DO: A Guide to Creating Your Own Unique Wedding Ceremony*, by Ms. Sydney Barbara Metrick.

Rituals need not be boring or solemn. They merely need to be meaningful to you personally, and structured into a meaningful process. Rituals employ symbols, words and actions that help you focus on the deeper meaning of a particular event. ✦ Romance Class participants have created a wide array of creative rituals, including: A TGIF ritual; dinner rituals; spiritual bedtime rituals; sexy fantasy rituals; "Quiet Time" rituals to quiet the kids; meditation rituals; greeting rituals; departure rituals; affirmation rituals; and "unwinding" rituals.

Resources

☆ *New Traditions: Redefining Celebrations for Today's Family*, by Susan Abel Lieberman
☆ *The Art of Ritual: A Guide to Creating and Performing Your Own Ceremonies for Growth and Change*, by Renee Beck & Sydney Barbara Metrick
☆ *Rituals For Our Times: Celebrating, Healing and Changing Our Lives and Our Relationships*, by Evan Imber-Black & Janine Roberts
☆ *Herbal Secrets*, by Letha Hadadi
☆ *The Well Seasoned Marriage*, by N.S. Fields
☆ *Myths to Live By*, by Joseph Campbell
☆ *Rituals in Psychotherapy*, by Onno van der Hart
☆ *Myth, Ritual & Religion*, by Andrew Lang

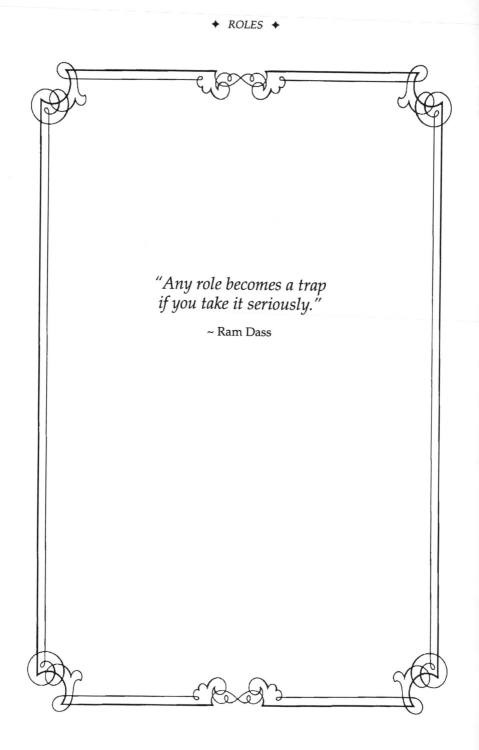

*"Any role becomes a trap
if you take it seriously."*

~ Ram Dass

Roles

Whether we like it or not, we're all part of a Grand Experiment that American culture is conducting. We're experimenting with our roles in a manner that is unprecedented in human history. We're in a transition: From an old paradigm of relationships based primarily on gender and traditional roles, to a new paradigm of relationships based on equality and individual aptitudes. ✦ This is why our relationships are so difficult, confusing and frustrating. This is why men don't know whether or not to open doors for women anymore. This is why women are struggling to balance careers and children. ✦ My guess is that it's going to take another 50 to 75 years before our culture settles into a new and relatively stable equilibrium. So where does this leave *us*? I think we've got three choices: 1) We can ride the wave, and experience all of its exhilaration as well as terror, 2) We can be swamped by the wave, and live in an overwhelmed frustration, or 3) We can sit on the shore, and hope it passes us by, leaving us unchanged and relieved. ✦ I don't know about *you*, but I'm waxing my surfboard!

I do *not* believe in equality. However, I *do* believe in equity. ✦ People who strive for equality are too busy "balancing the equation" of their relationship to *enjoy* it! If your squabbles center around issues like "I washed the dishes *last* week—it's now *your* turn!" I think you've lost sight of what your relationship is really all about.

FYI: Role Playing

As we mature, we tend to narrow our focus, and define ourselves by a very few roles that we play: Wife, Husband, Mother, Father, Breadwinner, Good Citizen, Volunteer, Friend. Don't forget about some of the *other* roles that you *could* play more often: Lover, Secret Admirer, Shoulder-To-Cry-On, Chef, Love Slave, Bride, Groom, Best Friend, Fantasy Lover. ✦ What other roles could you play?

Some of the roles we fill do not come from our conscious choices, but come about naturally as the result of our personalities and our up bringing. In some relationships, one person is just naturally more spontaneous and emotional, while the other is more reserved and logical. They complement, and enjoy, one another, as the spontaneous one finds security in the practical one . . . and the reserved one finds passion and joy in the emotional one. ✦ One danger, of course, is when these roles solidify, and fail to meet the changing needs of either one or both of the partners. Another danger is when you attempt to "complete" yourself through another. (Hint: It just doesn't work that way.) Find a copy of *The Missing Piece*, a great little book by Shel Silverstein.

If you want to be successful in *business*, there are many people—role models—you could emulate. If you want to be successful in *sports*, there are many athletes you could use as role models. And if you want a successful relationship, you could . . . you could . . . [*Uh-oh.*] ✦ Why are there so few role models for achieving successful, loving, intimate, long-term relationships? There are two reasons. ✦ First, very few people have successful, wonderful relationships that anybody else would want to model themselves after!—My guess is that the figure is somewhere around 1%. And secondly, those who *do* have wonderful relationships don't advertise the fact! Happy, contented couples make boring news stories. And besides, what do they care about the rest of the world? They've found heaven on earth! ✦ I *know* some of the members of the "One Percent Club." Some of them have attended my classes [and taught *me* more than I taught *them*]. Some of them may work with you. And others may be disguised as your neighbors down the street. They could be *anywhere!* (Although very few seem to have infiltrated the government, and they're extremely rare in Hollywood.) The lesson, I suppose, is that we all have to find our own path, our own Way. Perhaps we have to be our *own* role models.

If you don't redefine your relationship every five years or so, you're probably stuck in a rut. If you settle too comfortably into your respective roles, you invite laziness into your life. ✦ Some couples periodically re-evaluate their relationship. Some simply talk about it. Some do a variety of written exercises. Some sit down with a couples counselor for a "Relationship Check-Up." Some attend a workshop or seminar together.

Idea: Role Playing
✤ Who's your favorite TV character?
  ↦ Each of you choose a character.
  ↦ Go out on a date together and *stay in character for the entire time*! (Imagine a date between Captain Kirk and Edith Bunker; Jerry Seinfeld and Murphy Brown; Barnabas Collins and Maude.)
  ↦ Could you stay in character for a *whole day*?
✤ What about your favorite TV and movie stars?
  ↦ Katharine Hepburn and David Letterman; Marilyn Monroe and Jack Nicholson; Cher and Humphrey Bogart?
✤ What does your choice of characters reveal about your personality? Your fantasies? Your wishes? Your talents?

I'd like to acknowledge a woman who called me recently to express her feelings about my use of "gender stereotyping" in my first two books. (For example: My suggestion that you give your partner the gift of time by doing one of his/her chores: Guys—Wash the dishes. Gals—Cut the lawn.) ✦ I am very aware of the dangers of stereotyping, and I'm happy to have it brought to my attention, and I'm happy to have the opportunity to discuss it briefly. Here's my dilemma: I'm trying to communicate with a very diverse audience—people from all walks of life, with all kinds of backgrounds and beliefs. In order for a book to communicate effectively, the author must *first* meet people where they are, before he can suggest that the reader consider a different point-of-view. My decision has been to *mix together* the stereotypical and the unusual, and count on the context and my tone to convey my belief that our roles are not rigid. In fact, I strongly believe that it's healthy to experiment with different roles. It promotes creativity and understanding.

Resources
☆ *Becoming Partners*, by Carl Rogers
☆ *Games People Play: The Psychology of Human Relationships*, by Eric Berne
☆ *Intimate Partners: Hidden Patterns in Love Relationships*, by Clifford Sager & Bernice Hunt
☆ *The Cinderella Complex*, by Colette Dowling
☆ *Transformations: Growth and Change in Adult Life*, by Roger Gould
☆ *Homecoming: Reclaiming and Championing Your Inner Child*, by John Bradshaw

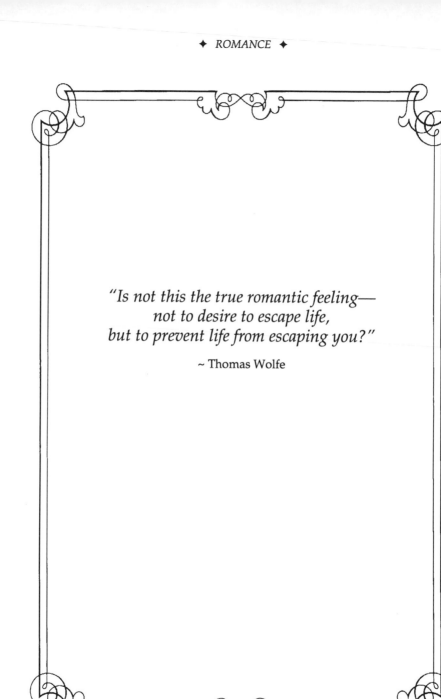

*"Is not this the true romantic feeling—
not to desire to escape life,
but to prevent life from escaping you?"*

~ Thomas Wolfe

Romance

"It's just plain unrealistic to expect romance to last more than a few years." "Romance inevitably fades in the face of everyday life." "Romance—it's just a passing phase we grow out of." ✦ I hear it in the Romance Class. I hear it in casual conversations. It drives me *crazy* every time. ✦ At least in the Romance Class I have the opportunity, if not the responsibility, to point out to people that they're strangling their own relationships with this kind of thinking. You see, romance isn't about flowers and candy and cute little notes. *Romance is the expression of love.* Without romance, love becomes just an empty concept. "I love you" becomes a meaningless, automatic phrase. ✦ Romance is not a thing separate from love. It's not something that you "grow out of" as you mature. If anything, one's love grows deeper as one matures, and the romance—the expression, the *action* of love—stays vibrant and creatively alive.

Creating romance is *easy*. It's *re*-creating romance that seems to give people a hard time. Most people come into the Romance Class with great romantic memories. "He used to bring me flowers *every week*." "She used to surprise me with breakfast in bed." What happened? No, they didn't "fall out of love"—Life just intruded, that's all. ✦ The good news is that they (and most of us) are *not* starting from scratch—we have a good romantic base to work from. The bad news is that Life won't stop intruding—you have to deal with kids and jobs and deadlines and taxes and chores and committees and relatives and neighbors and dogs and crabgrass.

Homework: Re-Creating Romance

Let's focus on the *positive* for a bit, shall we? Your relationship has many good points and strong qualities. What are they?

* List your three favorite qualities in your partner.
* List your three fondest memories of your life together.
* Essay Assignment: In 15 minutes, write on the topic of "The things I value most about our relationship."
* Go out to dinner together. Take along your answers. Discuss them. Bask in the glow of all the good things you've created together.

———————

Fiction can be a *great* source of romantic inspiration. From novels to short stories. From realistic to fantastic. From romances to erotica. ✦ Authors and poets and playwrights throughout history have used their imaginations to help them, and us, understand the joys and sorrows and mysteries of love. ✦ Have you ever thought of telling the story of your life and loves in fictional form? Have you ever considered writing something totally fanciful—to express yourself, to explore your feelings?

———————

Why do some people resist "settling-down"?
Why do they link security with monotony?
Why do they equate monogamy with boredom?
Why do they think long-term relationships lack excitement?
Why do they see commitment as incompatible with passion?

I believe that there's a common answer to all of these questions . . . And the link is *romance*—or rather, a misconception about the true nature of romance and its relationship to love. ✦ What happens is that people remove the concept of romance from love, *where it belongs,* and connect it to *other* things—things like being single; being infatuated; being immature and irresponsible; being forever moving and searching and unsettled. When this happens, the surface expressions of romance—passion, intensity, excitement—become linked with those states of being. You begin to believe, for example, that being single is exciting, and being married is boring; that security smothers passion; that monogamy means the end of passion. ✦ All of those statements are *beliefs*. If you *believe* them, *they are true for you.* Yes, of *course* you can create a boring, stuck-in-a-rut marriage. But that doesn't mean it's some kind of Rule that "All marriages are boring." And yet, this is what people *do!* It makes me so sad and frustrated to see people doing this to themselves and to each other. I want to shake them and yell *"It doesn't have to be that way! You can change your relationship by changing your beliefs!"* ✦ I know many people who have passionate 40-year marriages. I know several who have exciting affairs—*with their spouses.* I know retired couples who still date each other. These people all understand that they have control over whether or not romance is a part of their everyday lives. Romance is not some vague concept or elusive feeling that comes or goes of its own accord. Romance is the active part of love. Those who act on their love experience life-long excitement and passion. Those who don't act on their love are responsible for their own boredom.

———————

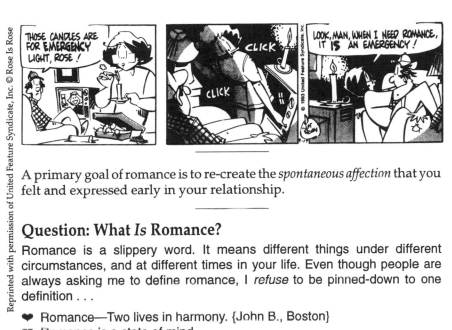

A primary goal of romance is to re-create the *spontaneous affection* that you felt and expressed early in your relationship.

Question: What *Is* Romance?

Romance is a slippery word. It means different things under different circumstances, and at different times in your life. Even though people are always asking me to define romance, I *refuse* to be pinned-down to one definition . . .

- ❤ Romance—Two lives in harmony. {John B., Boston}
- ❤ Romance is a state of mind.
- ❤ Romance is a state of being.
- ❤ Romance is the expression of love.
- ❤ Romance is joyful togetherness.
- ❤ Romance is *spontaneous affection*! {Kristen S., San Francisco}
- ❤ Romance is the process—Love is the goal.

Resources: Love In Fiction

- ✛ *The Bridges of Madison County*, by Robert James Waller
- ✛ *Slow Waltz in Cedar Bend*, by Robert James Waller
- ✛ *The Literary Lover: Great Contemporary Stories of Passion and Romance*, edited by Larry Dark
- ✛ *Griffin and Sabine*, by Nick Bantock
- ✛ *Sabine's Notebook*, by Nick Bantock (The story continues)
- ✛ *The Golden Mean*, by Nick Bantock (The story concludes)
- ✛ *Yellow Silk: Erotic Arts and Letters*, (the book) edited by Lily Pond & Richard Russo
- ✛ *Yellow Silk: Journal of the Erotic Arts*, (the magazine). Visit a good bookstore or write to P.O. Box 6374, Albany, California 94706.
- ✛ *Pleasures*—Erotica for women *by* women, edited by Lonnie Barbach

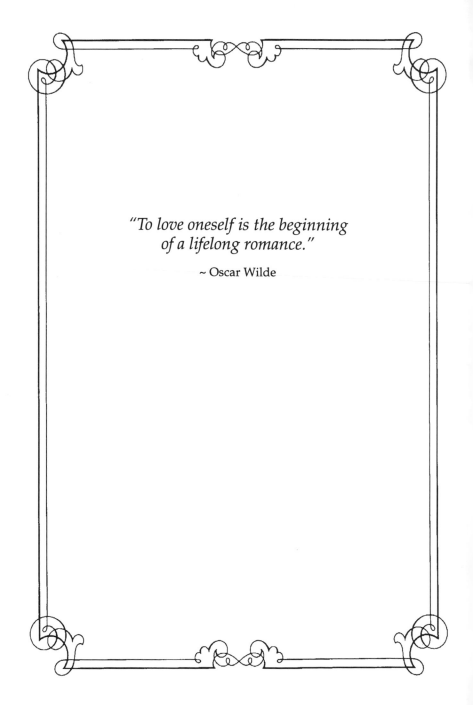

*"To love oneself is the beginning
of a lifelong romance."*

~ Oscar Wilde

Self-Esteem

Relationship problems almost always involve self-esteem problems: Either yours or his or both of yours. ◆ In order to love *another*, you must value *yourself*. To value yourself, you must have a sense of self-worth. Self-worth is built-up over time, and is a combination of how the important people in your life value you, and how you've internalized those messages into how you value yourself. Healthy self-esteem is a necessary foundation for intimate relationships.

The topic of self-esteem makes people *nervous*. (This is why it's the subject of so much humor—like *Saturday Night Live's* Stuart Smally: "I'm *good* enough... I'm *smart* enough... and doggone-it, people *like* me!") It makes us nervous because it strikes so close to home. We *all* have self-esteem issues. We *all* have doubts and insecurities and areas for growth.

Homework: Personal History

☞ Grab that pad and pen . . .
☞ In what areas of your life do you feel strong, confident?
☞ In what areas do you feel you don't measure up?
☞ Which of these areas are *important* to you? (You don't have to be great at *everything*!)
☞ When in your life did you feel the most confident and self-assured?
☞ How is your happiness diminished by feelings of inadequacy?
☞ Choose one skill that you'd like to improve—one that will, in some small way, improve your feeling of self worth.
☞ How can your partner help you? Do you need encouragement? Understanding? A little space? A non-judgmental listener?

Improving your self-esteem involves taking risks. It is accomplished by dealing with fear—fear of your limitations, fear of rejection, fear of failure, and a host of *other* fears. ◆ Give yourself (and your partner) time and patience and understanding.

The *worst* way to build-up your self-esteem is to do it at the expense of your partner's self-esteem. You'll *both* lose. Building yourself up by criticizing or belittling your partner is, in effect, emotional abuse. ✦ It's obvious that your partner will become resentful, dis-spirited and perhaps depressed. It may *not* be so obvious that your increase in self-esteem is on very shaky ground, as it is built not on your own abilities, but on someone else's shortcomings. At best, this strategy is misdirected and short-sighted. At worst, it is malicious and self-destructive.

We all have a continuously running conversation going on inside our heads. This "self-talk" is a normal part of our consciousness. It is also one area of our lives where we have *a great deal of control*. You can't control many outside circumstances in your life, but you *can* control many of your thoughts. And these thoughts have a direct impact on your self-esteem.

Homework: Self-Talk

✳ For the next week, keep a pad and pen with you at all times (at work, at home, in the car, in bed).
✳ Once an hour or so, jot jown a few phrases that capture the essence of your "self-talk" at that moment. Take a "snapshot" of your internal dialogue.
✳ Do you notice any patterns? Is your self-talk mostly positive or mostly negative? Does it sound a lot like one of your parents? Do you like what you're telling yourself?

Here's a quick way to tell whether a person has high self-esteem or low self-esteem: Determine whether he is a "giver" or a "taker." Is he giving or selfish? Is he open or closed? ✦ People with high self-esteem are secure in the knowledge of who they are; their sense of self-worth comes from inside themselves, so they are not overly dependent on others. This enables them to approach the world from a place of abundance. ✦ People with low self-esteem approach the world with a belief in scarcity. Basically, they're living in fear. Therefore, they tend to be selfish with material things as well as with feelings. They give little— and then only with strings attached. ✦ It's pretty clear that having high self-esteem is a prerequisite to being truly romantic. [I never *said* this was going to be *easy*!]

One of the very best ways to build self-esteem is also the simplest. Affirmations are an effective method for improving your "Self-Talk," and for influencing your unconscious mind. The use of positive affirmations is widespread among the most successful and happiest people in the world. ✦ A note to the practically-minded: Affirmations are not mystical or spiritual in nature—unless you choose to make them so. Affirmations are a logical and effective method of creating positive results in your life. The effectiveness of affirmations has been demonstrated by numerous psychological studies in additon to the flood of anecdotal evidence that people by the score are changing their lives positively through the use of affirmations.

Homework: Affirmations

There are many good books of affirmations. Or, you can create your *own* affirmations . . .

❖ Sit quietly/meditatively for 10 to 15 minutes, to still your mind.
❖ Now, think about the person you want to be . . .
   ✦ List the personal attributes you admire and aspire to.
   ✦ List your goals (personal and professional; short-term and long-term).
   ✦ Answer this question: "What is the essence I wish to project?"
❖ Now, write 3 to 5 statements based on your lists. Here's the format:
   ✦ Make each statement in the *present tense*, as if you *already* embody this quality. (Say "I am happy and confident"—not "I want to be . . .")
   ✦ Make each statement *personal*. (Say "I project warmth"—not "Warmth is a desirable characteristic.")
   ✦ Make each statement *positive*. (Say "I am a healthy non-smoker"—not "I don't want to smoke any more.")
❖ Write your affirmations on 3x5 cards and keep them with you at all times. Read them upon waking up in the morning, several times during the day, and just before you go to bed at night.
❖ Practice with these few affirmations for one month, and then evaluate your life, your state of mind, your moods, your relationships.

Resources

☆ *Self Esteem*, by Virginia Satir
☆ *The Psychology of Self-Esteem*, by Nathaniel Branden
☆ *Awaken the Giant Within*, by Anthony Robbins

Passion

*When everything tastes like **Champagne***
*When everything smells like **Freesia***
*When everything looks like **Christmas***
*When everything sounds like **Mozart***
*When everything feels like **Velvet***

~ Veronica M. Hay
From *In A Dream, You Can Do Anything, A Collection of Words*

Sensuality

Why aren't we more sensual? Why aren't we more attentive to the sensory inputs that we receive constantly through our five senses? Why don't we create more sensual environments for ourselves?

First, let's clarify the differences between *sensuality* and *sexuality* (the very next chapter, in case you're interested). ✦ Sensuality is a broader concept than sexuality. Sensuality is about arousing your senses or appetites. It often *does* have a sexual connotation to it, but not *always*. Sexuality is much more specific and focused on the genitals and on arousal in the service of orgasm. Being sensuous involves the conscious stimulation of a variety of your five senses. While sexuality involves your body interacting with another's body, sensuality is about you reacting to your environment. Sometimes that environment involves your partner, and sometimes it doesn't. ✦ Women, in general are closer to their sensual nature than men are. It probably has something to do with the biological fact that women's orgasms are more generalized, more diffused throughout their bodies; while men's orgasms tend to be highly localized. Call Dr. Ruth on this one!

Your immediate environment has a strong impact on your emotions and moods. It does so through your senses. Thus, one way to enhance your relationship is through the environment you create together. Is your home conducive to intimacy? How is your furniture arranged? What colors and fabrics surround you? How is your bedroom set-up? ✦ Do you use your environment to communicate with your lover? Do you give gifts that have a sensuous nature? Do you leave behind a perfume or cologne fragrance that will remind your partner of your presence?

Homework: Recognizing Sensuality

♠ What are your most sensual memories?
♠ When are you the most attuned to sensuous experiences?
♠ What kind of environments do you find sensuous?

Exercises: Experiencing Sensuality

Over the next month, make time for all of these experiences:

❋ Take a bubble bath. Alone. In water that is as hot as you can stand.
❋ Ask your lover to give you a one-hour sensual (not sexual) massage.
❋ Spend 5 minutes in every room in your house. Sit quietly, close your eyes, and focus on the way the room *smells* and "feels."
❋ Lie in bed naked with your lover. With the lights off. Explore your lover's body with your sense of smell and your sense of taste. Explore every square inch of his or her body. Take at least 20 minutes to do this. (At the end of 20 minutes you may make love if you wish.)
❋ For one entire day, focus on *color*.
❋ For one entire day, focus on *shapes*.
❋ For one entire day, focus on *sounds*. Not so much words and music, but sounds.

Who *says* Real Men aren't sensuous? In a famous letter, Napoleon told Josephine not to bathe during the two weeks that would pass before they would be together again—so that he could enjoy all her natural aromas!

FYI: Blocks to Sensuality

❒ Being preoccupied or distracted
❒ Over-reliance on one of our five senses, to the exclusion of the others
❒ Our conscious filters: Decisions to focus on certain things—and ignore other things
❒ Our *un*conscious filters: Habits, biases, prejudices, stresses
❒ Fear of feeling too good
❒ Lack of time: Rushing through our lives
❒ Focusing on the past or future, instead of on the *present moment*

Some of the things that prevent us from being more sensual are: Equating sensuality with femininity. Feelings of guilt. Religious misgivings about sensuality. Moving too quickly to notice. Being too busy to notice. Being overly-focused on one or two of your senses, to the exclusion of the others.

FYI: Sensuous Catalogs!

* *It's A Secret Lingerie.* Call for a free catalog: 800-390-3528.
* *Swimwear of the World*—Sexy swimwear *for men*! If you'd like to see your guy in one of those thong-things from Brazil or France, this is the place to shop! Just $2 from Shop At Home, Department 180, 2080 South Holly Street, P.O. Box 221050, Denver, Colorado 80222.
* *Barely Nothings*—Specializing in larger sizes. [Hey, not everybody's a size 4!] Call for a free catalog: 800-422-7359.

FYI: Sensuous Scents

Different scents have different effects on us. Laurel K. suggests that you combine the sensuous experience of a hot bath with specifically-scented bath beads:

* Relaxing & soothing: Ylang-ylang, bay, lavender
* Refreshing: Peppermint, rosemary, thyme
* Reviving: Juniper, bergamot
* Calming: Frankincense, sandalwood, patchouli

Resources

- ☆ *The Sensuous Man*, by M
- ☆ *The Sensuous Woman*, by J
- ☆ *A Natural History of the Senses*, by Diane Ackerman
- ☆ *The Book of Massage*, by Lucinda Lidell
- ☆ *Pamper Your Partner: An Illustrated Guide to Soothing and Relaxing Your Mate With the Sensual Healing Arts*, by Penny Rich

---

"Sex alleviates tension.
Love causes it."

~ Woody Allen

Sexuality

Sex. Ah, yes, the chapter that all the guys turn to first . . . ✦ Sexual energy is a strong, creative and magnetic force. It is positive and life-affirming. Things got messed-up when culture and religion twisted sex into something that often generates shame and guilt. How do we get back on track? One way is by re-connecting sex with love and romance. Sex—"communication without words"—can open the door to intimacy in a way that nothing else in the universe can. ✦ Sexuality and vulnerability go hand-in-hand. The more open you are, the more you will enjoy your sexual relationship. As a matter of fact, there is great excitement in vulnerability. This is the trade-off we make when we decide to stay with one partner, you see. We lose the excitement of newness, of conquest; but we gain the excitement of knowing and being known, of true freedom to be ourselves.

FYI: The Enemies of Sex

As compiled from a decade of responses in the Romance Class.

- ☛ Lack of respect for your partner's needs
- ☛ Confusing physical intimacy with emotional intimacy
- ☛ Lack of time
- ☛ Children!
- ☛ Timing: Leaving sex until too late at night
- ☛ Boredom and routines
- ☛ Myths and misinformation about sex
- ☛ Unrealistic expectations
- ☛ Selfishness and insensitivity

FYI: The Friends of Sex

As compiled from a decade of responses in the Romance Class.

- ☞ The right partner
- ☞ Time: Enough time
- ☞ Timing: The *right* time
- ☞ Creativity
- ☞ Honesty
- ☞ Dr. Ruth
- ☞ Generosity
- ☞ Open communication
- ☞ Romantic music
- ☞ Fantasy
- ☞ Victoria's Secret
- ☞ Locks on the bedroom door
- ☞ Lack of inhibitions
- ☞ Patience

Idea: "Take it off!"

I have to tell you straight-off that neither Tracey nor I have seen this video. But four women have written to me in the last year recommending it, so there must be something to it . . . ✦ . . . A tasteful, step-by-step video called *How to Strip for Your Man*. It will teach you the sexiest ways of walking, talking, posing and disrobing. Variety magazine says this video "promotes self-confidence, spontaneity and sensuality." ✦ At $29.75, it looks like a bargain to me. ["Hey *Trace*—hand me the phone and our charge card, would you?"] Call the Joan Cook catalog at 800-935-0971. Or write to 119 Foster Street, P.O. Box 6038, Peabody, Massachusetts 01961.

Homework: Take Your Choice

Choose among these exercises.

↔ Create an erotic fantasy that both of you find exciting. Act it out!

↔ Play "Give-And-Take":
  ❖ Plan a one-hour lovemaking session.
  ❖ Flip a coin to choose a "Giver" and a "Taker."
  ❖ The Giver's role is to give pleasure.
  ❖ The Taker's role is to receive pleasure. Nothing more!
  ❖ You trade places every 10 minutes.
  ❖ Ready—set—*go*!

↔ Plan a date for this Friday night. You're going to create a "Sensual Evening." The goal is to stimulate each other's senses and arouse one another, but *not* to have sex. General erotic enjoyment is the goal.

↔ Plan a second date for the following Wednesday night. We're going to balance the "Sensual Evening" with a "Sex, Sex—Nothing But Sex" date. I don't think I need to instruct you on this one.

Obviously, one does not *need* romance in order to be sexual. But by itself, sexuality only goes so far. Why? Because sexual energy is a wild, restless, mindless, short-lived thing (along with being an exciting, passionate, creative, joyful thing). ✦ Romance creates a context within which sexuality can be given more meaning. Romance focuses sexuality toward a loving purpose: The growth of intimacy. ✦ Without romance, sex is just seduction. Without romance, sex runs the risk of becoming manipulation or exploitation. Without romance, sex can turn into an empty habit or dull duty. ✦ *With* romance, sex becomes connected to love. *With* romance, sex becomes about *giving*, and not merely *taking*.

Even though we're bombarded with sexual messages in the media, in advertisements, and in our popular music, many of us go through our day-to-day lives devoid of true sexual feeling. Why? I think our modern lifestyle—with its focus on *quantity* instead of *quality*, and its messages of *image* instead of *content*—has dulled our senses. It has dulled our ability to sense our outside environment. It has *also* dulled our ability to sense our *inside* environment—our state of mind and our sense of our own bodies. The flood of messages and images coming at us, plus the fast pace of our lives, combine to mask the subtle stream of messages that emanate from within us. ✦ I suspect if we were to slow our lives down a little, and quiet ourselves a little bit, that we would probably have much more fulfilling, frequent, and satisfying sexual encounters!

"If orgasm is your only goal in having sex, you're missing 50% of the opportunity!" said Robert G., one night, in an all-men's version of the Romance Class. He set-off a lively discussion that consumed nearly an hour! [Where are the women when you need them??]

There is a challenge and an opportunity in every intimate relationship. The challenge is to maintain sexual passion in the face of daily responsibilities and routines that promote boredom. The opportunity is that the security created by your commitment to one another opens the door to deeper intimacy and a new level of self-disclosure that combine to stimulate sexual passion. ✦ Some people believe that when you're in a monogamous relationship *there's nowhere to go* when you feel bored or frustrated with your partner or your relationship. *This isn't true!* While your choice to be monogamous *does* mean you've decided not to look *outside* the relationship for gratification, it also means you've opened up the opportunity to look more deeply *inside* for gratification. Inside yourself and inside your relationship. ✦ Thus, a monogamous relationship becomes a unique vehicle for personal growth.

Resources

☆ *Becoming a Sexual Person*, by R.R. Francoeur
☆ *The Potent Self*, by Moshe Feldenkrais
☆ *For Each Other: Sharing Sexual Intimacy*, by Lonnie Barbach
☆ *Sexual Landscapes*, by J.D. Weinrich

*"When the going gets tough,
the tough go shopping."*

~ Bumper sticker wisdom

Shopping

True story: ✦ He wanted to get her a nice outfit for her birthday. She balked, pointing out that with four kids—two in college—money was tight. He had to think of a clever way to get past her logic. ✦ He invited her out to dinner, and asked her if she would trust him to select her outfit. She agreed. He set-out on the bed: Her raincoat and a pair of shoes! She, being a good sport, went along. He took her to a mall, saying that she had to be dressed *decently* if he was to take her out to dinner. She giggled throughout the whole evening. He loved every minute of it. ✦ She tried on several outfits, giggling and confounding salespeople throughout the mall. He bought her an outfit, cut off the tags, and she walked out of the store fully dressed. ✦ Years later, it's one of their favorite memories. {Thanks to J.T. and C.T., in Pennsylvania.}

Homework: A Shopping Spree
What could you buy for your lover in each of these stores?

❏ Victoria's Secret
❏ Radio Shack
❏ K-Mart
❏ Sharper Image
❏ True Value Hardware
❏ Toys-R-Us

❏ A hairstyling salon
❏ A grocery store
❏ An office supply store
❏ A lumber yard
❏ A candy store
❏ A fast food restaurant

If you view shopping as a *chore* and a *responsibility*, you'll have a hard time finding great gifts, and you'll have a miserable time doing it, too. Try shifting your mindset. View shopping as: 1) An expression of your love, 2) An exercise in creativity, 3) A way to express yourself, 4) A chance to get some exercise, 5) A chance to stock-up on gifts one and two years ahead of time—so you won't have to go shopping again anytime soon!

Go shopping for one blue gift and three red ones. ✦ Find two gifts for under $5—three gifts for $20-$25—and one gift for $50-$100. ✦ Get two sentimental gifts—one gag gift—and one practical gift.

Homework: Exercise Your Imagination

If money were no object, and you had all the time in the world . . .

☞ What would you buy for your lover *today*?
☞ What would you buy for yourself?
☞ Where would you go?
  ♥ How would you travel there?
  ♥ How long would you stay?
  ♥ What would you do there?
☞ Where *else* would you go?
☞ What is the *ultimate gift* you would buy for your partner?
☞ What would you build or design?
☞ What would you like to experience?
☞ What would you like to learn?

What could you do today/this month/this year to enable yourself to buy or create just a little piece—some of the *essence*—of one of the items above?

Suggestions: A Shopping List

1 bottle of expensive champagne
2 tickets to Paris
3 albums by George Winston: *Autumn, Winter Into Spring, Summer*
4 bags of confetti
5 colored Magic Markers
6 birthday cards
7 balloons
8 Hershey's Kisses
9 romantic greeting cards
8 romantic movies on videotape
7 candles
6 lottery tickets
5 different types of bubble bath
4 copies of *Yellow Silk* magazine—"The Journal of Erotic Arts"
3 red roses
2 albums by Enya: *Shepherd Moons* and *Watermark*
1 white, lacy garter belt with matching stockings

Resources

☆ The *Anyone Can Whistle* catalog—"A catalog of musical discovery." All *kinds* of interesting and offbeat musical instruments and other "things" that make noise. 800-435-8863, or P.O. Box 4407, Kingston, New York 12401.

☆ *Seasons* catalog—"Gifts that last for times that change." Gifts on the thoughtful, elegant side. 800-776-9677, or P.O. Box 64545, Saint Paul, Minnesota 55164.

☆ The *Current* catalog—All kinds of stuff, specializing in *personalized* products. Things like: Greeting cards with your name printed on them; stationery, cards and notes; notebooks; signs; stickers; various kinds of boxes, and more. Write for a catalog: Current, Express Processing Center, Colorado Springs, Colorado 80941.

☆ *Metropolitan Opera Guild* catalog—For opera lovers—from the afficionado to the neophyte. Recordings, collectibles, T-shirts and more! Call for a free catalog: 800-566-4646.

☆ *i ♥ barbra catalog*—For fans of Barbra Streisand! Yes, a whole catalog full of Streisand collectibles: Rare magazines, records, posters, scripts, photographs, autographs and more! Just $2, from Publisher Inquiry Services, 951 Broken Sound Parkway N.W., Building 190, P.O. Box 5057, Boca Raton, Florida 33431.

☆ *Hershey's Gift* catalog—For the chocolate lover in your life! Chocolate greeting cards personalized with your message; and all kinds of chocolates packed in tins, mugs and glassware. The catalog is just $2, from Shop At Home, Department 180, 2080 South Holly Street, P.O. Box 221050, Denver, Colorado 80222.

☆ *Cinema City* catalog—For movie buffs. Movie posters, photos, scripts, autographed items and more. The catalog is just $2, from Shop At Home, Department 180, 2080 South Holly Street, P.O. Box 221050, Denver, Colorado 80222.

☆ *Graceland Gifts* catalog—Good lord, an entire catalog of Elvis Presley memorabilia! *Elvis lives!* The catalog is just $1, from Shop At Home, Department 180, 2080 South Holly Street, P.O. Box 221050, Denver, Colorado 80222.

☆ The *Cheers* catalog—From the place "Where everybody knows your name." Just $2 from from Shop At Home, Department 180, 2080 South Holly Street, P.O. Box 221050, Denver, Colorado 80222.

☆ *Manny's Baseball Land* catalog—For all sports fans! Caps, jackets, jerseys (old and new) for pro football, baseball, hockey, basketball and college teams! A one-year subscription of 8 issues is free! Call 800-776-8326.

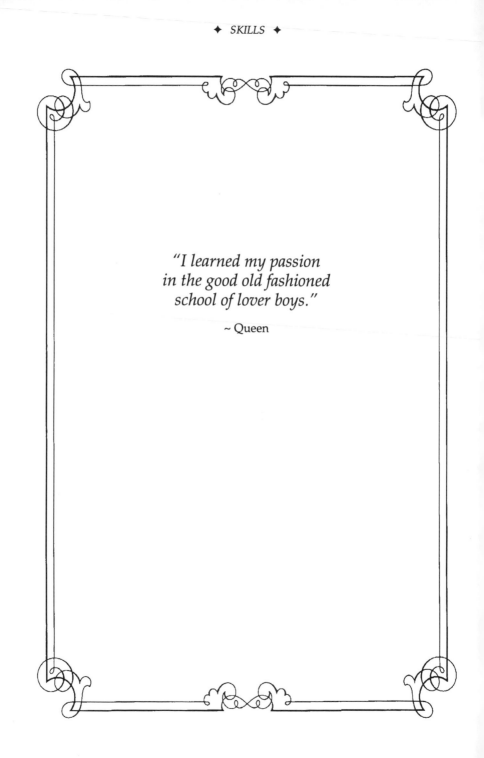

*"I learned my passion
in the good old fashioned
school of lover boys."*

~ Queen

Skills

You came into the world equipped with the full range of emotional resources needed to deal with anything and to accomplish your Purpose in life. [Isn't that comforting to know?] You don't need to *learn* love—it's already in there. You don't need to learn anger, passion or tenderness. ✦ What we *do* need are skills that will help us *access* these emotions and experience them when they are appropriate. Men often have difficulty getting to those tender and gentle emotions. —But rest assured, they're in there! Women often have difficulty accessing their anger and power. —But push the right buttons, and *pow!* ✦ Who's going to help you learn these skills? Sorry, it's not *me* . . . it's your *partner*. If you've chosen well, your lover is your teacher, and you are hers/his. It's not magic or even Fate. It's simply the nature of things.

(An unedited exchange in the Romance Class):

Him: *"I admit that these skills are useful. but this romance stuff isn't exactly brain surgery, is it?"*

Her: *"It may not be brain surgery, but some of you guys could sure use a personality transplant!"*

It is important to learn to recognize and respect *the lessons of your own experience*—as opposed to book-learning or someone else's advice (no matter how genuine or well meant). ✦ You don't *really* learn something until you've *experienced* it. This is why you can hear a suggestion or bit of wisdom repeatedly for *years*, feeling that it's an obvious, overused, trivial phrase . . . Until one day you *experience* the insight, and it suddenly becomes a Profound Truth. ✦ This is why no book (including this one) can change your life. Anything you read—no matter *how* profound, True, or inspiring—is only the first of *many* steps in helping you, affecting you, or changing you. It's *your* job to internalize the message, synthesize it and customize it into something that really *fits* for you. And then you've still got to *experience* it. Otherwise the greatest wisdom and insight in the *world* will remain merely theoretical.

FYI: Mindreading Skills

Mindreading is *not* assuming that you know what's on her mind—it's *knowing* what's on her mind! (Eighty percent accuracy is acceptable. Fifty percent is *not*.) Can you develop mindreading skills? Of *course* you can. You don't have to be psychic. You just have to . . .

✛ Listen more carefully. *Pay attention!*

✛ Respect what she's saying. *Your* opinion ain't relevant here!

✛ *Remember* what she's said. It doesn't do you any good if it's not in your memory banks.

Here's a mindreading exercise:

▲ First, remember that this is a *game*.

☐ You both win if you succeed in generating awareness.

☐ You both lose if you take this too seriously and end up getting mad.

▲ Flip a coin to choose one partner to be the mindreader.

▲ The mindreader then makes 5 to 10 statements that he or she believes are true about his or her partner. Things like . . . "I think you hate it when I play poker with the guys." "I think you love the toaster I bought for your birthday." "I feel you don't value the work I do around the house." "I believe that you resent the time I spend on the phone."

▲ The partner gives points for right and wrong answers:

☐ + 3 points = Absolutely True!

☐ + 2 points = Sort-of/Kind-of True (We Need to Talk)

☐ - 2 points = There's A *Grain* of Truth Here (But You've Twisted It Up)

☐ - 3 points = Wrong, Wrong, *Wrong*! (Are You Talking About *Me*?!?)

▲ Switch roles.

▲ Compare scores. Congratulate your partner for the correct statements. Discuss the incorrect statements.

▲ Don't expect to resolve everything right away! The point here is to raise awareness!

▲ Play this mindreading game again in three months. Have either of you become better mindreaders? Is your relationship more fun?

The subtle skills of mindreading and hinting don't always work. That's when you need to employ the much more direct tactic of *bartering*. Basically, the philosophy of bartering is "I'll do this for you, if you'll do that for me." This approach may seem rather blunt and unromantic to you . . . but hey, sometimes you just have to be ruthless! ✦ Save bartering for special favors and for having fun. (Bartering is especially effective when it comes to sex. Think about it!) But use bartering *selectively*. It's easy to fall into a *habit* of bartering, and that's not wise.

Suggestion: The Blame Game

The reason that nagging doesn't work is that it is based on blaming, finger-pointing and guilt-producing language. Here's a way out:

✳ Re-phrase your complaint into a caring statement that offers a solution to the dilemma.
✳ Make sure you include *yourself* as part of the solution.
✳ For example, you could change the first statement into the second one:
    ✳ **Old**: "When I come home from work, all you do is complain."
    ✳ **New**: "I value our time together, and I'm afraid we haven't been paying enough attention to each other. I've called a babysitter—let's go out for dinner!"
✳ Or how about this scenario?
    ✳ **Old**: "You used to be romantic when we were single!"
    ✳ **New**: "Let's take turns creating romantic dates—one-a-week. I'll go first . . ."
✳ This exercise breaks down the barriers that separate us.
✳ It also demonstrates goodwill, because you make the first move.
✳ You're not putting your lover on the defensive, which always backfires.

FYI: Skills You Need to Know

➤ How to be affectionate without being sexual.
➤ How to cook your lover's favorite meal.
➤ How to share your feelings without dumping them on your partner.
➤ How to be supportive without being controlling.
➤ How to listen *actively* instead of *passively*.
➤ How to be interdependent without slipping into dependency.
➤ How to keep in touch with your "Inner Child."
➤ How to say "*I love you*" in Hawaiian: "*Aloha wau ia oe!*"
➤ How to make love in that *special way* that your partner loves so much.
➤ How to grow together instead of growing apart.
➤ How to keep your relationship your #1 priority amid life's many demands.

Resources

☆ *Megaskills*, by Dorothy Rich
☆ *The Elusive Obvious*, by Moshe Feldenkrais
☆ *Human Options*, by Norman Cousins
☆ *Pulling Your Own Strings*, by Wayne W. Dyer
☆ *A Whack on the Side of the Head*, by Roger von Oech
☆ *Creative Gift Packagings*, by Yoko Kondo

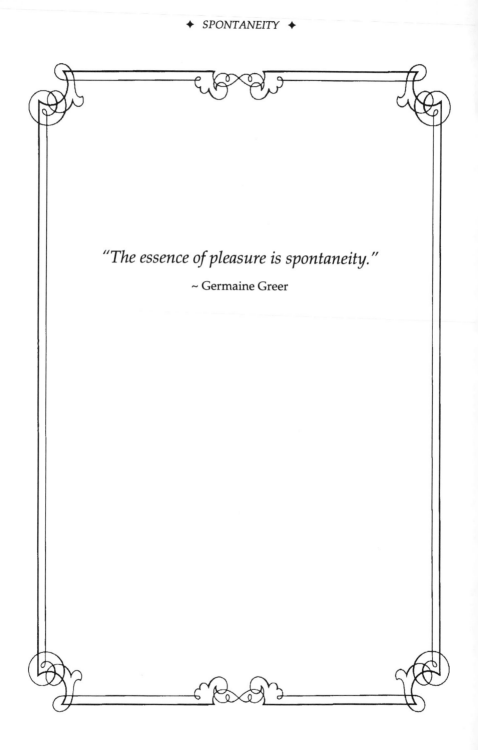

"The essence of pleasure is spontaneity."

~ Germaine Greer

Spontaneity

Big guy in the back of the class. He's been sitting with his arms crossed all evening, looking like he's swallowed something unpleasant. He suddenly brightens, and says, "Doesn't it kill the spontaneity in my relationship if I'm following pre-written lessons, or doing just what my wife instructs me to do?" With a smug look he settles back in his chair. [I should have expected this!]   ✦   Do you think spontaneity happens spontaneously? *Hah!* Spontaneity requires commitment, preparation, flexibility, creativity, time and purpose.   ✦   Think about the "spontaneous" creations of a jazz musician playing a solo, or a comedian doing improvisation. A lot of time and effort goes into creating these experiences. If you want to experience the fun, creativity and joy that spontaneity can bring to your relationship, you have to work at it. It's not *hard* work, but it does require *some* effort.

Exercises: Encouraging Spontaneity

How about some exercises to warm-up your spontaneity?

✳ Spontaneous Writing Exercise

  ✴ Grab a pad and pen. Sit down for 15 minutes and write continuously.
  ✴ Write whatever pops into your head. Simply transcribe your "stream of consciousness."
  ✴ If you can't think of anything to write, then write "I can't think of anything to write" over and over again, until some different thoughts spontaneously pop into your head. And I guarantee they will!
  ✴ This exercise encourages your spontaneity by helping you to recognize the constant flow of thoughts, ideas and insights that are constantly flashing through your brain. It also helps you overcome the natural censors in your head.

✳ Change a Pattern Exercise

  ✴ Sometime during the next week, when you catch yourself doing the same old thing you do every day at this time—*do something different!* If you're watching TV . . . Leap out of your chair, grab your partner, and go out dancing! If you're about to have dinner . . . pick up the whole table and move it into your back yard! If you're between crises at work . . . fake a minor illness, go home and make love with your partner!

Idea: Getting "Pinned"

Dan R. travels a lot. He's on planes four days a week. One day he was circling Chicago, he'd finished his reports and his paperback, he was missing his wife, and he was flipping aimlessly through the airline magazine . . . When an ad for corporate logo lapel pins caught his eye, and he had a spontaneous romantic brainstorm. He picked-up the Air Fone, called the company, and ordered a lapel pin that said

"I LOVE MY WIFE"

Cool, huh? But the story continues . . . The minimum order was 150 pins, at $4.32 each. That totaled $648—a lot of money. Here's how Dan rationalized the expense: $648 is equivalent to five elegant dinners plus four movie dates plus three dozen roses. He figured that 150 "I Love My Wife" pins were equivalent to all that—so he bought 'em! ✦ Not only does his wife love it, but Dan now gives out free pins to people on planes who ask him about his pin. Now *that's* what *I* call The Friendly Skies! ✦ You, too, can reach Lapel Pin, Inc. at 800-229-7467, or at 6381 Hollywood Boulevard, Suite 505, Hollywood, California 90028.

Many of us aren't very good at asking for what we want. We just want our partner to read our minds. {"Is that really so much to ask?" *Yes!*} I can't tell you how many times people in the Romance Class respond to me with, "If I have to ask for what I want, it doesn't count/it takes the fun and spontaneity out of the romance." Tain't true, folks! ✦ First of all, would you rather get what you want, or hold onto the myth that your partner is psychic, and continue harboring the resentment that's building inside you? C'mon, let go of that anger! ✦ Secondly, some people just need a romantic jump-start now and then! ✦ Thirdly, spontaneity ain't everything!

Idea: Global Awareness

Here's how one couple in the Romance Class told us they choose vacation destinations: They go to their local public library, where they have a world globe, three feet in diameter. One of them gives it a hefty spin, and the other closes his eyes and *points*. Wherever his finger lands, *that's where they go!* ✦ Some of their rules: Ocean spots can be either luxury cruises or sailing vacations. And only one ocean vacation every four years is allowed. If an already-visited spot is chosen, the spinner gets to choose any adjacent country. War zones may be skipped.

Controlling your partner runs counter to the spirit of loving relationships. Relationship control is usually accomplished through subtle but powerful manipulation. There are many problems with this approach to relationships. ✦ Manipulation leads to a lack of spontaneity. It puts a lot of pressure on you—being the "Puppet Master"— and it leads to sure disappointment when things don't go your way. ✦ Now let's look at the effects of manipulation on your *partner*. People who are manipulated feel devalued, not listened-to, and not understood. This adds up to feeling unloved. How do these people usually respond? By giving up, shriveling-up, shutting-up, or getting-up and leaving. None of which are great choices, are they?

One of the best ways to encourage your spontaneity is to think like a child. Approach situations with curiosity. See the world with a sense of wonder. Don't assume you know everything. Be willing to take a risk.

Resources

☆ *Flow: The Psychology of Optimal Experience*, by Mihaly Csikszentmihalyi

☆ *Human Options*, by Norman Cousins

☆ *Mindful Spontaneity*, by Ruthy Alon

"Any time that is not spent on love is wasted."

~ Torquato Tasso

Time

When you come right down to it, *time* is all you really *have* to give to another person. ✦ It's your most valuable resource. Your time is your *life!* ✦ If you give time with love, you create intimacy. If you give time in any other way, it causes problems, resentments, misunderstandings.

In the real world we trade time for money. We work *x* number of hours and we get paid *y* amount of dollars. We then use that money to provide for our basic needs—*and* to buy gifts that express our feelings. This is fine— but don't forget that gifts are merely symbols: They *represent* you. ✦ The best gift is the gift of *yourself*—your time and attention. That's what your lover *really* wants from you . . . more of *you!* ✦ Idea: Spend more *time* instead of more *money* on each other!

If you are an average American, and you live to be 75 years old, during your life *you will watch a total of 14 uninterrupted years of TV.*

Just *think* about this fact for a moment . . . ✦ I don't care if you're watching PBS, documentaries and *Masterpiece Theatre* the whole time— it's *still* not a great way to use-up your life, is it? ✦ Take a holiday from your TV for a week. [Okay, *okay* . . . You can tape your three favorite shows on the VCR for future viewing. Are you happy now? Can you please turn your attention back to your partner?] Many couples who try this experiment are pleasantly surprised to rediscover the art of conversation. And without the easy distraction of the boob tube, many of them rediscover each other.

Here's a guaranteed way to save time—as well as prevent problems: Make time to talk *regularly* about important relationship issues. If you put it off, not only will problems pile-up, but your skills at communicating intimately will get rusty, making the problems even *worse.* If you can anticipate problems and resolve issues as they arise, you'll avoid the time-consuming crises that cause so much heartache. ✦ Some couples hold weekly "Couple Meetings." Some talk over dinner. Some talk over cocktails. Some talk while they walk.

One evening in the Romance Class we were talking about time and its relation to *now*, when Howard S. nearly fell backwards in his chair. "It's so *obvious*—why've I never understood this before?" He was literally flushed with excitement. "There's a major but subtle difference between living *in* the moment—and living *for* the moment!" It took the class several minutes to get it all sorted out, but Howard had really hit upon something. ✦ Living *for* the moment is usually a selfish, irresponsible thing to do. There's no thought given to the consequences of your actions. (Although hedonism *does* have its place!) Whereas living *in* the moment is a focused, conscious choice to live with awareness and appreciation.

FYI: Time Facts

▼ Most couples spend less than 30 minutes a week sharing intimate feelings.

■ The average American spends more than 4 hours a day watching TV.

▲ Most people's lovemaking sessions take less than 25 minutes.

● Most couples leave lovemaking until the very end of the day, when they're tired, preoccupied and spent.

Are you giving your lover leftovers? Do you give her whatever time is "left over" from the rest of your life? If you don't consciously put her at the top of your priority list, she'll automatically drop to the *bottom* of the list. It's a Rule of Nature: "People take for granted those who are closest to them." ✦ Our culture is not structured in a way that supports love. As a matter of fact, much of society actively resists your efforts to make time for your partner. Your career could easily absorb all of your "free time" if you allowed it to. Your chores and other responsibilities will consume you—*if you let them.* ✦ Here's the secret: You must fight back. You must set boundaries. You must limit the encroachment of the rest of the world into your relationship.

> *"Time is precious and so are you.*
> *Time is fleeting but you are not.*
> *This is why I give my time to you."*
> ~ From the wedding vows of S.D. and B.C.

FYI: Time Facts/Time Questions

➤ There are 1,440 minutes in a day.
  * How many of those minutes do you spend near your partner?
  * How many minutes do you spend being loving?
  * How many minutes would you *like* to spend together?
➤ You will live for 25,567 days—if you live to be 70 years old.
  * What do you *really* want to do with those days?
  * When you look back on your life, *what will you regret not having made time for?* Take action *today* to prevent this from happening.
➤ If you live to be 70, that's 36,816,480 minutes.
  * We live our lives in *minutes*—not years.
  * Pay attention to those minutes—they have a way of slipping past unnoticed and unappreciated.

FYI: Saving Time the Yuppie Way

If you or your partner are high-powered, upwardly-mobile executive-types, you're always balancing how to use your time. Do you use the extra hour lounging in bed with your partner, or do you catch-up on all those business books you need to read in order to give you that competitive edge? [At this point the workaholics are scratching their heads, saying, "There's a *choice* here?!"] ✦ You can now do *both*! There's a service that reviews more than 1,000 books every year. An editorial board chooses two or three titles per month to review for subscribers. Professional business writers read and reread each book, then write a concise yet comprehensive eight-page summary for you. ✦ The cost is $110 for 30 summaries. Call Soundview Executive Book Summaries at 800-521-1277 or 802-453-4062, or write to 5 Main Street, Bristol, Vermont 05443.

Resources

☆ *Getting Things Done*, by Edwin C. Bliss
☆ *The 8-Day Week*, by John Ward Pearson
☆ *Dancing With Wu Li Masters*, by G. Zukav
☆ *Busy Bodies*, by Lee Burns

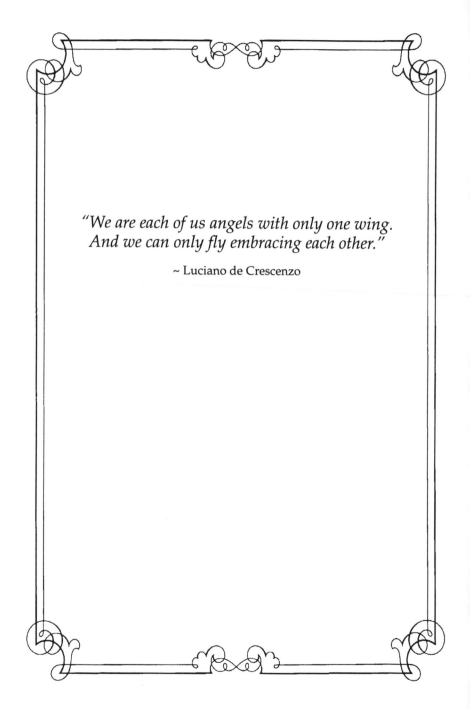

*"We are each of us angels with only one wing.
And we can only fly embracing each other."*

~ Luciano de Crescenzo

Togetherness

Another definition of "romance": *Joyful togetherness*. I like that.

"Isn't it possible to overdose on 'togetherness'? I mean, doesn't familiarity breed contempt?" If you view *togetherness* as simply "being in close proximity to one another," then sure, you can get tired of one another. But that's not what I mean when I say *togetherness*. ✦ To me, togetherness is "intimate sharing." Togetherness takes you to a deeper level of sharing your time and experiences together. Togetherness is about really *connecting* with your partner.

Exercises: Love In Action
* Make a list of specific things that your partner *already* does that make you feel loved. Thank her for those things.
* Make a list of specific things that you'd *like* your partner to do.
    * Be specific. Don't say, "I want you to pay more attention to me."
    * List at least 20 items.
* Trade lists with your partner.
* Each of you choose one item to act-on in the next week.

You don't *really* learn something until you've *experienced* it. This is why you can hear a suggestion or bit of wisdom repeatedly for *years*, feeling that it's an obvious, overused, trivial phrase . . . Until one day you *experience* the insight, and it suddenly becomes a Profound Truth. This is why no book (including this one) can change your life. Anything you read—no matter *how* profound, True, or inspiring—is only the first of *many* steps in helping you, affecting you, or changing you. It's your job to internalize the message, synthesize it and customize it into something that really *fits* for you. And then you've still got to *experience* it. Otherwise the greatest wisdom and insight in the *world* will remain merely theoretical.

> "*I do not want to make reasons for you to stay,*
> *Only reasons for you to return.*"
>
> ~ Jonivan

Togetherness doesn't mean smothering your partner. Togetherness is not motivated by jealousy. Togetherness must be freely chosen by each partner. Togetherness does not always involve physical proximity. Togetherness is expansive, not limiting.

It's not the journey of a thousand miles that is so daunting—
it's the pebble in your shoe that is driving you
to distraction.

Suggestion: Co-Meditation

Meditation is well-known for its ability to reduce stress, increase health, and focus one's mind. All of which, of course, can help your relationship, too. But the practice of meditation is a *solitary* activity. —*Except* in one unique Tibetan form of meditation. ✦ "Co-meditation" is a form of deep relaxation in which two people participate: The meditator and the co-meditator, who observes and responds to breathing cues with a variety of responses. The technique was created to help sick or dying people, but some who have experimented with it report that it is a great couple's exercise which promotes togetherness through its ability to help two people connect. ✦ Co-meditation is so new that there's not yet a book about it. If you find one, please drop me a note, and I'll include it in a future issue of the *Loveletter—The Newsletter of Romantic Ideas*. Until then . . .

❖ A co-meditation session takes 20 to 30 minutes.
❖ The meditator assumes a relaxed position, sitting or lying down.
❖ The co-meditator instructs the meditator to progressively relax the body.
❖ The meditator is asked to take several deep breaths, exhaling with an audible "Aaaaah."
❖ The co-meditator then counts the meditator's breaths out loud, and occasionally offers suggestions or ideas like,"Visualize your stress evaporating," or "You're feeling peaceful and at ease."
❖ The co-meditator finally recites a mantra chosen by the meditator.

Some couples trade roles every other day, making it a regular ritual. Others use co-meditation just once a week, as a way to re-connect and enhance their feelings of togetherness.

Being consistently romantic produces a cumulative effect: You life will be revitalized, your spirit will blossom, you partner will fall in love with you again.   ✦   A pretty good payoff for a little togetherness, wouldn't you say? This cumulative effect of romance counter-balances the negative effect of "Relationship Entropy," which is the natural tendency of couples to drift apart unless they actively work on their relationship.

Reprinted with permission of King Features Syndicate, Inc., Sally Forth © 1993

Resources

☆ *The Art of Staying Together*, by Michael Broder
☆ *American Couples*, by Philip Blumstein & Pepper Schwartz
☆ *Being Intimate; A Guide To Successful Relationships*, by John Amodeo and Kris Wentworth
☆ *Pairing*, by G. Bach and R. Deutsch
☆ *The Way of Marriage: A Journal of Spiritual Growth Through Conflict, Love and Sex*, by Henry James Borys
☆ *The Halved Soul: Retelling the Myths of Romantic Love*, by Judith Pintar
☆ *Embracing Each Other: Relationship as Teacher, Healer & Guide*, by Hal Stone & Didra Winkelman
☆ *Intimate Strangers: Men & Women Together*, by Lillian B. Rubin

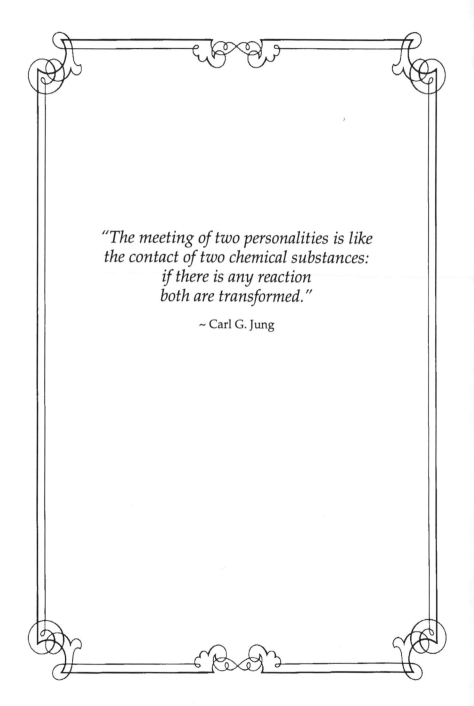

"The meeting of two personalities is like the contact of two chemical substances: if there is any reaction both are transformed."

~ Carl G. Jung

Touching

One of the things that distinguishes your love relationship from any other relationship in your life is the way you *touch* one another. There is, of course, *sexual* touching that is reserved for your lover. But there is *also* what I call "intimate touching," which is that special soft-but-electric touch that is shared between lovers. It's different from the hug you give your parents. It's different from the loving and healing way you touch your children. "Intimate touching" is a form of communication between two people who are connected on subtle, passionate levels of feeling and spirit. ✦ Don't panic if your intimate touching has lost some of its spark. It's more often caused by lack of time and attention than by lack of true feeling. Slow down. Pay attention. Listen. Talk. Re-connect.

Homework: Reach Out And Touch Someone

"People *always* think about touching when they're intimate and feeling close to one another, but they *rarely* think about touching when they're arguing and feeling angry with one another," said Mary T. in the Romance Class one evening. The simple act of holding hands while you're arguing could have a major impact on your relationship.

＊ The next time you're discussing one of your "hot topics," sit facing one another and hold hands while you're talking.

＊ Maintain eye contact, too! (This will be hard at times, but it's well worth the effort!)

＊ Why are we doing this? Because it will help you stay focused. It will help you remember you're talking with a *real person*, and not a stereotype that is easy to attack. It will help you communicate more clealy.

＊ This exercise keeps anger focused, and prevents your argument from wandering from topic to topic. It also takes rage and turns it into tears pretty quickly.

How often do you touch each other?
Couples in love touch each other more often than other people do.
Touching heals. Touching communicates.

You can touch your partner with your *eyes*. ✦ Research has shown that eye contact can be just as important and reassuring as physical touch. If you look carefully and sensitively, you can learn a *lot* about people just by looking into their eyes. And they, in turn—if they're paying attention— can learn a lot about *you*. ✦ There *is* such a thing as "The look of love"!

You can touch your partner with your *words*. ✦ Your words don't have to be eloquent. They just have to be true and heartfelt. We all know (but sometimes forget) that our words touch and evoke emotions in our loved ones. No one ever gets tired of hearing "I love you."

You can touch your partner with your *actions*. ✦ Loving gestures and the gift of time go a long way in communicating your feelings for your lover. It's okay to be a person of few words—*if* your actions speak clearly and loudly enough.

You can touch your partner with *gifts* and *presents*. ✦ Items are *symbols* of love. They represent you. They can capture a moment in time. ✦ Note: In the Romance Class we make a distinction between *gifts* and *presents*. See the Gifts chapter for an explanation.

Note: There's Touching . . . And Then There's *Touching*
What do these types of touching mean to you?
- 👅 A kiss on the cheek/the neck/the lips.
- 👅 A touch on the shoulder/knee/thigh/hand.
- 👅 A pat on the shoulder/fanny/leg.

A new skill for men: The Non-Sexual Touch. {"*Yeah, right!*"} ✦ Intimate touching does not—*should not*—be equated with sexual touching. We all have need to be touched in a caring, loving manner that carries no sexual overtones. {"*Uh-huh!*"} When *all* of your touching is oriented around sex, you actually produce the opposite result: Your partner shuts-down in order to protect herself. ✦ Here's the paradox: The more non-sexual touching you engage in, the more it enhances your sexual life! {"Well, I'll try it for a day and see what happens."} Give it a month, okay?

Does your lover anticipate your need to be touched? If so, you're lucky—and in the distinct minority. Most of us have to take on the responsibility for asking for what we want. It ain't fair to get angry at your partner for not knowing exactly what you need. For many of us, it's difficult to ask to be touched/hugged/kissed/loved. We feel we "Shouldn't have to ask for it." We feel it "Destroys the spontaneity." We feel disappointed because the fairy tale isn't turning out right. ✦ You might take a lesson from your dog or cat. When your dog wants to be petted, he just trots right up, wags his tail frantically, and looks at you with those big, soulful eyes. When your cat wants cuddling, she simply jumps into your lap and forces you to pet her. Maybe *we* should practice our tail-wagging and lap-sitting skills.

FYI: Point/Counter-Point

■ Anonymous man in the Romance Class: "Why do women complain that men aren't subtle, and just want to get right down to sex—and then turn around and complain that we like them in lingerie?"

● Anonymous woman in the Romance Class: "Why do men expect women to dress in lingerie—when they themselves lounge around in tattered sweat pants?"

Resources

☆ *Touching: The Human Significance of the Skin*, by A. Montahue
☆ *Massage and Loving*, by Anne Hooper
☆ *Moments of Engagement*, by Peter D. Kramer
☆ *The Massage Book*, by George Downing

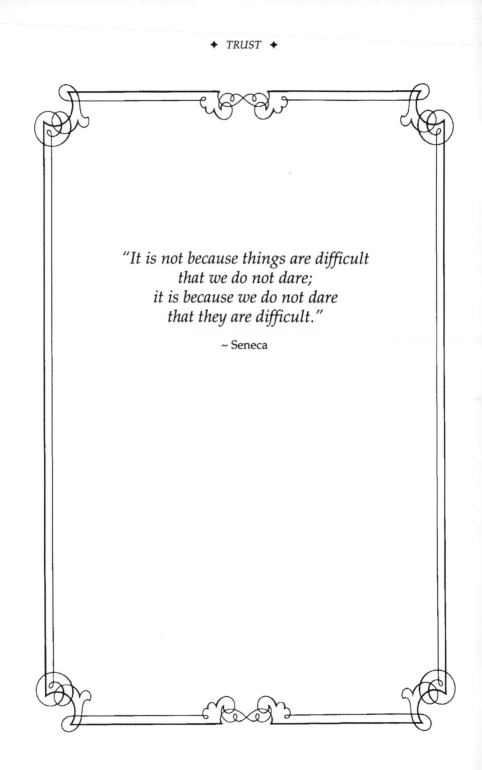

*"It is not because things are difficult
that we do not dare;
it is because we do not dare
that they are difficult."*

~ Seneca

Trust

Relationships are built on trust. This isn't just a nice-sounding phrase or a pompous platitude from some know-it-all psychologist. It is the Truth. Years of research reflects this; religious teachings agree; and people in the Romance Class confirm this again and again. Relationships built on trust can withstand an *unbelievable* amount of adversity. These relationships are also full of fun and adventure, because each partner is comfortable with change and open to growth.

Homework: Building Trust

Open, intimate communication builds trust. Trustworthy behavior is the *only* way to maintain it. I can help you with the communication part... The behavior part is up to *you*. ✦ Practice this exercise every day for a month. Every morning before you get out of bed:

■ Talk together for 10 to 15 minutes. Include:
 ▲ **Appreciation**: Why are you glad you're with him or her? Make it specific. We're looking for genuine feelings, not simple compliments.
 ▲ **Worries**: What concerns (about work, the world, *anything*) are you harboring? We're not looking for solutions, just a sympathetic ear.
 ▲ **Questions**: What's going on in your life that your partner should know about? Trivial details or major happenings—it's all important.
 ▲ **Needs & wants**: What do you need from your partner? What do you want? Emotionally. Practically. Short-term. Long-term.
 ▲ **Promises & wishes**: Make a specific promise to your partner. Make a wish for the two of you.
■ Repeat this exercise every evening, in bed, before going to sleep.

The only realistic basis for a mature, intimate relationship is *trust*. You must trust your partner *implicitly*. Nothing else *works*! ✦ If one of you is truly untrustworthy, it is impossible to build a solid relationship on that weak, shifting foundation. If, on the other hand, your partner *is* trustworthy, and you *still* don't trust her, what you have is either an immaturity problem or a lack of self-esteem. Give yourself time to deal with these issues. They're major.

FYI: Benefits of Trusting

♥ Trusting allows you to be more spontaneous.
♥ Trusting frees energy that otherwise would be expended in protecting yourself.
♥ Trusting is a requirement for intimate communication.
♥ Trusting allows you to be yourself.

Idea: A Ritual of Rage

Do you trust one another enough to bear the other's anger, frustration and rage? It is very difficult to face these negative feelings head-on in a loving relationship. Here's a unique and helpful exercise from the PAIRS Program, a fantastic 16-week seminar for couples. (PAIRS stands of Practical Application of Intimate Relationship Skills).

The Vesuvius

➢ Named after the volcano, this exercise allows you to "blow up"!
➢ It helps you deal with very strong anger—rage and fury.
➢ Ritualizing your anger allows you to get it out of your system effectively and safely.
➢ Here's what you do:
    ↦ The angry person: First asks permission of his partner to "blow up." You set a time limit ("I need about three minutes.") Then you just *let loose*! Yell and scream. Rant and rave. Be loud! Be unreasonable! Blame and call names! About *anything* that's got you steamed.
    ↦ The partner: Simply listens. No response is called for. No solutions are necessary. You're just the audience, watching the volcano explode!
➢ When you've finished, you hug and thank your partner.
➢ The Vesuvius allows you to express rage and other miscellaneous "unacceptable" emotions directly—instead of letting them infect your relationship.

This is just a brief description of an exercise discussed in detail in *Passage To Intimacy*, by Lori H. Gordon, Ph.D., founder of the PAIRS Program. You can reach the PAIRS Foundation at 3705 South George Mason Drive, Suite C-8, Falls Church, Virginia 22041; 703-998-5550 or 800-842-7470.

Do you trust *yourself*? Do you listen to yourself? Are you acquainted with the quiet Voice inside you? Do you trust your own experiences?—Even when those experiences run counter to conventional wisdom or other's advice? Do you trust your feelings? Do you trust your intuitions?

> *"Trust life, my friends.*
> *However far afield life seems to take you,*
> *this trip is necessary."*
>
> ~ Emmanuel/Pat Rodegast

A modest proposal: Trust your partner completely. Trust him to love you, support you, listen to you and come through for you. And make sure that he knows that you trust him. Wait and see what happens. ✦ Most people strive to live up to their loved one's expectations of them.

Resources

☆ *You Learn By Living*, by Eleanor Roosevelt
☆ *The Art of Loving*, by Erich Fromm
☆ *The Couple's Journey*, by Susan Campbell
☆ *Emmanuel's Book: A Manual for Living Comfortably in the Cosmos*, by Pat Rodegast & Judith Stanton
☆ *Intimate Strangers: Men & Women Together*, by Lillian B. Rubin
☆ *Embracing Each Other: Relationship as Teacher, Healer & Guide*, by Hal Stone & Sidra Winkelman

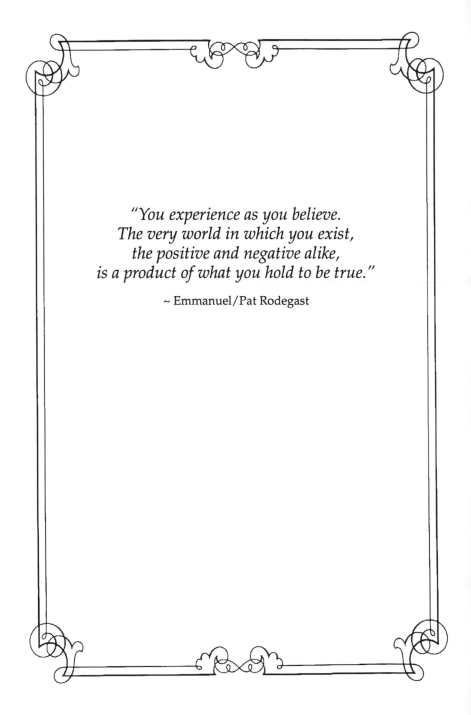

*"You experience as you believe.
The very world in which you exist,
the positive and negative alike,
is a product of what you hold to be true."*

~ Emmanuel/Pat Rodegast

Truth

Throughout the ages, wise men and women have taught—by word and by example—that our Purpose here is to learn Love.

*"Let the disciple cultivate love
without measure toward all beings."*
~ Buddha

*"A new commandment I give to you,
that you love one another."*
~ Jesus

*"Love is constant, it is we who are fickle.
Love does guarantee, people betray.
Love can always be trusted, people cannot."*
~ Leo

When are we going to *listen*? The Truth is staring us in the face, and we look away—distracted or too busy or afraid. Afraid of love? Who, me??

It's not only the poets, prophets and sages who speak the Truth. Sometimes you need look no further than your morning newspaper. ✦ Beverly Beckham, a very insightful and thoughtful yet practical newspaper columnist for the *Boston Herald* recently wrote: "Love doesn't make you miserable . . . Love doesn't break your heart every other day. Love makes life better, not worse. Love builds you up, it doesn't tear you down. If it doesn't do these things, it's not love. It's invention or habit or loyalty or devotion. but it's not love. And it's not worth a lifetime of tears."

Many of the concepts in this book are Universal Truths. I can't take credit for them—they simply *are*. Many people write and teach these truths. We use different words and different approaches. You may hear the same advice for *years* without it sinking in . . . Until one day someone puts a slightly different twist on it, and suddenly you *get it*. Keep searching until you get it. Be patient. Be persistent. It's worth it.

There is one place where the Truth can *always* be found: It's in the *Now*. You can find hints, advice and great quotes in the Past. But Truth isn't simply an idea—it's an experience. And experiences happen *now*. Truth must be re-created, re-experienced and re-understood all the time.

What's the truth about how much control you have in your life? Do we have much control, or are we at the mercy of outside events? Do you decide your own fate, does someone else, or does some higher power? Many people who have lived through some truly devastating experiences are able to rise above them and live fulfilling, happy and love-filled lives. How do they do it? ✦ They do it through a seemingly simple belief: How you feel is *not* the result of what's happening in your life—it's your *interpretation* of what's happening. This gives you *tremendous* control over your life—more control than most people believe is possible. ✦ Have you ever heard this phrase . . .

"It's not what happens to you—
It's what you do about it!"

This is the life philosophy and message of motivational speaker W Mitchell. Mitchell was burned over 65% of his body in a motorcycle accident. He underwent 32 sessions of plastic surgery to reconstruct his face and body. He rebuilt his life . . . only to become paralyzed four years later in an aircraft accident. "Before I was paralyzed, there were 10,000 things I could do. Now there are 9,000. I can either dwell on the 1,000 I lost, or focus on the 9,000 I have left." ✦ You, too, have tremendous inner resources with which to deal with the circumstances of your life. I believe that any relationship can be turned around and made to sparkle—as long as you both have just a little willingness. If you do, the courage and the creativity will come along naturally. ✦ [Note to the Typo Brigade: W Mitchell spells his name *without* a period. So you *haven't* caught an error!]

"There are many truths of which the full meaning cannot be realized
until personal experience has brought it home."

~ John Stuart Mill

Scenario: You're reading a book or listening to an inspirational speaker, when suddenly a certain phrase *grabs your attention and won't let go.* You experience a flash of insight, and several pieces of the puzzle that is your life click into place. You have what's known as an "*Ah-ha!*" experience. You feel lighter, more at peace, happier for several days . . . until . . . You tell someone about your experience, and they say, "Oh heck, *everybody* knows *that!*" You feel deflated and a bit like a fool for having been so profoundly affected by such a trivial bit of everyday advice. ✦ *What happened?!* You stopped trusting your own experience. You let someone else's opinion or judgment turn you away from a personal Truth. It sometimes takes a lot of internal strength to hold onto something that is meaningful and profound to you. Treasure and protect the words that speak to your heart!

Homework: Searching for Truth

Where does the Truth get lost in your life?

✢ In the myriad details of everyday life?
✢ In the rush of getting things done?
✢ In other goals that seem more important?
✢ Have you given responsibility to someone else?
✢ Have you simply forgotten about it?
✢ Are you too tired? Too depressed? Too confused?
✢ Are you worried about the future? Guilty over the past?
✢ Have you simply abandoned the search?

Talk this over with your lover. It's important stuff.

❖ Set aside an entire evening to talk about these issues.
❖ What changes would you like to make in your lives?
❖ How can you help each other?
❖ List some specific Truths about your individual lives.
❖ List some Truths about your relationship.

Resources

☆ *The Road Less Traveled*, by Scott Peck
☆ *Getting the Love You Want: A Guide for Couples*, by Harville Hendrix
☆ *Trances People Live*, by Stephen Wolinsky
☆ *The Prophet*, by Kahlil Gibran
☆ *Illusions*, by Richard Bach

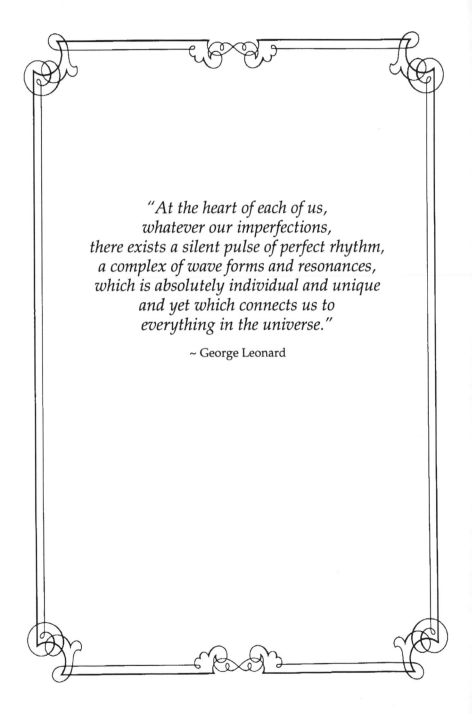

*"At the heart of each of us,
whatever our imperfections,
there exists a silent pulse of perfect rhythm,
a complex of wave forms and resonances,
which is absolutely individual and unique
and yet which connects us to
everything in the universe."*

~ George Leonard

Uniqueness

How is it we can marvel at the uniqueness of a snowflake, and then turn around and say, "*Men*—They're all alike!" or "Just like a *woman.*" Our uniqueness as individual people is marvelous and mysterious. Couples who continue to appreciate each other's uniqueness are still busy discovering one another after 50 years of marriage . . . While the couples who feel they "know each other inside-out" are puzzled by their boredom. ✦ Romance is a celebration of uniqueness.

FYI: The 7 Kinds of Intelligence

The more you understand your own uniqueness, the better able you are to *be yourself*, to *express yourself*, and to *love yourself*. The more you appreciate your *lover's* uniqueness, the better able you are to *appreciate, understand* and *love* him or her. ✦ A wonderful book that will give you a whole new perspective on our uniqueness is *7 Kinds of Smart* by Thomas Armstrong. He shows that there are at least *seven* distinct ways of being smart—not just the verbal and logical/mathematical know-how measured by IQ tests and SAT scores. ✦ When we talk about this concept in the Romance Class, most people gain a newfound respect for some talent/ability/quirk—intelligence!— of their partner that they had been ignoring or belittling. Here, very briefly, are the seven kinds of smart:

1. "Word Smart"—Expressing your verbal intelligence
2. "Picture Smart"—Thinking with your mind's eye
3. "Music Smart"—Making the most of your melodic mind
4. "Body Smart"—Using your kinesthetic intelligence
5. "Logic Smart"—Calculating your mathematical and scientific abilities
6. "People Smart"—Connecting with your social sense
7. "Self Smart"—Developing your intrapersonal intellect

How are you smart? (Notice that this is a different question from "How smart are you?") How is your partner smart? Do you capitalize on your strengths? Which kinds of smart would you like to develop? How can each of the seven kinds of intelligence be used to enhance your relationship?

Not only are *you* unique—your *relationship* is unique, too. Treat it like the precious, one-of-a-kind thing it truly is.

An Exercise: Explore Your Uniquenesses

Explore these aspects of yourself with your partner. Are you both familiar with the uniqueness of each other's characteristics? Do you respect your differences? Or do you try to mold her to conform to your preferences? Or do you compromise yourself in seeking to be the person you think he'll like?

- ■ **Work**: Do you work to live—or live to work? Do you have a *job* or a *career* or a *passion*? Do you work efficiently? Do you *enjoy* your work? Do you work best alone or with others? What kind of work do you want to be doing 10 years from now?
- ▲ **Play**: Do you make time to play? How do *you* define play? Who do you play with? How well do you balance *work* and *play*? How much playing do you need in your life?
- ● **Energy Level**: Are you a tireless dynamo? Or do you need to conserve your energy for when you need it most? Are you a morning person or a night person?
- ■ **Sleep**: Do you need your eight hours per night *or else*? Or will five hours do just fine? Are you a light sleeper or do you go comatose the second your head hits the pillow? Do you need perfect silence in order to fall asleep? Window open or closed? Are you a bed hog? Are you a cover-stealer?
- ▼ **Time**: Are you always on time? Or are you perpetually late? Are you a clock-watcher, or do you just saunter along?
- ◆ **"Velocity"**: Do you *leap* on ideas/make detailed Action Plans (even for vacations?!)/do five things at one time? Or do you take things as they come/let Nature take its course/work slowly and methodically? {Thanks to Jim Cathcart, an awesome professional speaker, for coining the term Velocity as an important descriptor of personalities.}
- ● **Sex**: Once-a-month or twice-a-day? Fast or slow? Quiet or loud? Physical and sweaty or tender and sweet? Meaningful or casual? Romantic or routine? Physical release or spiritual connection?
- ▲ **Togetherness**: Quantity of time? Quality of time? What kind of activities do you like to do together?—Tennis or backgammon? Attending parties or sitting quietly reading? [Watching TV together *does not* count as "togetherness time"!!]
- ■ **Eating**: Gourmet or simple? Do you enjoy the *process* of preparing meals, or do you just like to *eat*? Do you sit and savor your meals, or do you eat-and-run? How often do you like to/need to eat out? What's your favorite type of restaurant? What does food *mean* to you?
- ◆ **Passions**: What are your passions/interests/hobbies? Do you pursue them alone/as a couple/with others?
- ● **What *else*** makes you unique?

Homework: An Attitude Survey

✣ Where do your attitudes *really* come from? Your parents? Oprah? *Cosmo*? The newspaper? Your friends? (I'm not saying that there's anything wrong with picking-up attitudes from others. But knowing and acknowledging their source is often helpful. Sometimes we pick-up attitudes, and repeat opinions that we haven't really thought through.)

✣ What's the difference between an *attitude* and an *opinion*? How do they differ from *convictions* and *beliefs*?

✣ How *strongly held* are your attitudes?

✣ List your attitudes about a variety of topics (such as Money, Sex, Children, Work, Chores, Holidays, etc.).

✣ Rate them according to whether they're "core" or "peripheral" attitudes.

   ✗ "Core" attitudes and beliefs are those that *define* us. They're an integral part of who we are. They are non-negotiable.

   ✗ "Peripheral" attitudes and beliefs, on the other hand, are more like *preferences*. They often change depending on our mood.

✣ We're not looking for *essays* here—just some short, bulleted phrases that express your attitudes and feelings—so don't be intimidated by this exercise.

✣ Compare your list with your partner's.

✣ Possible insight: Many of your disagreements and problems stem from attitudes/opinions/beliefs that aren't really that important to you!

✣ Possible insight: Different opinions can co-exist in one relationship!

Your uniqueness is one of your strengths. It makes you attractive to others. Growth and change are necessary and desirable, but don't try to change yourself for another, or you'll compromise your uniqueness and lose yourself.

Resources

☆ *Honoring the Self: The Psychology of Confidence and Respect*, by Nathaniel Branden

☆ *Personhood*, by Leo Buscaglia

☆ *The New Male-Female Relationship*, by Herb Goldberg

☆ *The Power Is Within You*, by Louise Hay

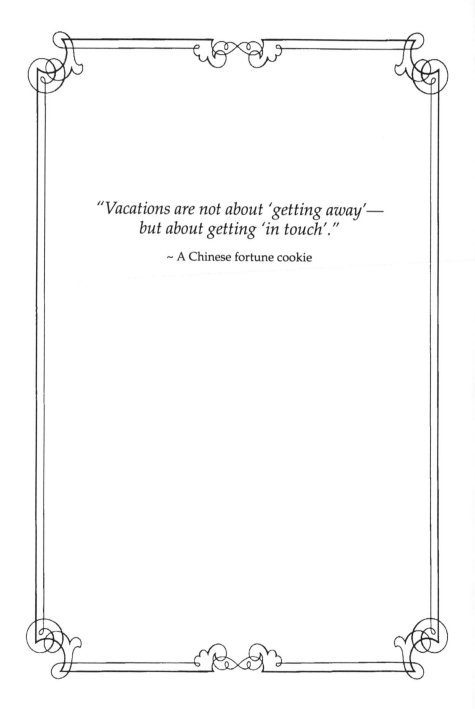

"Vacations are not about 'getting away'—
but about getting 'in touch'."

~ A Chinese fortune cookie

Vacations

Being on vacation is much more about a *state of mind* than it is about location. Why? For one thing, you deal with *time* differently than you do in your day-to-day life. Most of us automatically toss our watches aside while on vacation. We consciously—*desperately*—want to escape from the tyranny of the clock. What we are *unconsciously* doing is shifting into a mode of living in the *now*. ✦ Think about it. In your daily life, much of your time is spent thinking about, planning for, and anticipating the future. In addition, we worry about the past, and are often stuck in bad habits from the past. We live in the *past*, we live in the *future*—and rarely do we live in the *present moment*! This is what I think vacations are really for: To remind us of the importance of the *now*. ✦ Here's a secret that's not a secret: The more you live in the now, the more vital you'll be; the more alive you'll feel; the more energy you'll have for all of the large and small tasks in your life. Will it make you more romantic? You betcha!

FYI: Budget Holidays

Some vacation strategies for s t r e t c h i n g your dollars:

♥ "Go to the most expensive place and get the least expensive room!" {Thanks to Eileen Buchheim, who *definitely* knows how to plan a romantic holiday . . . as she runs Celebrate Romance, which has a toll-free Romantic Tips Hotline (800-368-7978) among other romantic goodies!}

♥ Travel *off-season* to popular vacation spots.

♥ "If you're flexible and love surprises, plan your vacation around the *lowest airfare* instead of aiming for a specific destination! Go wherever your money will take you the farthest! Using this strategy we vacationed one year in *Pittsburgh*, and the next year in *Greece*!" {Thanks to Julie Z.}

♥ Charter a yacht with a group of good friends.

♥ Tack-on mini-vacations to your business trips.

♥ Travel to countries where the exchange rate is favorable. Your dollars will go much farther.

There are three phases to every vacation: 1) Anticipation, 2) Vacation, and 3) Recollection. Do you experience and enjoy each phase to its fullest? If you don't, you didn't get your money's worth. ✦ *Anticipation.* There is an art to looking forward to a vacation without making yourself miserable that you're not there yet. If you have the right mindset, the anticipation can be a great phase. I know people who have nearly as much fun perusing travel brochures and planning travel itineraries as being on the vacation itself! ✦ *Vacation.* Being on vacation should be a *natural* and easy thing, but I've discovered that most adults have lost the knack. Remember when you were a kid? —Summer vacation was the Natural State of Things, and school was a rude intrusion. Well, as adulthood wears on, this mindset gets reversed: Work becomes the Natural State of Things, and vacation becomes a strange and foreign time. Many people rob themselves of their vacations by being unable to relax and let-go. It may take some practice. So *practice!* ✦ *Recollection.* Vacations come and go, but good memories can last a lifetime! I know people who are still enjoying vacations they took 25 years ago! Do you take photos during vacations? Do you save seashells, ticket stubs, menus and matchbooks? Do you have scrapbooks of your vacations?

Suggestion: Visit "Sweetheart City, USA"

I mentioned Loveland, Colorado in my previous book—because it's known worldwide as the ultimate place to have your valentine card postmarked from, and then sent on to your love . . . But Tracey and I have since visited the town, and I'd like to tell you about it. ✦ Loveland, 50 miles north of Denver, is a great off-the-beaten-path destination. Loveland is home to one of the most *romantic* bed and breakfasts in the world. Loveland is also home to many artists—especially sculptors. The many art galleries will enthrall you.

➤ The Lovelander Bed and Breakfast has nine guest rooms. All are furnished with comfortable antique furniture. Some have jacuzzis. Some have stained glass windows. *All* are romantic. Owners Marilyn and Bob Wiltgen are the *ultimate* hosts. Call them at 303-669-0798.

➤ Here's how the Valentine Mailing Program works: Seal, stamp and address your valentine card; enclose it in a larger envelope and mail it to: Postmaster, Attn: Valentine, Loveland, Colorado 80538. (It must be received in Loveland by February 8th in order to give them time to stamp it with the special Loveland postmark and yearly-updated poem!)

➤ For more info, call the friendly folks at the Loveland Chamber of Commerce at 303-667-6311.

Tip: Rocky Mountain High

The ultimate skier's high is a mountain of knee-deep, untracked powder. Several Colorado ski areas now offer snowcat transportation to pristine mountain tops! And, unlike heli-skiing in Canada's Bugaboos at $4,000 a week, snowcat tours run about $200 per day. Call these folks for more info:

❀ Irwin Lodge: 303-349-5308
❀ Aspen Powder Tours: 303-925-1227
❀ Jupiter Jones's Steamboat Powder Cats: 303-879-5188

Here's some vacation reading that will help you maintain a vacation mindset even after you return home: Linda Weltner's wonderful book *No Place Like Home: Rooms and Reflections from One Family's Life.* It's a collection of her thought-provoking and insightful newspaper columns. Here's a sampling: "People today prefer showers to tubs, sex to courtship, columns like this one to books. For most of us, time is worth too much to waste it drawing water, sending love letters or turning pages. We value nothing more than the most efficient way to get things done."

Reprinted with permission of NEA, Inc., Arlo & Janis © 1993

Resources

☆ *The Weekend Camper,* by Dan & Inez Morris
☆ *The Complete Guide to America's National Parks,* from the National Park Foundation
☆ *The Complete Guide To Bed & Breakfast Inns and Guesthouses,* by Pamela Lanier
☆ *Trouble-Free Travel with Children,* by Vicki Lansky

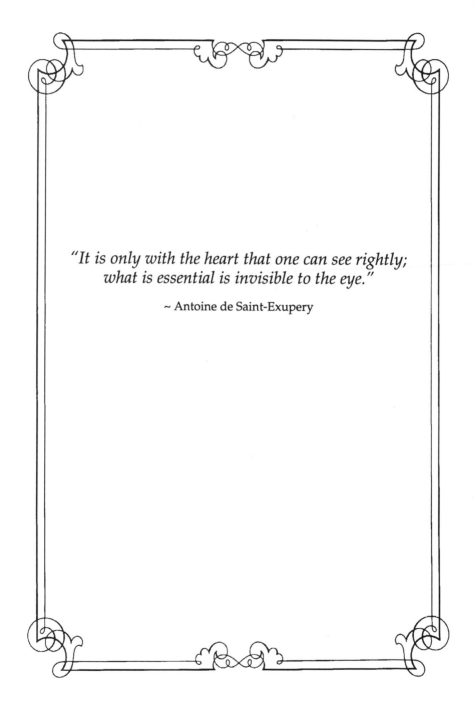

"It is only with the heart that one can see rightly; what is essential is invisible to the eye."

~ Antoine de Saint-Exupery

Vision

The word vision—with a small *v*—is about eyeballs. With a capital *V* it's about imagination, inner sight, and the expression of love. ✦ Do you have a Vision for your life? Do you have a Vision for your relationship?

Your life is either an *expression* of your Vision, or a *search* for your Vision. Having a Vision helps crystalize your hopes and dreams. It also helps move you from theory into action. ✦ A Vision is more than a plan. A Vision is broader than a goal. A Vision goes beyond vague hopes. A Vision encompasses your beliefs and values. A Vision is a synthesis of all these characteristics into a coherent vision of your ideal future.

Homework: Exploring Your Vision

● Which phrases sum-up your beliefs—your "Philosophy of Life"? Choose one or more of these, or write-in your own:
  - ❐ "Love makes the world go round."
  - ❐ "Money makes the world go round."
  - ❐ "The Lord helps those who help themselves."
  - ❐ "Carpe diem"—"*Seize the day!*"
  - ❐ "Live each day as if it were your last."
  - ❐ "When the going gets tough, the tough get going."

  ❐ _____

● How do these beliefs affect your day-to-day life in a positive way? How do they limit you?
● How are your core beliefs reflected in your relationship?
● How do *your* core beliefs compare with your *partner's* beliefs?

Vision has to do with what direction you take in life. —Are you on a spiritual Path? ✦ Vision affects the decisions you make. —Are your decisions based on fear, and the avoidance of pain, or on love, and the creative expression of your life? ✦ Vision is a kind-of inner light that guides your actions. —Are your actions consistent with your beliefs and values?

The Gospel According to Godek, Revisited

✤ You can compromise without compromising *yourself*.
✤ You can change without losing your uniqueness.
✤ You can grow without growing apart.
✤ You can give without losing *anything*.
✤ You can open-up without being judged.
✤ You can disagree without arguing.
✤ You can feel without losing control.
✤ You *can* keep the passion alive in a long-term relationship.
✤ You can be mature without losing the child inside of you.

✱ You cannot be known unless you open your heart.
✱ You cannot love without being vulnerable.
✱ You cannot be intimate without taking a risk.
✱ You cannot share feelings in a non-supportive environment.
✱ You cannot enter a relationship demanding a guarantee.
✱ You cannot be interdependent unless you're first independent.
✱ You cannot be controlling and spontaneous at the same time.
✱ You cannot live without making mistakes.
✱ You cannot realize your dreams if you don't have well defined goals.
✱ You cannot grow unless you learn from your mistakes.
✱ You cannot forgive another until you've forgiven yourself *first*.
✱ You cannot heal a broken heart until you risk it again.

■ You have the power to choose how your feelings affect you.
▲ You have the ability to alter your reality with your beliefs.
● You have all the talents and capabilities to fulfill your Purpose.

I recently had an insight that helped me connect the three realms of our lives: The physical, emotional and spiritual. The physical/emotional connection and the emotional/spiritual connection have long been obvious to me. But connecting the *physical* with the *spiritual* has been a dilemma. ✦ What I realized is that there is a Way, a Path, that is available only to couples in committed relationships: Long-term physical intimacy combined with long-term emotional intimacy promotes a unique state of inner peace, wholeness, *spirituality*.

There are five key personality attributes that combine to produce your personal Vision: They are your opinions, attitudes, beliefs, values and philosophies. ✦ Are you clear about what you believe and what you stand for? Do you know what your core values are—versus your peripheral opinions? Are your philosophies well-reasoned—or are they really just opinions masquerading as philosophies? ✦ To help us understand these important personalitity attributes, I've arranged them in a hierarchy, ranked in order, from simple and peripheral to complex and core:

Philosophies
Values
Beliefs
Attitudes
Opinions

To elaborate briefly: Our philosophies underly all of the other attributes. Philosophies form a solid core for our personalities. They're comprised of a coherent and complementary network of values and beliefs. Our philosophies are core—they're unshakeable; whereas our opinions are peripheral—they're changeable, flexible and influenced by fads and trends. Overall, our values and beliefs are more firmly held than our attitudes and opinions. ✦ The point of all this is to show you what's behind the formation of your personal Vision. You can't have a focused Vision if you're unclear about these attributes.

I believe that a romantic's life is guided by a Vision of shared values and expanding love with an intimate partner. The expression of this Vision can take a *million* different forms, as we are all magnificently different and endlessly creative individuals. ✦ What joins us is a belief, a faith, in the power of love. Through romance—the expression of love—we give, we create, we learn, we grow, we fulfill ourselves and our role in the world.

Resources

☆ *The Search for Oneness*, by Lloyd H. Silverman & Frank M. Lachmann
☆ *Illusions*, by Richard Bach
☆ *The History of the Future*, by Peter Lorie and Sidd Murray-Clark
☆ *Notes On Love And Courage*, by Hugh Prather

Romantic Things To Do Today

_____

_____

_____

_____

_____

Lessons To Review

_____

_____

_____

_____

_____

Romantic Plans for Next Week

_____

_____

_____

_____

_____

Personal Affirmations

_____

_____

_____

_____

_____

Romantic Plans for Next Month

_____

_____

_____

_____

_____

Romantic Shopping List

_____

_____

_____

_____

_____

Romantic Plans for Next Year

_____

_____

_____

_____

_____

Misc. Romantic Ideas

_____

_____

_____

_____

_____

Romance 101
Love Coupon

This coupon entitles the holder to
2 hours of *totally uninterrupted time* together with
the issuer of this coupon . . .
to be used in any way you choose to use it!

A gift to _____

With love from _____

Romance 101
Love Coupon

Good for one *Romantic Escape Weekend!*

A gift to _____

With love from _____

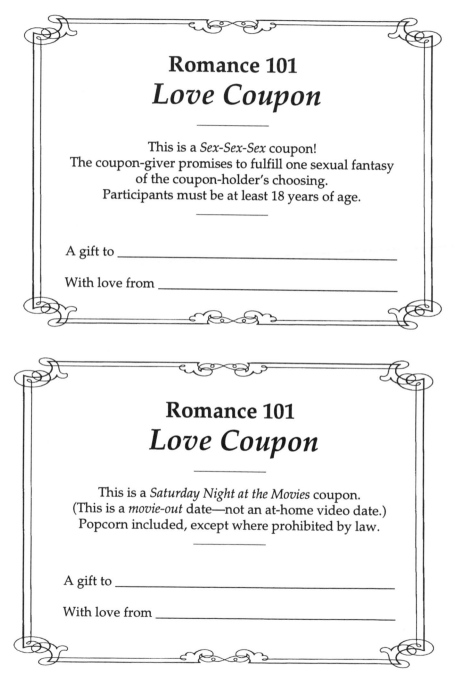

Romance 101
Love Coupon

This is a *Sex-Sex-Sex* coupon!
The coupon-giver promises to fulfill one sexual fantasy
of the coupon-holder's choosing.
Participants must be at least 18 years of age.

A gift to _____

With love from _____

Romance 101
Love Coupon

This is a *Saturday Night at the Movies* coupon.
(This is a *movie-out* date—not an at-home video date.)
Popcorn included, except where prohibited by law.

A gift to _____

With love from _____

An Invitation

These books and seminars are part of the Grand Conversation, as Greg calls it. He sees his books as "The beginning of a *dialogue*, and not merely another long-winded *monologue* by some so-called 'expert'." We would like to hear from *you*. ✦ You are invited to write to us with your romantic ideas and your romantic stories—whether sentimental, outrageous, or creative. They may end up in the *LoveLetter* newsletter, or perhaps in a future book. We will credit you by name or protect your anonymity, as you wish. —Or just write to say *Hi!*

Gregory J.P. Godek
Casablanca Press, Inc.
P.O. Box 226
Weymouth, Massachusetts 02188-0001
617-340-1300

Romance 101
Love Coupon

This is a *Romantic Brainstorming Session* coupon.
The coupon-holder and coupon-giver agree
to spend at least 2 hours brainstorming
ideas for enhancing their
love affair!

A gift to _____

With love from _____

Romance 101
Love Coupon

An *Evening of Dancing* coupon.
The coupon-holder may choose between
an evening on the dance floor, or
an evening of "dancing between the sheets"!

A gift to _____

With love from _____

Romance Seminars

Gregory J.P. Godek presents keynote speeches and seminars for a variety of organizations nationally and internationally. ✦ Greg's speeches range from 30-minute motivational talks to hour-long inspirational keynote lectures. Every presentation is custom-tailored to the audience he is addressing. ✦ Greg's seminars range from 2-hour sessions to day-long workshops, depending on the organization's needs. The seminars are high-energy, interactive sessions that are designed specifically for each different situation. ✦ For more information, please write or call Greg at:

LoveTalks
Casablanca Press, Inc.
P.O. Box 226
Weymouth, Massachusetts 02188-0001
617-340-1300

MEMBER

NATIONAL
SPEAKERS
ASSOCIATION

Romance 101
Love Coupon

One romantic dinner.
Prepared by the coupon-issuer.

A gift to _____

With love from _____

Romance 101
Love Coupon

_____
_____
_____

A gift to _____

With love from _____

Index

N

O

P

Q

R

Order Form

Books

✦ Softbound: *1001 Ways To Be Romantic* ($11.95)
✦ Hardbound: *1001 Ways To Be Romantic* ($18.95)
✳ Softbound: *1001 More Ways To Be Romantic* ($11.95)
✳ Hardbound: *1001 More Ways To Be Romantic* ($18.95)
➤ Softbound: *Romance 101*: ($12.95)
➤ Hardbound: *Romance 101*: ($18.95)

Call Toll-Free
800-444-2524
Extension 65

Major credit cards accepted.
Overnight delivery & regular delivery available: Different shipping charges apply.
For book orders only.

Newsletter

❤ A free one-year subscription to newsletter of romantic ideas—
The LoveLetter—is now available for the asking.
❤ It's a $25 value, and it's full of creative, unusual and wonderful ideas, gifts and gestures.
❤ Sign-up yourself, your spouse, your boyfriend/girlfriend, your parents, your friends—anyone who needs a good swift kick-in-the-pants, or would simply appreciate receiving lots of great romantic ideas on a regular basis.
❤ And as long as you're writing, why don't you send-in your favorite creative ideas, great gift finds, special gestures. You'll be credited by name! Join the ongoing "Romance Conversation."
❤ Write to: *LoveLetter*, P.O. Box 226, Weymouth, Massachusetts 02188.
